Lecture Notes in Computer Science 11389

Commenced Publication in 1973
Founding and Former Series Editors:
Gerhard Goos, Juris Hartmanis, and Jan van Leeuwen

More information about this series at http://www.springer.com/series/7410

Begül Bilgin · Jean-Bernard Fischer (Eds.)

Smart Card Research and Advanced Applications

17th International Conference, CARDIS 2018
Montpellier, France, November 12–14, 2018
Revised Selected Papers

 Springer

Editors
Begül Bilgin
Rambus - Cryptography Research
Rotterdam, Zuid-Holland, The Netherlands

Jean-Bernard Fischer
Nagravision
Cheseaux-sur-Lausanne, Vaud, Switzerland

KU Leuven
Leuven-Heverlee, Belgium

ISSN 0302-9743   ISSN 1611-3349 (electronic)
Lecture Notes in Computer Science
ISBN 978-3-030-15461-5   ISBN 978-3-030-15462-2 (eBook)
https://doi.org/10.1007/978-3-030-15462-2

Library of Congress Control Number: 2019933892

LNCS Sublibrary: SL4 – Security and Cryptology

This Springer imprint is published by the registered company Springer Nature Switzerland AG
The registered company address is: Gewerbestrasse 11, 6330 Cham, Switzerland

Preface

These proceedings contain the papers selected for presentation at the 17th Smart Card Research and Advanced Applications Conference (CARDIS 2018), which was held in Montpellier, France, during November 12–14, 2018, and organized by the Montpellier Laboratory of Informatics, Robotics and Microelectronics (LIRMM).

Since 1994, CARDIS has provided a forum for experts from industry and academia to exchange ideas on the security of smart cards and related applications. The smart card object has been part of our daily life for so many years in the form of personal devices (banking cards, SIM cards, electronic IDs, etc.) that we do not remember a life without it. In relation to smart card security, the root of trust of embedded solutions is becoming key as Machine-to-Machine (M2M) and Internet of Things (IoT) applications are increasing massively. This increased exposure naturally widens the attack space, whether physical or logical, local or remote. It is more important than ever to understand how smart cards and other embedded devices can be secured by discussing all aspects of their design, development, deployment, evaluation, and application.

This year, CARDIS received 28 valid submissions from 12 countries. Each paper was double-blind reviewed by at least three independent reviewers. We selected 13 papers based on 102 written reviews from the 30 members of the Program Committee with the help of 35 external reviewers. The technical program also featured three invited talks: Frank Piessens from KU Leuven in Belgium presented "Security Specifications for the Hardware/Software Interface"; Benoit Feix from eshard in France presented "Exploiting a New Dimension in Side-Channel Analysis: Scatter on Symmetric and Asymmetric Embedded Cryptography"; and Wyseur Brecht from Nagravision in Switzerland presented "Challenges in Securing Industrial IoT and Critical Infrastructure." A free tutorial was held co-located with the conference: "Understanding Leakage Detection" organized by the REASSURE Consortium.

We would like to thank the general chair, Philippe Maurine, for the great venue and smooth operation of the conference. We would also like to express our gratitude to the Program Committee and the external reviewers for their thorough work, which enabled the technical program to be of such high quality, and the Steering Committee for giving us the opportunity to serve as program chairs at such a prestigious conference. The financial support of all the sponsors was highly appreciated and greatly facilitated the organization of the conference; we thank the sponsors: ANSSI, CNRS, Gemalto, Nagra-Kudelski, LETI-CEA, LIRMM, Rambus, STMicroelectronics, University of Montpellier. Last but not least, we would like to thank all the authors who submitted their work to CARDIS 2018.

January 2019

Begül Bilgin
Jean-Bernard Fischer

Organization

General Chair

Philippe Maurine   University of Montpellier, France

Program Chairs

Begül Bilgin   Rambus-Cryptography Research, The Netherlands
                  and KU Leuven, Belgium
Jean-Bernard Fischer   Nagravision, Switzerland

Steering Committee

François-Xavier Standaert (Chair)	UC Louvain, Belgium
Thomas Eisenbarth	Worcester Polytechnic Institute, USA
Aurélien Francillon	EURECOM, France
Edouard de Jong	De Jong Frz. Holding BV
Marc Joye	NXP Semiconductors, USA
Konstantinos Markantonakis	Royal Holloway University of London, UK
Amir Moradi	Ruhr University Bochum, Germany
Svetla Nikova	KU Leuven, Belgium
Pierre Paradinas	Inria and CNAM, France
Jean-Jacques Quisquater	UC Louvain, Belgium
Francesco Regazzoni	University of Lugano, Switzerland
Yannick Teglia	Gemalto, France

Program Committee

Josep Balasch	KU Leuven, Belgium
Guillaume Barbu	IDEMIA, France
Alessandro Barenghi	Politecnico di Milano, Italy
Sonia Belaïd	CryptoExperts, France
Thomas De Cnudde	KU Leuven, Belgium
Jeroen Delvaux	Nanyang Technological University, Singapore
Thomas Eisenbarth	Universität zu Lübeck, Germany
Benoix Feix	eshard, France
Domenic Forte	University of Florida, USA
Aurélien Francillon	Eurecom, France
Elke De Mulder	Rambus-Cryptography Research, USA
Hannes Gross	TU Graz, Austria

Vincent Grosso   Radboud University, The Netherlands
Annelie Heuser   CNRS/IRISA, France
Marc Joye   NXP Semiconductors, USA
Kerstin Lemke-Rust   Bonn-Rhein-Sieg University, Germany
Roel Maes   Intrinsic ID, The Netherlands
Oliver Mischke   Infineon, Germany
Amir Moradi   Ruhr University Bochum, Germany
Debdeep Mukhopadhyay   IIT Kharagpur, India
Axel Y. Poschmann   DarkMatter, UAE
Emmanuel Prouff   ANSSI, France
Francesco Regazoni   ALaRi, Switzerland
Kazuo Sakiyama   University of Electro-Communications, Japan
Erkay Savaş   Sabanci University, Turkey
Tobias Schneider   UC Louvain, Belgium
Yannick Teglia   Gemalto, France
Yuval Yarom   University of Adelaide, and Data61, Australia
Carolyn Whitnall   University of Bristol, UK
Marc Witteman   Riscure, The Netherlands

Additional Reviewers

Alberto Battistello   Erdinc Ozturk
Ryad Benadjila   Jungmin Park
Shivam Bhasin   Sikhar Patranabis
Manuel Bluhm   Thomas Pöppelmann
Olivier Bronchain   Bastian Richter
Giovanni Camurati   Debapriya Basu Roy
Nicolas Debande   Okan Seker
David El-Baze   Rémi Strullu
Berk Gulmezoglu   Shahin Tajik
Christoph Herbst   Benjamin Timon
James Howe   Lucille Tordella
Malika Izabachene   Rei Ueno
Angshuman Karmakar   Aurelien Vasselle
Elif Bilge Kavun   Nikita Veshchikov
Albert Levi   Junwei Wang
Marco Martinoli   Felix Wegener
Ahmet Can Mert   Jan Wichelmann
Marius Muench

Contents

Convolutional Neural Network Based Side-Channel Attacks in Time-Frequency Representations

Guang Yang[1,2], Huizhong Li[1,2], Jingdian Ming[1,2], and Yongbin Zhou[1,2(✉)]

[1] State Key Laboratory of Information Security,
Institute of Information Engineering, Chinese Academy of Sciences, Beijing, China
{yangguang2,lihuizhong,mingjingdian,zhouyongbin}@iie.ac.cn
[2] School of Cyber Security, University of Chinese Academy of Sciences,
Beijing, China

Abstract. Profiled attacks play a fundamental role in the evaluation of cryptographic implementation worst-case security. For the past sixteen years, great efforts have been paid to develop profiled attacks from Template Attacks to deep learning based attacks. However, most attacks are performed in time domain – may lose frequency domain information. In this paper, to utilize leakage information more effectively, we propose a novel deep learning based side-channel attack in time-frequency representations. By exploiting time-frequency patterns and extracting high level key-related features in spectrograms simultaneously, we aim to maximize the potential of convolutional neural networks in profiled attacks. Firstly, an effective network architecture is deployed to perform successful attacks. Secondly, some critical parameters in spectrogram are studied for better training the network. Moreover, we compare Template Attacks and CNN-based attacks in both time and time-frequency domain with public datasets. The heuristic results in these experiments provide a new perspective that CNN-based attacks in spectrograms give a very feasible option to the state-of-the-art profiled attacks.

Keywords: Side-Channel Attacks · Time-frequency analysis ·
Spectrogram · Convolutional neural networks · Deep learning

1 Introduction

Side-Channel Attacks (SCAs), introduced in 1996 by Paul Kocher [16], have become a serious threat to practical security of cryptographic devices. They exploit side-channel leakages, such as power consumption and electromagnetic radiation, to recover the secret information of cryptographic algorithm implemented in a physical device. Side-Channel Attacks can be divided into two classes: non-profiled attacks, such as Differential Power Analysis (DPA) [17], Correlation Power Analysis (CPA) [4] and Mutual Information Analysis (MIA) [11],

© Springer Nature Switzerland AG 2019
B. Bilgin and J.-B. Fischer (Eds.): CARDIS 2018, LNCS 11389, pp. 1–17, 2019.
https://doi.org/10.1007/978-3-030-15462-2_1

and profiled attacks, such as Template Attacks (TA) [6] and Stochastic Attacks (SA) [30].

Among all the SCAs, profiled attacks are recognized as the most powerful ones and play a fundamental role of security evaluation of cryptographic algorithm implementations. A profiled attack consists of two phases: the profiling phase and the attack phase. For the profiling phase, the attacker procures a copy of the target device and learns the unique physical leakage characteristics with known keys. For the attack phase, the attacker attempts to recover the unknown key in the target device with the help of profiled leakage details. Among profiled attacks, TA is the most popular profiling approach. But in real profiled attacks, the dependency of preprocessing (need trace alignment), difficulties of numerical problems (need careful calculation) and curse of dimensionality (need dimension reduction) together affect the performance of TA [8].

Recently, a line of machine learning (ML), especially deep learning (DL) based attacks, raises SCA community's concern [5,14,21,24–26,28]. In 2016, Maghrebi et al. conducted the first analysis of deep learning techniques for profiled attacks [21]. In 2017, Cagli et al. found that convolutional neural network (CNN) based profiled attacks are robust to trace deformation like jitter due to CNN's translation invariance [5]. In 2018, Prouff et al. studied how hyperparameters affect deep learning based attacks in the presence of masking and desynchronization [26]. Picek et al. considered the class imbalance problem when training ML/DL models [24]. Robyns et al. proposed a Correlation Optimization method to improve Correlation Electromagnetic Analysis (CEMA) [28].

Generally, the SCAs including TA and deep learning based attacks are usually performed in the time domain and less in frequency domain. Because the side-channel measurements (traces) are usually acquired in waveform, most attacks focus on analysing raw traces. But there are still several works proving that SCA in frequency has its own advantages in non-profiled attacks [10,20,22,28]. Normally, directly analysing traces in time domain is less efficient while the traces are misaligned. To transform traces from time domain to frequency domain, a Fourier transform is performed. But the Fourier transform is only able to retrieve the global frequency content of a signal, thus more irrelevant information will be included and the time information is lost [10]. To overcome this shortcoming, short-time Fourier transform (STFT) is an optional approach. STFT computes the Fourier transform over windowed trace segmentation and shifts window over the trace. Previous work shows that CPA can be used on spectrograms (squared magnitude of STFT) [15]. In the field of image processing, CNN processes 2D signal better because it handles features in two dimension (2D) simultaneously. We inspire by the success of CNN in these areas and aim to perform successful profiled attacks based on CNN in spectrograms.

In this paper, we propose a novel deep learning based SCAs method with raw traces in time-frequency representations. In our work, we transform traces into spectrograms as the first step, then use CNN to learn time-frequency 2D patterns and extract high level key-related features. Effective network architecture is deployed to perform successful attacks. Furthermore, we study the relationship between some critical parameters (leakage patterns and window size) in spectrograms and the network performance. Finally, we demonstrate the effectiveness of our proposed method by comparing TA and CNN-based attacks in both time and time-frequency domain with public datasets.

2   Preliminaries

2.1   Notations

Let $\mathbf{x} = \{\mathbf{x}_i | i = 1, 2, \ldots, N\}$ denote side-channel leakage acquisitions (traces) from a certain physical device, where $\mathbf{x}_i$ denotes a single trace corresponding to one cryptographic calculation. Notice that $\mathbf{x}_i$ is an one-dimension (1D) time sequence vector and the i-th entry of the vector $\mathbf{x}$ is denoted by $\mathbf{x}[i]$. Let $\mathbf{X} = \{\mathbf{X}_i | i = 1, 2, \ldots, N\}$ denote the spectrogram representation of $\mathbf{x}$. Notice that $\mathbf{X}_i = \text{STFT}(\mathbf{x}_i)$ is a two-dimension (2D) time-frequency image metrix and the i, j-th entry of the matrix $\mathbf{X}$ is denoted by $\mathbf{X}[i, j]$. During the acquisition, a target sensitive variable $V = f(T, K)$ is handled, where T denotes plaintext or ciphertext, K the part of secret key the attacker aims to retrieve and f some transform functions (not mainly concerned in this paper). T is uniformly distributed which guarantees the randomness of corresponding measurement $\mathbf{x}$.

2.2   Spectrogram

The short-time Fourier transform (STFT) is a ubiquitous tool for signal analysis and processing. As the signal is analysed in the frequency domain, it overcomes the time-domain limitations. Moreover, STFT can provide a precise time-frequency resolution within a specified window of the fixed size. In practice, the procedure for computing STFT is to divide a long time signal into several shorter segments of equal length and then compute the discrete time Fourier transform (DTFT) separately on each segment. Indeed, the STFT is usually computed with overlapping analysis windows, which introduces dependencies between adjacent windows and reduce artifacts at the boundary. In the discrete case, STFT function could be expressed as Eq. (1):

$$\text{STFT}\{x[n]\}(m, \omega) \equiv X(m, \omega) = \sum_{n=-\infty}^{\infty} x[n]w[n - mH]e^{-j\omega n}, \qquad (1)$$

where $X(m, \omega)$ is DTFT of windowed data, $x[n]$ is input signal at time n, $w[n]$ is window function, ω is phrase, m is position of window and H is an overlap constant between successive windows. In time-frequency signal processing, it is a common practice to work only with the magnitude of the STFT of a signal, so the phase information is ignored as in Eq. (2):

$$\text{spectrogram}\{x[n]\}(m, \omega) \equiv |X(m, \omega)|^2. \qquad (2)$$

In other words, spectrogram is the visual representation of the energy of a signal expressed as a function of frequency and time. For the sake of clarity, an illustration of trace and spectrogram is shown in Fig. 1, the spectrogram in (b) is the energy of STFT function.

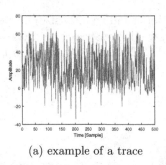
(a) example of a trace

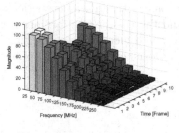
(b) example of a spectrogram

Fig. 1. An example of trace and spectrogram. The spectrogram is the magnitude of STFT (A bar graph is used here to show the 2D spectrogram intuitively).

2.3   Profiled Side-Channel Attacks

A profiled attack consists of two phases: an offline profiling phase (training in machine learning context), and an online attack phase (testing respectively).

In profiling phase, the attacker has a device with knowledge about the secret key implemented and acquires a set of N side-channel traces $\mathbf{x}_{profiling} = \{\mathbf{x}_i | i = 1, 2, \ldots, N\}$. Each trace $\mathbf{x}_i$ is corresponding to $v_i = f(t_i, k)$ in one encryption or decryption with known key k. Usually the traces are measured from power consumption or electromagnetic radiation using probes with an oscilloscope. Once the acquisition is done, the attacker builds suitable models and computes the estimation of probability:

$$\Pr[\mathbf{x}|V = v], \tag{3}$$

from a profiling set $\{\mathbf{x}_i, v_i\}_{i=1,2,\ldots,N}$.

In the attack phase, the attacker acquires a small new set of traces $\mathbf{x}_{attack} = \{\mathbf{x}_i | i = 1, 2, \ldots, M\}$ with a fixed unknown key k^*. With the help of the established models, the attacker can easily calculate the estimated posterior probabilities among k guesses following the Maximum Likelihood Criterion:

$$d_k = \prod_{i=1}^{M} \Pr[v_i = f(t_i, k) | \mathbf{x} = \mathbf{x}_i] = \prod_{i=1}^{M} \frac{\Pr[\mathbf{x} = \mathbf{x}_i | v_i = f(t_i, k)] \cdot \Pr[v_i = f(t_i, k)]}{\Pr[\mathbf{x} = \mathbf{x}_i]}. \tag{4}$$

Equation (4) stands only when acquisitions are independent which is a practical condition in reality.

The most widely used profiled attacks are Template Attacks (TA) [6] and its modified version Efficient Template Attacks (ETA) [9]. In TA, the attacker estimates conditional probability Eq. (3) by assuming that $\mathbf{x}$ follows a multivariate Gaussian distribution and estimating the mean trace $\bar{\mathbf{x}}_{t_i,k}$ and the covariance matrix $\Sigma_{t_i,k}$ for each possible (t_i, k) pair. Equation (3) then turns into:

$$\Pr[\mathbf{x}|V = v] = \frac{\exp(-\frac{1}{2} \cdot (\bar{\mathbf{x}} - \mathbf{x})^T \cdot \Sigma^{-1} \cdot (\bar{\mathbf{x}} - \mathbf{x}))}{\sqrt{(2\pi)^N \cdot |\Sigma|}}. \tag{5}$$

In ETA, the attacker replaces the covariance matrixes with one pooled covariance matrix to cope with some statistical difficulties [9].

2.4   Convolutional Neural Networks

Convolutional Neural Networks (CNN) are a category of neural networks with advantages including being similar to the human visual processing system, being highly optimized in structure for processing images, and being effective at learning and extracting abstractions of features [2]. In this section, we will introduce basic concepts of CNN.

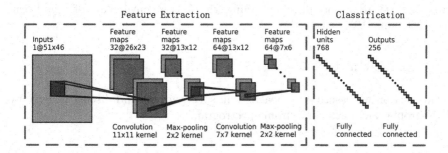

Fig. 2. The overall architecture of CNN

Figure 2 shows an overall architecture of CNN with two main parts: feature extractor and classifier. Feature extractor is composed of stacked operations of convolution, activation, pooling and sometimes normalization layers. The classifier is composed of several fully-connected layers of neurons. Each layer of the network receives the output from its immediate previous layer as its input, and passes its output as the input to the next layer, as it is called forward propagation. Higher-level features are derived from features propagated from lower level layers and finally calculate classification probabilities in the last output layer (for a classification task, usually the output layer is activated by softmax function as detailed in [5]).

Convolutional Layer. Convolutional layer is locally connected with shared weights in learnable kernels. Convolutional operation can be defined as:

$$s(t) \equiv (x * w)(t) = \sum_{a=1}^{n} x(a)w(t - a),\qquad(6)$$

where x are digital signals, w is the kernel function. Stride also affects Eq. (6) by controlling the step length of convolutional operation. The convolutional operations bring sparse connectivity and weight sharing. These properties reduce parameter amounts and computing time. The output of convolutional layers finally go through a non-linear activation function to simulate a biological neuron functionality. The activation adopted in this paper is Rectified Linear Unit (ReLU): $y = max(0, x)$ [18].

Pooling Layer. Pooling layer performs the downsampled operations to keep useful features and discard unnecessary details [3]. It helps represent translation invariance. The pooling kernel also slides window on the signal. For example, if a 2×2 max-pooling kernel with 2×2 strides is used, it outputs the maximum values within the window. Finally, the output size will be half of the input size.

Through training CNN, Backward Propagation algorithm is used with optimizer, such as SGD, Adagrad, AdaDelta, RMSprop, and Adam [29]. In this paper, we use Adam for efficient training with better convergence of deep learning algorithms [19].

3   Our Method

In this section we describe the leakages in spectrograms and discuss how to use CNN profiling and attacking from spectrograms.

3.1   Leakages in Spectrograms

In Sect. 2.2 we describe the mathematical definition of STFT and show a quick look of spectrogram. As STFT indicates the spectral content of the signal at each short time segment, it is a function of time and frequency that indicates how the spectral content of a signal evolves over time. Sliding windows are moved to obtain the spectral content of the signal over different time intervals, and the window length affects the time frequency resolution of the STFT. A small window results in a fine time resolution but a coarse frequency resolution because small windows have a short time duration but a wide bandwidth. A large window, on the contrary, results in a fine frequency resolution but a coarse time resolution because large windows have a long time duration but a narrow frequency bandwidth.

In profiling phase, as the sensitive value $V = f(T, K)$ is related to the secret key, the attacker often uses statistical tools to locate the sensitive value position among discrete digital sample points. Such tools include Pearson correlation coefficient: $\rho_{x,v} = \frac{\text{cov}(x,v)}{\sigma_x \cdot \sigma_v}$ and Signal Noise Ratio (SNR): $snr_{x,v} = \frac{\text{Var}[\text{E}[x|v]]}{\text{E}[\text{Var}[x|v]]}$. By repetitively computing above equations through all sample points over raw trace set $\mathbf{x}_{profiling}$, leakage points (points of interest, PoI) stand out from sample points with high ρ or snr.

We transfer these statistical tools detecting leakages in 2D spectrograms and find leakage existing in spectral-temporal patterns within expectation. Specifically, we calculate ρ and snr through each sample point (pixel) in the 2D spectrogram. For example, spectrogram set $\mathbf{X} = \{\mathbf{X}_i | i = 1, 2, \ldots, N\}$ is first calculated using Eq. (1) from raw trace set $\mathbf{x} = \{\mathbf{x}_i | i = 1, 2, \ldots, N\}$, where $\mathbf{X}_i$

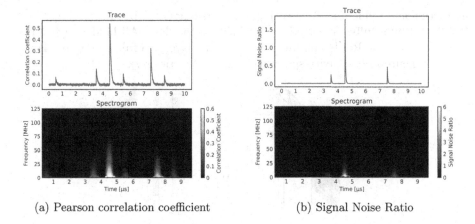

(a) Pearson correlation coefficient   (b) Signal Noise Ratio

Fig. 3. Leakage detection of traces and spectrograms in Grizzly dataset (Color figure online)

is a matrix. After pixel-wise leakage detection, correlation coefficient matrix and SNR matrix can be obtained.

Figure 3 shows the leakage characteristics in traces and spectrograms from Grizzly dataset (detailed in Sect. 4.1). In both subfigures, the upper part is the normal leakage detection result of traces, the lower part is the result of spectrograms in the form of heat map. In heat maps, connected regions in white and yellow are dramatically distinguished from others in black, where brighter color corresponds to high numerical value of ρ and snr. Leakage in spectrogram is detected in warm regions, which reveals the fact that spectrogram contains the time-frequency leakage simultaneously. Time synchronization can be found in the upper and lower parts of the figure, while the difference between the raw trace and spectrogram leakages is that the leakages on the spectrogram form clusters on the two-dimensional plane. This simultaneity reflects in unique 2D image patterns which is quite suitable for CNN to classify.

3.2 Builds CNN with Spectrograms

In this section, the 2D CNN network architecture is described in detail. We refer to some classic CNN architectures such as AlexNet [18] and VGGNet [31] to build our network. As shown in Fig. 4, the spectrograms are fed to the network, and the label of the spectrogram is the key-related sensitive variable. It is passed through a 2D convolutional layer, where we use filters with a small receptive field to extract features. In order to minimize information loss in the time and frequency dimensions, we set the convolution kernel size of equal width and height. The convolution operation extract patterns simultaneously on time and frequency. After the convolutional layer, a max-pooling layer is added with stride 2×2 to downsample the time-frequency feature map. Then the combination of convolutional layer and pooling layer is performed once more for further feature extraction and reduction of network parameters amount. The max-pooling layer is followed by a fully-connected layer to flatten the data. All hidden layers are equipped with the ReLU non-linearity. The final layer is a fully-connected layer with 256 neuron nodes, corresponding to 256 categories respectively.

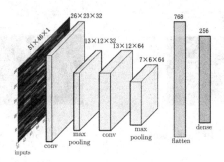

Fig. 4. A base network architecture for 2D CNN with spectrograms

4   Experiments

In this work, all experiments are conducted on an Intel(R) Xeon(R) CPU E5-2667 v3 @ 3.20 GHz 32 core machine, one NVIDIA Tesla K80 GPU and two NVIDIA Titan Xp GPUs. We use the Keras library [7] (version 2.1.3) with TensorFlow library [1] (version 1.4.1) as backend for CNN linked to NVIDIA CuDNN.

4.1   Datasets

We consider three public datasets which mainly differ from implementations. All the datasets are made public exclusively for SCA research. We use these datasets for reproducibility of our results.

DPA contest V4.1 (DPAv4.1) provides measurement of a masked software implementation of AES-256 on an Atmel ATMega-163 smart-card [34]. For the acquisitions, we have 125 points per clock. We preselect consecutive 500 points for each trace. In our experiment, we use the first round S-box output as the label to train CNN:

$$V = \text{Sbox}[P \oplus k^*] \oplus M, \tag{7}$$

where P is a plaintext byte, M is a known mask byte. Since all AES intermediate variables are defined in Galois field $GF(2^8)$, label V contains 256 classes.

Grizzly provides measurement of an unprotected implementation of the 8-bit CPU Atmel XMEGA 256 A3U [23]. In our experiments, we have 1000 points per clock. We preselect consecutive 2500 points for each trace. Our goal is to determine the success of the profiled attacks in recovering the byte k processed. The S-box output V is the label to train CNN, which is provided in the dataset.

DPA contest V2 (DPAv2) provides measurement of an unprotected hardware implementation of the AES-128 algorithm on SASEBO GII FPGA board [33]. There are roughly 213 points per clock. We preselect consecutive 1000 points for each trace. Since the parallel block cipher encryption is implemented, DPAv2 is a difficult dataset to attack. Previous works showed the most suitable leakage operation is the register writing in the last round:

$$V = \text{Sbox}^{-1}[C_1 \oplus k^*] \oplus C_2, \tag{8}$$

where C_1 and C_2 are two ciphertext bytes. In our experiments, C_1 is the 12-th ciphertext byte and C_2 is the 8-th one according to [25].

4.2   Evaluation Method

In this paper, evaluation metrics like top-1 accuracy (Acc), top-3 accuracy (Top3 Acc), success rate (SR) and guessing entropy (GE) are used to evaluate the effectiveness of key retrieval. For SR and GE as detailed in [32], we run the attack 100 times with randomly selected sub-samples of $\mathcal{D}_{validate}$ or $\mathcal{D}_{attack}$ to find the average number of traces to achieve GE<1 bit and SR>80%. We run a 10-fold cross-validation on $\mathcal{D}_{profiling}$ to determine the STFT window size, and a normal training and attack on $\mathcal{D}_{profiling}$ and $\mathcal{D}_{attack}$ to compare different profiled attacks.

4.3   Preprocessing

For each dataset, we preselect a continuous segmentation of all sample points to reduce computing complexity. Then we perform STFT on each dataset with customized window size through exhaustive search for better attacking performances, detailed in Sect. 4.5. Just as the normal SCA and deep learning approach, we split each dataset into 2 distinct part $\mathcal{D}_{profiling}$ and $\mathcal{D}_{attack}$. While in training phase, the $\mathcal{D}_{profiling}$ is further divided into 2 parts $\mathcal{D}_{train}$ and $\mathcal{D}_{validate}$, where the validation set $\mathcal{D}_{validate}$ serves as an indicator of early stopping to avoid overfitting. Table 1 shows the data splitting size in each dataset.

Table 1. Data splitting size in 3 datasets

Dataset	Profiling	Attack
DPAv4.1	9000	1000
Grizzly	51200	10000
DPAv2	90000	10000

Finally, before training the networks, a Min-max normalization $\frac{X - X_{min}}{X_{max} - X_{min}}$ is performed to scale features into $[0, 1]$ range, which will avoid gradient problems in network training phase. Notice that data augmentation [5,24,27] is not performed in our experiments, because the purpose of our experiments is to determine the validity of utilizing spectrograms, not to solve misalignment or jitter problems. And also there are no class imbalance issues since we consider identity function to generate the label.

4.4   CNN Architecture

The signal, represented by 1D raw traces or 2D spectrograms, is feed-forwarded through CNN layers. The feature extraction part includes one or more operations: convolutional filter, activation, batch normalization and pooling [5,21]. Convolutional stride is set to 1 and zero-padding is used to prevent valid operation in the edge of feature map. The pooling stride is set to 2 for downsampling layer input size and the parameter amount of next layer. The classification part contains a stack of layers followed by several fully-connected layers with ReLU. A dropout rate of 50% is between the last 2 fully-connected layers to prevent overfitting. Sometimes a global max-pooling is used to downsample feature map in each channel to reduce the parameter size of fully-connected layers. The last fully-connected layer contains 256 neurons activated by softmax function, calculating the classification score. The cross-entropy is used as loss function.

The 2D CNN basic architecture is illustrated in Sect. 3.2. The design of neural architecture is under an overall consideration among previous works [5,18,21,26]. The detailed architecture is slightly different between 3 datasets in the number of convolutional layers and pooling layers. For DPAv4.1 and Grizzly, since they are software implementations and the data amount is small, fewer convolution operations and small filters (size 3 and 5) are performed. For DPAv2, since it is an FPGA implementation, more convolutional operations and large filters (size 11) are used to enlarge receptive field against high sampling rate, and improve the feature extracting robustness against noises.

To train a proper network, several techniques are used to prevent overfitting and get better network generalization. The Adam optimizer with reduced learning rate is used to minimize the cross-entropy corresponds to maximize the likelihood of the right label. A mini batch of 200 is employed. The learning rate is initially 0.001 and reduced to half when the loss doesn't decrease for 10 epochs with a threshold of 0.0001. We set 200 epochs for the training, but also set an early stopping threshold of 40 epochs (which monitors the validation loss and stops the training if the loss doesn't fall). During the training, the network kernel weights are recorded for the best validation loss. Once the training is done we reconstruct the neuron network with the best recorded weights. With higher values for training epochs, overfitting occurs and no improvements have been noticed. The weight of filters activated by ReLU is randomly initialized with Gaussian distribution $N(0, \sqrt{\frac{2}{n_l}})$ according to [12], where n_l is the neuron number of previous layer.

4.5   Spectrogram Parameters

In this work, a single trace is segmented in several windows with overlap of 90%. We set the overlap for 90%, because it doesn't impact the real time-frequency resolution and more importantly would benefit for software implementations which have stronger but sparser leakage signals [35], such as Grizzly. The Hanning window is used to segment traces as a common choice. The STFT of each window is calculated in order to find square of the magnitude of dominating frequency. Then we scale the spectrogram images to $[0, 1]$ range for the convenience of network training as described before.

In STFT, small window size results in high time resolution but low frequency resolution, and vice versa in large window size scenario. Because of the trade-off between time and frequency in STFT, spectrogram can not guarantee both high time and frequency resolution. As each dataset is measured in different implementations running frequencies and sampling rates, we introduce both absolute window size (window length) and relative window size (percentage of one clock) to represent window size. To find an optimal window size for SCA on spectrogram, an exhaustive search is used to determine window size, evaluated by a 10-fold cross-validation on the profiling set $\mathcal{D}_{profiling}$. We evaluate the robustness of window size configuration by calculating the average evaluation metrics on 10 validation sets.

Table 2 shows the cross-validation evaluation results on $\mathcal{D}_{profiling}$ with the help of 2 NVIDIA Titan Xp GPUs. It takes 3 h for DPAv4.1, 6 h for Grizzly and 8 h for DPAv2 to run the cross-validation algorithms, roughly 3 min, 6 min and 8 min for a single training. In DPAv4.1, a window size of 64 (1/2 of a clock) achieves the best accuracy where a single spectrogram (Spc for short) has an average success rate of 95.9%. Since DPAv4.1 is a software implementation on a smart card, the noise is much lower than other two datasets. The leakages distribute in large range of time and frequency with high SNR. Window size influences the attack so little that similar accuracy is achieved with various window sizes. In Grizzly, when the window size is set to 125 (1/8 of a clock), the network loss converges to 3.74 and 8.49% accuracy is achieved. It takes only 3 traces for GE under 1 bit and 4 traces for SR more than 80%. When the window goes larger or smaller, more traces are needed accordingly. Same phenomenon occurs in DPAv2 dataset where proper windows size (100, 1/2 of a clock) results in better performances—averaging 700 traces to achieve SR over 80%. Large window (200 or 300) brings a coarse time resolution which explains the decline in performances. Furthermore, small window (less than 50) leads to profiling failure, thus no guarantee of successful key recovery.

As a matter of fact, the choice of window size is conditioned by two limitations: (1) the window length should be small enough (better within a clock length) so that the windowed trace segmentation is essentially stationary over the window interval, (2) the window length should be large enough (better more than 64) so that the DTFT of the windowed trace segmentation provides a reasonable frequency resolution. Considering both two constraints empirically, we think window size from 64 to 256 suits most cases in practice. Specifically, balanced

Table 2. Cross-validation averaging results for different window sizes of STFT to perform a 2D CNN-based attack

Window@Percentage		Spc size	Loss	Acc	Top3 Acc	GE < 1	SR > 80%
DPAv4.1	8@1/16	(4,494)	0.159	95.3%	99.6%	1	1
	16@1/8	(8,243)	0.168	94.9%	99.7%	1	1
	32@1/4	(16,181)	0.153	95.2%	99.7%	1	1
	64@1/2	(32,63)	**0.142**	**95.9%**	**99.7%**	1	1
	125@1	(63,29)	0.199	94.1%	99.6%	1	1
	187@3/2	(94,17)	0.195	94.5%	99.5%	1	1
Grizzly	62@1/16	(32,349)	4.08	6.56%	16.86%	5	5
	125@1/8	(63,183)	**3.74**	**8.49%**	**21.28%**	**3**	**4**
	250@1/4	(126,91)	3.76	8.28%	21.07%	3	4
	500@1/2	(251,41)	5.00	2.95%	7.40%	>10	>10
	1000@1	(501,16)	5.51	0.51%	1.53%	>10	>10
	1000@3/2	(751,7)	5.01	1.98%	5.55%	>10	>10
DPAv2	12@1/16	(6,495)	5.544	0.43%	1.29%	>1500	>1500
	25@1/8	(12,326)	5.544	0.43%	1.30%	>1500	>1500
	50@1/4	(25,191)	5.536	0.62%	1.63%	750	750
	100@1/2	(50,91)	**5.536**	**0.65%**	**1.67%**	**700**	**700**
	200@1	(100,41)	5.538	0.60%	1.58%	950	900
	300@3/2	(300,48)	5.538	0.63%	1.60%	950	950

time and frequency resolutions lead to a balanced spectrogram image width and height. On the one hand, a balanced spectrogram size takes both time and frequency into consideration in STFT. On the other hand, a "square" spectrogram image is more suitable for convolution and pooling operations because the filter size and stride are usually designed with same width and height. For example, when the window is 1000 long in Grizzly, the spectrogram size is 501×16, namely high time but low frequency resolution, after 4 convolution layers and pooling layers with downsampling rate 2, the spectrogram size becomes 32×1 which implies redundant frequency information but exhausted temporal information. The imbalance in information utilization probably leads to information loss and profiling failure.

4.6   Attack Comparisons

In this section, by applying the proper STFT window size and network architecture in previous sections, we represent traces into spectrograms and compare different profiled attacks in raw and time-frequency representations.

To exploit leakages in spectrogram and confirm the effectiveness of CNN-based attacks, we evaluate several CNN-based attacks and Template Attacks (as baseline method) in raw traces and spectrograms on each dataset. For clarity, Efficient Template Attacks (ETA) in both spectrograms and traces are performed after a PoI selection (5,25,50 points with highest correlation coefficient). Furthermore, Principal Component Analysis (PCA) [13] is also used before ETA and serves as a reference feature extractor of raw traces and spectrograms. We select top $5, 10, 20, 30$ eigenvectors picking by correlation coefficient to perform ETAs. For CNN-based attacks, to take the most of the profiling set, we random split a small ratio of the data as validation set when training in case of overfitting. Similar network architecture is used for 1D CNN as the same as 2D CNN by replacing 2D operations into 1D operations. 200 epochs (recording the best validation loss during training) are deployed for better convergence.

Table 3. Attack results of our method and baseline methods

Method		DPAv4.1			Grizzly			DPAv2		
		Acc	GE < 1	SR > 0.8	Acc	GE < 1	SR > 0.8	Acc	GE < 1	SR > 0.8
Spc	2D CNN	95.5%	1	1	8.47%	3	4	**0.82%**	**400**	**550**
	ETA,5poi	15.0%	4	3	2.46%	7	5	0.67%	600	550
	ETA,25poi	58.4%	2	2	2.85%	6	6	0.61%	650	750
	ETA,50poi	82.5%	1	1	3.64%	5	5	0.65%	1000	1050
	PCA-ETA	82.5%	1	1	5.75%	5	4	0.59%	650	650
Trc	1D CNN	**96.5%**	1	1	**9.52%**	3	4	0.63%	750	650
	ETA,5poi	1.9%	9	7	2.08%	8	7	0.59%	1500	1500
	ETA,25poi	32.1%	2	2	2.76%	7	6	0.61%	950	1000
	ETA,50poi	63.5%	2	2	2.59%	7	6	0.57%	750	850
	PCA-ETA	86.9%	1	1	4.48%	6	5	0.60%	850	750

The results we obtained are summarized in Table 3 and Fig. 5 (without DPAv4.1 brevity). As for DPAv4.1, CNN-based attack in spectrograms can achieve more than 95% accuracy with a single spectrogram to recover the key byte, which proves the soundness of attacks in spectrograms. Next, we test our methods on Grizzly, an 8 bit MCU software implementation. As it is shown in Table 3 and Fig. 5, ETA in spectrograms get higher accuracy than in raw traces with same PoI number. PCA-ETA also works better in spectrograms than in traces with top 5, 10, 20, 30 eigenvectors picking by correlation coefficient. Meanwhile, CNN-based attacks significantly outperform ETA in both time and time-frequency domain, gaining GE<1 bit with only 3 traces. Finally we challenge our method in DPAv2, which is much more difficult to attack. The result shows that attacks in spectrogram are more effective than in raw traces with same profiling techniques. There, only 400 spectrograms are needed for GE less than 1 bit with the 2D CNN in spectrograms, compared with more than 750 traces with attacks (including 1D CNN) in raw traces. Since in this experiment more traces/spectrograms (nearly all profiling set $\mathcal{D}_{profiling}$) are used for training, and evaluation is performed on $\mathcal{D}_{profiling}$, the neuron network trains with more data than in Sect. 4.5 and gets better performances.

Naturally, spectrogram is a combined representation of time domain and frequency domain. Compared with raw traces in time domain, spectrograms lose

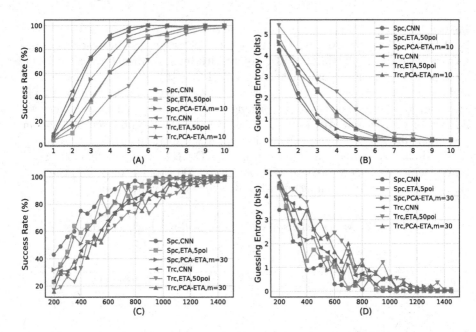

Fig. 5. Results of Grizzly (A, B) and DPAv2 (C, D)

little time resolution but gain frequency resolution. A single pixel in spectrogram contains both time-frequency information than a point in raw traces with higher ρ and snr. This peculiarity shows its advantage if time information is not good enough for a successful attack. Last but not least, as it is observed in Sect. 3.1, PoI in spectrogram show patterns, gathered in clusters along time domain and expanded in low frequency domain. Patterns hide local time-frequency high level features in spectrogram. CNN extracts feature through recognizing patterns, which explains CNN-based attacks exceed ETA because PoI selection destroys 2D time-frequency patterns and ETA itself can't handle these 2D patterns. Therefore, CNN is naturally the choice of attacks in spectrograms.

5   Conclusions

In this paper, we investigate the side-channel leakage in time-frequency representations and propose a new profiling strategy using CNN. Experiments show that by analysing temporal-frequency transformation in spectrogram representation, 2D time-frequency patterns can be utilized for extracting high level features and classified for key recovery. Effects of different window sizes on CNN-based attacks are studied. Compared with classic profiled attacks in 1D raw traces, CNN-based attacks in 2D spectrograms achieve better performances than Template Attacks and at least same effectiveness (sometimes better) as CNN-based attacks in raw traces.

Despite results shown here, there is still room for improvement. Side-channel countermeasures, masking and hiding, are not considered in this work, as this paper focus on pioneering a new profiled side-channel strategy. As STFT is calculated on each independent single trace, masking and hiding are completely reflected in single spectrogram. In other words, leakage existing in high order and random spatial positions, which can be analysed by CNN due to its feature extraction and transformation invariance. Future works will study CNN based attacks in time-frequency representations in the presence of masking and hiding countermeasures.

Acknowledgment. This work is supported in part by Natural Science Foundation of China (No. 61632020, 61472416 and 61602468), National Key Research and Development Program of China (No. 2017YFB0802705) and the National Cryptography Development Fund under Grant MMJJ 20180223.

References

1. Abadi, M., et al.: Tensorflow: a system for large-scale machine learning. OSDI **16**, 265–283 (2016)
2. Alom, M.Z., et al.: The history began from alexnet: a comprehensive survey on deep learning approaches. CoRR abs/1803.01164 (2018)
3. Boureau, Y., Ponce, J., LeCun, Y.: A theoretical analysis of feature pooling in visual recognition. In: Proceedings of the 27th International Conference on Machine Learning (ICML-2010), 21–24 June 2010, Haifa, Israel, pp. 111–118 (2010)
4. Brier, E., Clavier, C., Olivier, F.: Correlation power analysis with a leakage model. In: Joye, M., Quisquater, J.-J. (eds.) CHES 2004. LNCS, vol. 3156, pp. 16–29. Springer, Heidelberg (2004). https://doi.org/10.1007/978-3-540-28632-5_2
5. Cagli, E., Dumas, C., Prouff, E.: Convolutional neural networks with data augmentation against jitter-based countermeasures. In: Fischer, W., Homma, N. (eds.) CHES 2017. LNCS, vol. 10529, pp. 45–68. Springer, Cham (2017). https://doi.org/10.1007/978-3-319-66787-4_3
6. Chari, S., Rao, J.R., Rohatgi, P.: Template attacks. In: Kaliski, B.S., Koç, K., Paar, C. (eds.) CHES 2002. LNCS, vol. 2523, pp. 13–28. Springer, Heidelberg (2003). https://doi.org/10.1007/3-540-36400-5_3
7. Chollet, F., et al.: Keras (2015). https://keras.io
8. Choudary, M.O., Kuhn, M.G.: Efficient, portable template attacks. IEEE Trans. Inf. Forensics Secur. **13**(2), 490–501 (2018). https://doi.org/10.1109/TIFS.2017.2757440
9. Choudary, O., Kuhn, M.G.: Efficient template attacks. In: Francillon, A., Rohatgi, P. (eds.) CARDIS 2013. LNCS, vol. 8419, pp. 253–270. Springer, Cham (2014). https://doi.org/10.1007/978-3-319-08302-5_17
10. Debande, N., Souissi, Y., Elaabid, M.A., Guilley, S., Danger, J.: Wavelet transform based pre-processing for side channel analysis. In: 45th Annual IEEE/ACM International Symposium on Microarchitecture, MICRO 2012, Workshops Proceedings, Vancouver, BC, Canada, 1–5 December 2012, pp. 32–38 (2012). https://doi.org/10.1109/MICROW.2012.15
11. Gierlichs, B., Batina, L., Tuyls, P., Preneel, B.: Mutual information analysis. In: Oswald, E., Rohatgi, P. (eds.) CHES 2008. LNCS, vol. 5154, pp. 426–442. Springer, Heidelberg (2008). https://doi.org/10.1007/978-3-540-85053-3_27

12. He, K., Zhang, X., Ren, S., Sun, J.: Delving deep into rectifiers: surpassing human-level performance on imagenet classification. In: 2015 IEEE International Conference on Computer Vision, ICCV 2015, Santiago, Chile, 7–13 December 2015, pp. 1026–1034 (2015). https://doi.org/10.1109/ICCV.2015.123

13. Jolliffe, I.: Principal component analysis. In: Lovric, M. (ed.) International Encyclopedia of Statistical Science, pp. 1094–1096. Springer, Heidelberg (2011). https://doi.org/10.1007/978-3-642-04898-2_455

14. Kim, J., Picek, S., Heuser, A., Bhasin, S., Hanjalic, A.: Make some noise: unleashing the power of convolutional neural networks for profiled side-channel analysis. IACR Cryptology ePrint Archive 2018, 1023 (2018)

15. Kim, M., Han, D., Ryoo, J.C., Yi, O.: CPA performance enhancement based on spectrogram. In: IEEE International Carnahan Conference on Security Technology, ICCST 2012, Newton, MA, USA, 15–18 October 2012, pp. 195–200 (2012). https://doi.org/10.1109/CCST.2012.6393558

16. Kocher, P.C.: Timing attacks on implementations of Diffie-Hellman, RSA, DSS, and other systems. In: Koblitz, N. (ed.) CRYPTO 1996. LNCS, vol. 1109, pp. 104–113. Springer, Heidelberg (1996). https://doi.org/10.1007/3-540-68697-5_9

17. Kocher, P., Jaffe, J., Jun, B.: Differential power analysis. In: Wiener, M. (ed.) CRYPTO 1999. LNCS, vol. 1666, pp. 388–397. Springer, Heidelberg (1999). https://doi.org/10.1007/3-540-48405-1_25

18. Krizhevsky, A., Sutskever, I., Hinton, G.E.: Imagenet classification with deep convolutional neural networks. In: Advances in Neural Information Processing Systems 25: 26th Annual Conference on Neural Information Processing Systems 2012, Proceedings of a Meeting Held 3–6 December 2012, Lake Tahoe, Nevada, United States, pp. 1106–1114 (2012)

19. Le, Q.V., Ngiam, J., Coates, A., Lahiri, A., Prochnow, B., Ng, A.Y.: On optimization methods for deep learning. In: Proceedings of the 28th International Conference on Machine Learning, ICML 2011, Bellevue, Washington, USA, 28 June–2 July 2011, pp. 265–272 (2011)

20. Longo, J., De Mulder, E., Page, D., Tunstall, M.: SoC It to EM: electromagnetic side-channel attacks on a complex system-on-chip. In: Güneysu, T., Handschuh, H. (eds.) CHES 2015. LNCS, vol. 9293, pp. 620–640. Springer, Heidelberg (2015). https://doi.org/10.1007/978-3-662-48324-4_31

21. Maghrebi, H., Portigliatti, T., Prouff, E.: Breaking cryptographic implementations using deep learning techniques. In: Carlet, C., Hasan, M.A., Saraswat, V. (eds.) SPACE 2016. LNCS, vol. 10076, pp. 3–26. Springer, Cham (2016). https://doi.org/10.1007/978-3-319-49445-6_1

22. Mateos, E., Gebotys, C.H.: A new correlation frequency analysis of the side channel. In: Proceedings of the 5th Workshop on Embedded Systems Security, WESS 2010, Scottsdale, AZ, USA, 24 October 2010, p. 4 (2010). https://doi.org/10.1145/1873548.1873552

23. Omar Choudary, M.G.K.: Grizzly: power-analysis traces for an 8-bit load instruction. https://www.cl.cam.ac.uk/research/security/datasets/grizzly/. Accessed Oct 2017

24. Picek, S., Heuser, A., Jovic, A., Bhasin, S., Regazzoni, F.: The curse of class imbalance and conflicting metrics with machine learning for side-channel evaluations. IACR Trans. Cryptogr. Hardw. Embed. Syst. **2019**(1), 209–237 (2019). https://doi.org/10.13154/tches.v2019.i1.209-237

25. Picek, S., Samiotis, I.P., Kim, J., Heuser, A., Bhasin, S., Legay, A.: On the performance of convolutional neural networks for side-channel analysis. In: Chattopadhyay, A., Rebeiro, C., Yarom, Y. (eds.) SPACE 2018. LNCS, vol. 11348, pp. 157–176. Springer, Cham (2018). https://doi.org/10.1007/978-3-030-05072-6_10
26. Prouff, E., Strullu, R., Benadjila, R., Cagli, E., Dumas, C.: Study of deep learning techniques for side-channel analysis and introduction to ASCAD database. IACR Cryptology ePrint Archive 2018, 53 (2018)
27. Pu, S., et al.: Trace augmentation: what can be done even before preprocessing in a profiled SCA? In: Eisenbarth, T., Teglia, Y. (eds.) CARDIS 2017. LNCS, vol. 10728, pp. 232–247. Springer, Cham (2018). https://doi.org/10.1007/978-3-319-75208-2_14
28. Robyns, P., Quax, P., Lamotte, W.: Improving CEMA using correlation optimization. IACR Trans. Cryptogr. Hardw. Embed. Syst. **2019**(1), 1–24 (2019). https://doi.org/10.13154/tches.v2019.i1.1-24
29. Ruder, S.: An overview of gradient descent optimization algorithms. CoRR abs/1609.04747 (2016)
30. Schindler, W., Lemke, K., Paar, C.: A stochastic model for differential side channel cryptanalysis. In: Rao, J.R., Sunar, B. (eds.) CHES 2005. LNCS, vol. 3659, pp. 30–46. Springer, Heidelberg (2005). https://doi.org/10.1007/11545262_3
31. Simonyan, K., Zisserman, A.: Very deep convolutional networks for large-scale image recognition. CoRR abs/1409.1556 (2014)
32. Standaert, F.-X., Malkin, T.G., Yung, M.: A unified framework for the analysis of side-channel key recovery attacks. In: Joux, A. (ed.) EUROCRYPT 2009. LNCS, vol. 5479, pp. 443–461. Springer, Heidelberg (2009). https://doi.org/10.1007/978-3-642-01001-9_26
33. TELECOM ParisTech SEN Research Group: DPA Contest (2nd edition) (2009–2010). http://www.DPAcontest.org/v2/
34. TELECOM ParisTech SEN Research Group: DPA Contest (4th edition) (2013–2014). http://www.DPAcontest.org/v4/
35. Zhang, L., Ding, A.A., Fei, Y., Luo, P.: Efficient 2nd-order power analysis on masked devices utilizing multiple leakage. In: IEEE International Symposium on Hardware Oriented Security and Trust, HOST 2015, Washington, DC, USA, 5–7 May 2015, pp. 118–123 (2015). https://doi.org/10.1109/HST.2015.7140249

A Systematic Study of the Impact of Graphical Models on Inference-Based Attacks on AES

Joey Green[(✉)], Arnab Roy, and Elisabeth Oswald

Department of Computer Science, University of Bristol,
Merchant Venturers Building, Woodland Road, Bristol BS8 1UB, UK
{joey.green,arnab.roy,elisabeth.oswald}@bristol.ac.uk

Abstract. Belief propagation, or the sum-product algorithm, is a powerful and well known method for inference on probabilistic graphical models, which has been proposed for the specific use in side channel analysis by Veyrat-Charvillon et al. [14].

We define a novel metric to capture the *importance* of variable nodes in factor graphs, we propose two improvements to the sum-product algorithm for the specific use case in side channel analysis, and we explicitly define and examine different ways of combining information from multiple side channel traces. With these new considerations we systematically investigate a number of graphical models that "naturally" follow from an implementation of AES. Our results are unexpected: neither a larger graph (i.e. more side channel information) nor more connectedness necessarily lead to significantly better attacks. In fact our results demonstrate that in practice the (on balance) best choice is to utilise an acyclic graph in an independent graph combination setting, which gives us provable convergence to the correct key distribution. We provide evidence using both extensive simulations and a final confirmatory analysis on real trace data.

Keywords: Belief propagation · Factor graphs · AES ·
Inference based attacks · Side channel attacks · Template attacks

1 Introduction

Side channels in the form of power or EM traces are a significant source of information for adversaries. Extracting as much as possible of this information is clearly desirable, and the utilisation of graphical models for this purpose was early on described in publications such as [3,6,12]. These papers represented the algorithm under attack as a Markov model and inferred information about the underlying hidden state by using statistical inference, e.g. the max-product algorithm.

The key idea in such types of attacks is that the graphical model defines how variables (observed and hidden) depend on each other. By using different types

B. Bilgin and J.-B. Fischer (Eds.): CARDIS 2018, LNCS 11389, pp. 18–34, 2019.
https://doi.org/10.1007/978-3-030-15462-2_2

of algorithms it is possible to infer information about the hidden variables. The use of the sum-product algorithm (aka belief propagation, BP) on a factor graph was proposed recently in [14] as a way to utilise graphical models for complex algorithms such as AES. It proved to be very powerful: in comparison to other profiled attacks, this method can cope with very noisy side channel traces, and even combine information from many traces effectively. In follow on works this type of attack was compared to other types of DPA style attacks [4], and used in different contexts [13]. Although the method performed well in all these papers, it is well known that there are no guarantees for convergence, or even for the inferred distributions to be at all meaningful. This is due to the nature of the factor graphs that result from a typical implementation of e.g. AES. Thus like many other analysis methods it is possible that the method completely fails in some contexts, but is strong in other contexts.

In this submission we set out to determine how to best configure a graphical model to ensure attack success. We focus our study around the AES algorithm that was also chosen by the seminal papers introducing this method. Our results challenge in particular the intuition that "more" leakage makes for stronger attacks. This is interesting because more leakage intuitively implies more potential information: even if multiple leakages may provide redundant information (it is well known that AES achieves full diffusion after two rounds), this redundant information could be hoped to implicitly improve the signal quality. Consequently, one could expect that the more leakage information about AES is included in a factor graph, the more of this information can propagate to the key bytes.

1.1 Outline of This Paper

We review the necessary background on using (loopy) belief propagation in Sect. 2. Thereafter in Sect. 3 we explain two improvements of the sum-product algorithm. In Sect. 4 we give a novel definition that captures the *importance* of a variable node. We also define several variations of factor graphs of particular interest for attacks on AES. These variations essentially represent progressively smaller graphs, whereby the smallest is an acyclic graph requiring the least memory. For this graph the results guarantee convergence of the sum-product algorithm without any loss of success rate and efficiency. We also spell out three methods for combining multiple traces. Sections 5, 6, and 7 present results of experiments using simulated (we simulate leakage according to a weighted bit model, and add Gaussian noise) and real trace data. We observe that except for the noisiest of cases the acyclic graph with the most pragmatic trace combination method is on par with more complex variations. We conclude with recommendations for practice in Sect. 8.

To aid the flow of the paper we opted to supplying comprehensive tables and figures primarily in the appendix. The text however does summarise the most important findings from both tables and figures. There is also a full version of this work available on the IACR Eprint archive [2].

2   Preliminaries

The key ingredients for the attacks that we aim to study are a suitable graphical model and an algorithm for inference. We review these briefly using and relating them to AES as appropriate (for a more in-depth description we refer the reader to [7]). At the end of this section we provide the necessary details about our simulation environment.

2.1   Inference on Graphical Models

A factor graph is a bipartite graph $G = (\mathcal{V}, \mathcal{F}, \mathcal{E})$ where $\mathcal{V}, \mathcal{F}$ are two finite sets of vertices and $\mathcal{E}$ ($\subset \mathcal{V} \times \mathcal{F}$) is a set of undirected edges. We will refer to the vertices in $\mathcal{V}$ as variable nodes and the vertices in $\mathcal{F}$ as factor nodes. We will use the i, j, k to denote the variable nodes and f, g, h to denote the factor nodes. Given $i \in \mathcal{V}$, the set ∂i is defined as $\partial i := \{f \in \mathcal{F} : (i, f) \in \mathcal{E}\}$. For any $f \in \mathcal{F}$ the adjacent vertices ∂f is defined in the same way.

A factor graph gives the joint distribution of the random variables $\mathbf{X}_{\mathcal{V}} := (X_1, \ldots, X_{|\mathcal{V}|})$ where each X_i corresponds to a vertex in $\mathcal{V}$. For any subset of variable nodes $\mathcal{I} := \{i_1, i_2, \ldots, i_m\} \subset \mathcal{V}$ we will denote the corresponding random variables as $\mathbf{X}_{\mathcal{I}} := (X_{i_1}, X_{i_2}, \ldots, X_{i_m})$. The values of these random variables $\mathbf{x}_{\mathcal{I}}$, are also defined in a similar way. For our application each random variable X_i can have values $x_i \in \mathcal{X} := \{0, 1\}^n$. For the rest of this article $\mathcal{X}$ will denote the set $\{0, 1\}^n$ unless specified otherwise. For the definition of the joint distribution we refer to the full version [2].

Constructing a Factor Graph. A factor graph can be constructed from (the implementation of) any iterative function F[1]. The input variables, intermediate variables used in the iterative function, and the output variables are represented as the variable nodes of the factor graph. The factor nodes correspond to the basic functions/operations used to define (or implement) F. A factor node is usually connected to two or more variable nodes which represent the inputs and outputs of the function.

In practice an AES assembly implementation can be easily translated to a factor graph. The sixteen plaintext bytes and key bytes are represented as variable nodes. Parsing the (assembly) code, whenever an arithmetic operation is performed we add a factor node for this operation, and a new variable node to represent the output of the operation, and connect these elements to the existing graph. Although leaky, we excluded memory operations, such as `ldr` and `str` operations from our factor graph (so we do not artificially inflate leakages). Our AES factor graph thus includes the following factor operations: `XOR`, `SBOX`, and `XTIMES`.

---

[1] A factor graph can also be constructed for non-iterative functions but this is not necessary for our work.

The Sum-Product Algorithm. The sum-product algorithm, also known as the belief propagation (BP) algorithm, is an iterative "message" passing algorithm where the messages are the probability distributions over the single variable space $\mathcal{X}$. For each edge in $\mathcal{E}$ there are two such distributions $\nu_{i \to f}(\cdot)$, which is the message from variable node to factor node and $\tilde{\nu}_{f \to i}(\cdot)$, which is the message from a function node to variable node. The messages at the tth iteration are denoted as $\nu_{i \to f}^{(t)}$ and $\tilde{\nu}_{f \to i}^{(t)}$.

For the definition of the sum-product algorithm, we refer the reader to the full version [2] of this article. When the factor graph is acyclic, the algorithm converges after a fixed number of iterations. When the factor graph contains cycles, it becomes *loopy belief propagation* and no longer has guaranteed convergence. A frequently used heuristic to stop the BP algorithm in such cases is to terminate after t_{max} iterations which is a fixed parameter to the algorithm. Typically one chooses t_{max} in line with the size (i.e. diameter) of the graph. For further details on factor graphs and BP algorithm we refer the interested readers to [7,11].

In our implementation, all variable nodes send their initial distribution along all their connected edges in the first round of the algorithm. Once completed, the factor nodes send their messages, by selecting an adjacent variable node, then collecting all incoming messages (excluding the one from the target variable node) and applying their own 'function' on these messages. They do this for all adjacent variable nodes. Upon termination of the algorithm, the marginal distributions of all sixteen key bytes are computed. This is done by taking the product of each key's initial distribution with all incoming messages to the respective key byte. To judge success of an attack, the keys are ranked according their probability.

2.2   Attack Setup and Implementation Details

The work presented in this paper uses an adaptation of AES FURIOUS (originally written for Atmel's AVR) written in the ARM Thumb assembly language. Our lab setup consists of custom host board with an ARM Cortex-M0 of the LPC series. The board has an on board signal amplifier and filter. We utilise a stable external clock running at 125 MHz. The data is recorded by a PicoScope 2000 Series instrument. We took 150000 traces, of which 120000 were used for template building and 30000 for doing repeat attacks. In any attack the result of the template matching is utilised as the input probability distributions for the (leaky) variable nodes.

Because real trace data implies a fixed device leakage model and a corresponding signal-to-noise ratio (SNR), we also performed two types of simulations with varying SNRs. The first simulation was via using the tool ELMO [10], which emulates the leakage of a Cortex-M0. The emulator was built by profiling a different type of M0, manufactured by ST Micro. Thus we would expect the simulation results (when appropriate levels of Gaussian noise is added) to match our real trace results. We also performed Hamming weight (HW) based simulation, which turned out to give identical results to the ELMO simulations hence we opted to not include them in our tables.

In our implementation we set the value of t_{max} (used by the BP algorithm) to be 50. This value was chosen because it is greater than the diameter of the largest graph G (which has a diameter of 42), and thus gives room for propagation around the loops. For the calculation of first-order success rates (SR) and key ranks, we follow the recommendation of [9] and compute average key ranks over 200 repeat experiments.

3   Improving Loopy Belief Propagation

Different variations of the (loopy) BP algorithm are proposed in the literature. We add our own improvements and explain the resulting algorithm in this section.

3.1   Epsilon Exhaustion

One of the parameters for the Belief Propagation Algorithm is how many iterations to run. This is represented by the value t_{max}. In this paper we propose an additional termination criterion, which allows the algorithm to terminate early, if certain conditions are met. As the BP algorithm is a message passing algorithm, there may come a point after a number of iterations where the messages being updated have received most of the information in the graph, and will not change significantly. If this is detected over a series of consecutive rounds, we can deduce that the factor graph has reached a stable equilibrium, and we can therefore terminate the algorithm without being at risk of discarding useful information.

We implement this by having two user defined parameters, ε and ε_s. After each iteration of the BP algorithm, we observe the incoming messages at the sixteen key byte nodes. If the Euclidean distance between the message from the current iteration and the message from the previous iteration is greater than the threshold ε, we conclude that the current round did not provide the key bytes with enough new information. If this occurs over ε_s consecutive rounds, we conclude that as enough information has propagated, further rounds would not benefit the key bytes, and it is safe to terminate the BP algorithm early.

We used the Euclidean distance metric to measure the difference between two probability distributions after considering other possibilities, see also Sect. 4.1.

3.2   Ground Truth Checking

One open problem encountered in template-based DPA style attacks is differentiating a 'good' trace from a 'bad' one, when it is not simply characterised by a large variance. For instance, even a small clock jitter can slightly misalign a trace in relation to the template values, which typically means that template matching gives very poor results. Due to the nature of the Belief Propagation algorithm, we compute the marginal distribution of the key bytes by taking the product of all their incoming messages (Sect. 2.1). If an erroneous trace is computed in an

---

Algorithm 1. BP algorithm with epsilon exhaustion and ground truth check

---

1 **function** BPA $(\mathcal{G}_{aes}, \varepsilon, \varepsilon_s, \varepsilon_g, t_{max}, k^*, i_p)$

        `/* ` k^*, i_p ` are the variable nodes corresponding to the key and plaintext respectively */`

2   Initialize the messages as i.i.d uniform random variables

3     $count := 0$

4   **foreach** $t \in \{1, \ldots, t_{max}\}$ **do**

5   **foreach** $(i, f) \in \mathcal{E}$ **do**

6   update $\nu_{i \to f}^{(t)}$ with incoming messages

7   **end**

8   **foreach** $(i, f) \in \mathcal{E}$ **do**

9   update $\tilde{\nu}_{f \to i}^{(t)}$ with incoming messages

10   **end**

11   **if** $(k^*, f) \in \mathcal{E}$, $\|\tilde{\nu}_{f \to k^*}^{(t)} - \tilde{\nu}_{f \to k^*}^{(t-1)}\|_\infty < \varepsilon$ **then**

12             $count = count + 1$

13   **if** $count == \varepsilon_s$ **then**

                        `/* Epsilon Exhaustion check */`

14   break

15   **else**

16                 $count = 0$

17   **end**

18   **end**

19   **if** $\|\nu_{f \to i_p} - \mu_{\mathcal{L}}[i_p]\|_\infty < \varepsilon_g$ **then**

                        `/* Ground truth check */`

                `/* ` $\mu_{\mathcal{L}}[i_p]$ ` is the leakage distribution at node ` i_p ` */`

20   **return** 0;

21   **else**

22   **return** -1 `/* Discard trace */`

---

attack, an erroneous distribution sent to a key byte can detrimentally alter the marginal; in a worst case scenario, if the erroneous message has probability 0 for the correct key byte value, the attack will *never* successfully recover the key. In this paper we present a way of detecting an erroneous trace, by considering a known plaintext attack against AES.

Assuming we know the plaintext values, the idea is to check the "belief" about them *after* BP has terminated. We would expect that for a good trace, once all information has propagated through the graph, the belief about the plaintext values would be consistent with what we know to be the true values. If this is not the case, then BP is unlikely to have converged to a meaningful key distribution either. We measure the consistency between the initial distribution of the plaintext bytes and the distribution after BP using the Euclidean distance (as with the termination criterion).

For the ground truth check to work we need to assume some leakage on the key bytes in the graph (this may come from the key schedule for instance).

If the probability distribution on the key bytes was uniform (i.e. we assume no information on the key bytes), then, because the key byte nodes are connected to the plaintext byte nodes via an XOR factor node, we could not infer any information about the plaintext byte nodes. This is due to the XOR "locking effect": XOR the acts like a one-time pad if one of the two inputs is uniform.

4   Studying AES FURIOUS Factor Graphs

Previous work already explored the effect of some choices regarding the actual construction of the factor graph for implementations of AES. We are interested whether or not there is a trade-off between the number of included factor nodes and the efficiency of an attack. Utilising fewer nodes is advantageous in practice not only because fewer profiles have to be created (and therefore fewer profiling traces are required) but also because having to correctly match fewer templates during an attack leads to more robust attacks (in practice traces are not perfectly aligned).

Our "base" graph G takes into account all intermediate steps, and we also assume some leakage via the key schedule on the key bytes. We then introduce a measure that is novel in the context of Belief Propagation in the context of side channels to judge the "importance" of a node in relation to the key bytes in Sect. 4.1, and then study reduced graphs systematically in Sect. 4.2.

4.1   Importance of a Variable Node

We want to assess whether or not it is necessary to include all the nodes of the factor graph from the full AES. More specifically, one could wonder what "effect" the information from nodes from the second and further rounds of AES have on the key. It is known that AES reaches full state diffusion after two rounds of AES, but there is no implication that nodes from future rounds provide more or less information than nodes in the first two rounds.

To quantify the "effect" of a node we somehow want to consider its contribution in the detection of the (unknown) key. For an important node we would expect that any change in it's input distribution would result in a change in a key byte(s) distribution.

The effect or importance of a node in the factor graph is quantified by the "distance" of it's distribution from the key node distribution. In the graphical model the variable nodes have an associated (discrete) distribution. Thus it seems natural to look for a suitable distance metric in relation to (discrete) distributions.

We determine the marginal distribution of the key node say K, given the distribution of the other nodes: we thus determine $\mu(K) = \sum_{X_i} \Pr(K, X_1, X_2, \ldots)$ where X_i is the random variable corresponding to the variable node in the factor graph. In the AES factor graph these nodes correspond to the different intermediate variables e.g. k_1, t_1 etc in Fig. 3. In the following paragraph we will refer to a node by the associated random variable.

For a (randomly) fixed unknown key and a fixed plaintext the value of the intermediate variable at the node X_i is also fixed. Suppose we have a perfect leakage corresponding to the different values of the intermediate variable at X_i. This can be described by fixing a value of the random variable $X_i = x$ and $\Pr(X_i = x) = 1$ whereas $\Pr(X_i \neq x) = 0$. For the correct value of X_i, the distribution $\mu_x(K) = \sum_{X_j} \Pr(K, X_1, X_2, \ldots, X_i = x, X_{i+1}, \ldots)$ is expected to be "closer" to μ compared to the distribution obtained by fixing an incorrect value of X_i. For defining this notion of distance between two distribution we use *Hellinger* distance. The Hellinger distance is a well known measure to quantify the similarity of two distributions. In contrast to other (similar) measures it is directly related to the Euclidean distance metric (in the discrete case) and thus is an actual distance metric.

Definition 1. *The importance of a node X is defined as*

$$\mathcal{I}(X) = \{D(\mu(K), \mu_{X=x}(K))\}$$

where $D(\cdot, \cdot)$ is the Hellinger distance between the distributions.

Note that $\mathcal{I}(X)$ is a set of "distances" for different values x of X.

Definition 2. *(**Hellinger Distance**) For two discrete distributions $\{p_i\}$ and $\{q_i\}$ the Hellinger distance is defined as*

$$D(p, q) = \frac{1}{\sqrt{2}} \sqrt{\sum_i (\sqrt{p_i} - \sqrt{q_i})^2}. \tag{1}$$

Because we are in a profiled scenario, we know all the necessary distributions to compute this distance metric for any node in the graph.

4.2   AES Factor Graphs

We now detail the graphs that we study. They range from a "full graph", including nodes for intermediates across all ten AES rounds, to a very sparse graph, including only a few intermediates from the first round. The larger the graph is, the more memory it requires. The memory requirements can be derived based on the number of nodes and edges. All variable nodes store an initial distribution, and each edge has two probability distributions, corresponding to incoming and outgoing messages from the connected variable node. Because AES FURIOUS essentially is byte oriented implementation of AES, all distributions in our graph are represented by 256 floating point values. The exact memory requirements are thus dependent on the specific implementation/use of a float. In the following description we assume the use of a C style floating point data type (four bytes).

G : corresponds to the full AES encryption algorithm. It requires $\approx 6.6\,\mathrm{MB}$ of memory per trace.

G_1 : corresponds to the first encryption round only, excluding the key schedule. We provide (part of) this graph in Fig. 3, which shows the first column of the first round. It requires ≈ 0.7 MB of memory per trace. Several factor nodes are drawn in red in this graph. Removing them leads to G_1^A.

G_2 : corresponds to G_1, with the addition of the Add Round Key step and the SubBytes output of the second round. It requires ≈ 0.9 MB of memory per trace.

G_1^A : corresponds to an acyclic factor graph of the first encryption round, as shown by removing the red nodes in Fig. 3. It requires ≈ 0.54 MB of memory per trace.

G_1^{KS} : corresponds to G_1, with the addition of the key schedule variables. It requires ≈ 0.84 MB of memory per trace.

As an example, to mount a 200 trace BPA attack against graph G, one would require ≈ 1.3 GB memory. To mount an attack using the graphs G_1 and G_1^A one would only need ≈ 140 MB and ≈ 108 MB memory respectively.

Considerations Regarding Node Removal for G_1^A. To convert the one round AES factor graph G_1 into an acyclic graph G_1^A we choose to remove a set of factor nodes which are marked in red in Fig. 3. One obvious reason to choose this set of nodes is that in the AES algorithm these nodes are part of the diffusion layer. Since the diffusion layer causes the cyclic structure of the AES factor graph, removal of these nodes leaves the factor graph acyclic. Removal of any node naturally is followed by the removal of the edges to that node, along with any leaf nodes (which would otherwise be disconnected from the rest of the graph and thus not contributing any messages).

4.3   Combining AES Factor Graphs

In many real world settings adversaries may gain access to several leakage traces. These traces may correspond to different inputs for instance. In any case so far we have only discussed factor graphs that take input (e.g. the plaintext) and thus we now look at ways in which we can process multiple inputs.

Large Factor Graph (LFG) Method. In [14] they approach the problem of combining graphs from different inputs by associating each input with a dedicated graph, and then they produce a "large factor graph" by connecting all factor graphs through some common nodes. In the particular case of AES (the same would apply to other algorithms too), the nodes representing the key bytes are common (because all traces would be for the same unknown secret key). We call this method the LFG Method.

The potential advantage of this method is that information from one trace can propagate through the common nodes into the "adjacent' graph, which may (positively) affect the attack outcome. However, the clear downside to this method is that it potentially incurs a large memory overhead (unless one swaps "subgraphs" in and out of memory but this clearly implies a performance penalty and potentially some limitations on the message passing). It is also difficult to apply our ground truth check in this case because our intuition of "discarding" traces is made challenging due to all traces being interconnected; as information can propagate from one trace to another, it is not possible to pinpoint which trace affected the plaintext bytes. Finally there are a large number of cycles in such a graph, which means that it is impossible to make any statements about convergence or any meaningful outcome.

Independent Factor Graph (IFG) Method. In contrast to assembling one large graph, we could also treat each leakage trace independently and only have one copy of the graph in memory. Each trace then produces a set of distributions for the unknown key bytes, which can be combined using Bayes theorem.

The advantage for this method is that it can be executed in parallel (distributed over different cores) or sequential, allowing an easy speed-memory trade-off. Also, no further cycles are added, thus for our acyclic graphs we can be assured of convergence even in a multiple trace setting. The disadvantage may be that information cannot propagate from one leakage trace (associated graph) to another. It is possible to use the ground truth check here.

Sequential Factor Graph (SFG) Method. An easy tweak to the IFG method that enables information to "propagate" from one graph to another, would be to use the key distribution that is derived from the $i - 1$th leakage trace as prior distribution for the graph with the i−th leakage trace. This turns the IFG method into a strictly sequential method (thus SFG); it thus retains IFG's memory efficiency, convergence for acyclic graphs, and the possibility to implement a ground truth check.

5 Studying the Effect of Reduced Graphs in a Single Trace Setting

In the remainder of this paper we discuss experiments that aim to determine the impact of our tweaks to the BP algorithm, the variations of graphs and graph combination methods. We start in a single trace setting, and first consider the effects of nodes in later rounds, then we examine the effectiveness of our improvements on the BP algorithm, followed by an enquiry into the impact of using reduced graphs (in particular G_1 and G_1^A) on the attack outcomes.

5.1 Effect of Nodes in Later Rounds

We previously defined a metric that enables us to judge the effect that a node in the graphical model has on the key bytes. To use this metric practically we set up an experiment on the full graph G in which we supply simulated, HW based leaks with minimal noise (SNR = 2) and we let the BP algorithm run for the full $t_{max} = 50$. As implied by the definition, we first let BP run and produce a key distribution. Then we fix the input for the node that we are computing the effect of and fix this to a value (running through all input values of this node one by one), which enables us to compute the effect as defined in Sect. 4.1.

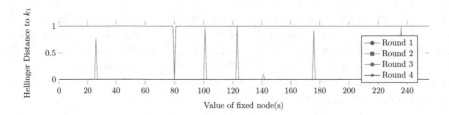

Fig. 1. Hellinger distance of k_1 to different fixed value s nodes

Our findings are that variable nodes from later rounds have no effect on the
key distribution. To provide some evidence for this, we include one graph that
is representative for all results. Figure 1 visualises the result from the variable
node s (which corresponds to the Sbox output) in different rounds of AES to
key byte k_1. Recall that our definition is based on the Hellinger distance metric:
any number that is close to zero indicates that a node has no effect. Figure 1
demonstrates then that this particular node as a great effect in round one, and
some small effect in round two, but thereafter it has no effect on this key byte.
Other variable nodes show the same behaviour: first round nodes have an effect,
second round nodes have a very small effect, and from round three onwards our
metric indicates that they have no effect.

5.2   Effectiveness of Our Improvements to the BP Algorithm

We investigated the effect of our epsilon exhaustion technique on by running
repeat experiments using ELMO simulations. These showed that in cases of high
and low noise, the information can be exhausted before reaching t_{max} iterations
(nearly all experiments terminated via the epsilon exhaustion rather than t_{max}).
Interestingly having more noise does not mean that the algorithm is more likely
to run up to t_{max} iterations. In fact often the epsilon exhaustion was considerably
earlier, e.g. in for SNR $= 2^1$ on average around 20 Belief Propagation iterations
are required before reaching a stable point.

We also investigated how often the ground truth check kicks in. We configured
our criterion to reject only "extreme outliers". Unsurprisingly, we found that it
is much harder to detect such cases in high noise settings, where the information
from a single trace is insufficient for any meaningful result. We note that in such
cases, where one would require multiple traces anyway, the ground truth check
could be applied to consecutive traces and we noticed in our implementation
that if there are two "bad" traces fed into BP consecutively, then our ground
truth method would pick this up. The experiments also indicate that cycles
in the graph may "amplify" unhelpful information, because in the experiments
on graphs without cycles our ground truth check criterion was never met; the
ground truth method spotted erroneous traces after BP had iterated for more
than 15 rounds, but as the acyclic graph is run for a maximum of 8 iterations,
these erroneous messages did not appear.

5.3   Impact of Graphs on Attack Success

As measures for the success of attacks we look at the (first-order) success rate, as well as the lowest (i.e. best) rank for the key. For the specific purpose of this experiment, we elected not to invoke our termination criterion for the cyclic graphs and instead allow BP to run up to 50 iterations (for G we did experimentally verify that increasing t_{max} did not lead to better success). We did this for a range of SNR's. In both settings, the high signal and the high noise, the performance of the attack using G_1 is nearly identical to the performance of the attack using the whole AES graph, or when including the key schedule, or when looking at two rounds, whereas there is a clear gap to the performance when using G_1^A. This shouldn't come as a huge surprise: we know from works such as [1,8] on SPA attacks on block ciphers, that the information from either the key schedule or just the encryption round goes a long way to recovering the key.

With such little difference in performance between the whole graph and G_1, it seems reasonable to utilise only the first round. This has not only the advantage of dealing with much smaller graphs, crucially it implies that also less profiling effort is necessary, which could be a practical advantage. For instance, if traces become increasingly misaligned (e.g. because the clock frequency of the processor is changeable), having to only profile the beginning (or end) round of an implementation could be more feasible than having to profile across the entire trace. With respect to G_1^A, although we see a large performance gap in the success rate (when compared to the whole graph and G_1), the 'Best Rank' results show that the G_1^A method is still effective as an attack. The advantage G_1^A has in this attack scenario is that convergence is guaranteed after 8 BP iterations.

Our results also showed, surprisingly, that better SNRs do not imply that fewer BP iterations are required. We observed that for SNR $= 2^1$, we needed 20 BP iterations; but for SNR $= 2^{-3}$ we needed fewer iterations, namely 15. We also noticed that, for SNR $= 2^1$ in the case of G, there was a success rate drop when using 50 iterations over 25. We speculate that this is due to the large number of cycles in the graph. From these results clear that there is no simple way of choose t_{max} optimally. However, by using our Epsilon Exhaustion improvement (see Sect. 3.1) we can terminate BP when the information updating the key has reached a stable equilibrium.

6   Studying the Effect of Different Graph Combination Methods

Having established that attack results based on using the whole graph or just G_1 are nearly identical in a single trace setting, we now turn our attention to attacks that utilise multiple leakage traces. We now compare the performance of the G_1 and the G_1^A graphs specifically to see if the performance difference between them persists across different trace combination methods.

We ran simulations ranging from high signal to high noise scenarios. In the high signal scenarios there were no differences between the graphs w.r.t different combination methods. Only in noisy scenarios did we observe differences. For our discussion we include two particularly striking sets of results in Figs. 4 and 5 in the appendix. In the high noise scenario we provided more traces than in the high signal case. The figure shows attack outcomes for the different graph combination methods as applied to different graphs.

In the case of SNR of 2^{-1} we see, surprisingly, that the acyclic graph G_1^A can outperform G_1 across different combination methods, and that LFG for G_1^A isn't strictly the best method. When we use ten or more traces, G_1^A has a constant success rate, compared to G_1 when using IFG and SFG for the same number of traces. We saw the same results for an SNR of 2^{-3}. Only when decreasing the SNR to 2^{-6}, G_1 performed better than G_1^A and LFG is the best combination for G_1. The IFG method with G_1 only starts to succeed after 45 traces, when the LFG method has over a 90% success rate. We also observe here that although IFG is favoured over SFG when the SNR is high (2^{-1}), SFG becomes more effective when the SNR is lower, needing around 70 traces to have an 80% success rate. When using G_1^A in a low noise scenario, the graph connecting method seems to have little effect on the results, and we see no signs of success until we use 60 or more traces. We hypothesise that in a low SNR setting having more dependent variables helps to compensate for the noise, an observation that has been made elsewhere in the same context [5]. However it would appear that in the context of a relatively large graph that takes into account "sufficient" leakage from the first round, extra information from later rounds is not as important. These results show that neither more rounds nor more intermediates or more connected graphs necessarily make for a more effective attack overall.

7 Studying the Effect of Reduced Graphs in a Multiple Traces Setting

As a final experiment we simulated multiple trace attacks (with IFG) using reduced graphs. We studied different noise levels (low, medium, and high), and provide Fig. 6 in the appendix. In short, only when moving to high noise settings the larger graphs proved to be slightly advantageous (in line with the observations in the previous section) in terms of first-order success rate. However, if we consider the median ranks of the experiments, we see the effectiveness of the acyclic methods is still comparable to the cyclic methods; when using 90 traces, the acyclic graphs ranked the correct key with the second highest probability.

For confirmation purposes we also ran these attacks on our real trace set. We determined the SNR on those traces and reran the simulations with a matching SNR $(=2^{-5})$. Figure 2 shows the outcomes of these experiments. In the left pane we visualise the comparison based on using G_1 between real and simulated traces. The right pane shows the same comparison using G_1^A. Clearly the simulation results are a very good match with the real traces. We can also see that the performance of G_1^A is again nearly identical to G_1.

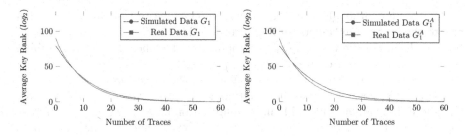

Fig. 2. Comparison of a BP attack on real trace data against simulated data (SNR 2^{-5}), using graphs G_1 and G_1^A.

8 Conclusions and Recommendations for Practical Use

The approach of using a belief propagation algorithm on a factor graph that describes an implementation under attack leads to a very powerful attack strategy. However there are many options to concretely instantiate this idea, and these options are expected to have an impact on the performance of concrete attacks. So far there exist very few publications about this important attack vector and none of them has drilled into the details related to building a graph for a specific implementation.

Our submission makes the first step into developing an understanding how choices in instantiating this attack vector impact on the resulting attacks. We specialise our investigation to AES FURIOUS, and look at the attack performance when reducing elements from the graph as it would "immediately" follow from the AES FURIOUS implementation. Alongside our experiments we provide a new metric to capture the effect of a variable node, and introduce two improvements to the (loopy) Belief Propagation algorithm that are useful specifically in the context of side channel analysis.

Our findings show that assumptions that might have been made in previous work, and that seem to naturally follow from the intuition about the working principle of Belief Propagation on factor graphs are not always met in practice. E.g. including more leakage does not always make a significant difference (our findings show that only in very noisy settings there is a slight advantage for our full factor graph). Combining multiple traces into a large factor graph is also not necessarily the best option. In fact our experiments suggest that the best option (except for the noisiest of settings) is to use an acyclic graph (which is guaranteed to converge to a correct result) in either the independent or sequential combination method because this will guarantee attack success at the expense of marginally more traces (in medium noise settings the approach works in fact as well as the best other approach). This is particularly interesting for the potential use of such a method in an evaluation setting: as a configuration is possible that guarantees convergence, and we have theoretical understanding about the necessary number of Belief Propagation iterations, we can avoid the attack failing with no explanation.

Our results, although derived by focussing on one algorithm/implementation are, to the best of our understanding, transferrable to other implementations of block ciphers. For the vast majority of popular block ciphers the cyclic attribute (typically related to a diffusion layer) of the algorithm leads to having to use loopy belief propagation. The nodes that cause the cycles are often related to simple transformations on variables that do not leak any "new" key information. Therefore they do not truly add "new" information into the graph, and thus we suggest to remove them and thereby remove the cycles and run the attack on a reduced graph. To not solely rely on intuition, we have introduced the Hellinger Distance metric to measure the 'importance' of each node in the graph. Therefore one approach in practice would be to derive the importance of candidate nodes for removal (either via some initial attacks or simulations). The user can then carefully select the desired factor graph for the implementation. Upon finding the optimal structure of the graph, the user then has a choice for the graph connection method. The graph connection method is largely independent of the structure of the graphs to be connected. We propose using the Independent Graph connection method, as it does not incur a large memory overhead when dealing with multiple traces (the noisier the trace set, the more traces will be required for the attack phase). However, if the user has access to a large amount of memory and computational power, they may instead opt to use the Large Factor Graph method, as we show in our results it performs marginally better over other graph connection methods.

Acknowledgements. Joey Green has been funded by an NCSC studentship. Arnab Roy and Elisabeth Oswald were funded in part by EPSRC under grant agreement EP/N011635/1 (LADA) and the ERC via the grant SEAL (Project Reference 725042).

Appendix

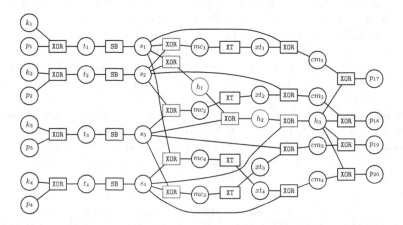

Fig. 3. Factor graph representing the computation of a column in the first round of AES FURIOUS. (Color figure online)

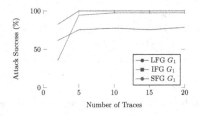
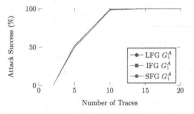

Fig. 4. Graph combination methods using graphs G_1 and G_1^A, SNR 2^{-1}

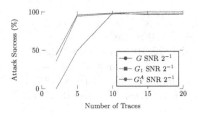
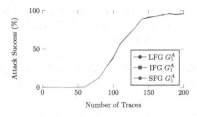

Fig. 5. Graph combination methods using graphs G_1 and G_1^A, SNR 2^{-6}

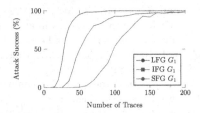
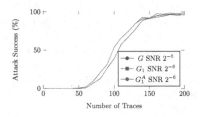

Fig. 6. Reduced graph comparison using SNRs 2^{-1} and 2^{-6} respectively

References

1. Banciu, V., Oswald, E.: Pragmatism vs. elegance: comparing two approaches to simple power attacks on AES. In: Constructive Side-Channel Analysis and Secure Design - 5th International Workshop, COSADE 2014, Paris, France, 13–15 April 2014, Revised Selected Papers, pp. 29–40 (2014)
2. Green, J., Roy, A., Oswald, E.: A systematic study of the impact of graphical models on inference-based attacks on AES. Cryptology ePrint Archive, Report 2018/671 (2018). https://eprint.iacr.org/2018/671
3. Green, P.J., Noad, R., Smart, N.P.: Further hidden markov model cryptanalysis. In: Rao, J.R., Sunar, B. (eds.) CHES 2005. LNCS, vol. 3659, pp. 61–74. Springer, Heidelberg (2005). https://doi.org/10.1007/11545262_5
4. Grosso, V., Standaert, F.-X.: ASCA, SASCA and DPA with enumeration: which one beats the other and when? In: Iwata, T., Cheon, J.H. (eds.) ASIACRYPT 2015. LNCS, vol. 9453, pp. 291–312. Springer, Heidelberg (2015). https://doi.org/10.1007/978-3-662-48800-3_12

5. Grosso, V., Standaert, F.-X.: Masking proofs are tight (and how to exploit it in security evaluations). Cryptology ePrint Archive, Report 2017/116 (2017). http://eprint.iacr.org/2017/116

6. Karlof, C., Wagner, D.: Hidden markov model cryptanalysis. In: Walter, C.D., Koç, Ç.K., Paar, C. (eds.) CHES 2003. LNCS, vol. 2779, pp. 17–34. Springer, Heidelberg (2003). https://doi.org/10.1007/978-3-540-45238-6_3

7. MacKay, D.J.C.: Information Theory, Inference, and Learning Algorithms. Cambridge University Press, New York (2003)

8. Mangard, S.: A simple power-analysis (SPA) attack on implementations of the AES key expansion. In: Lee, P.J., Lim, C.H. (eds.) ICISC 2002. LNCS, vol. 2587, pp. 343–358. Springer, Heidelberg (2003). https://doi.org/10.1007/3-540-36552-4_24

9. Martin, D.P., Mather, L., Oswald, E., Stam, M.: Characterisation and estimation of the key rank distribution in the context of side channel evaluations. In: Cheon, J.H., Takagi, T. (eds.) ASIACRYPT 2016. LNCS, vol. 10031, pp. 548–572. Springer, Heidelberg (2016). https://doi.org/10.1007/978-3-662-53887-6_20

10. McCann, D., Oswald, E., Whitnall, C.: Towards practical tools for side channel aware software engineering: 'grey box' modelling for instruction leakages. In: 26th USENIX Security Symposium, USENIX Security 2017, Vancouver, BC, Canada, 16–18 August 2017, pp. 199–216 (2017)

11. Mezard, M., Montanari, A.: Information, Physics, and Computation. Oxford University Press Inc., New York (2009)

12. Oswald, E.: Enhancing simple power-analysis attacks on elliptic curve cryptosystems. In: Kaliski, B.S., Koç, K., Paar, C. (eds.) CHES 2002. LNCS, vol. 2523, pp. 82–97. Springer, Heidelberg (2003). https://doi.org/10.1007/3-540-36400-5_8

13. Primas, R., Pessl, P., Mangard, S.: Single-trace side-channel attacks on masked lattice-based encryption. In: Fischer, W., Homma, N. (eds.) CHES 2017. LNCS, vol. 10529, pp. 513–533. Springer, Cham (2017). https://doi.org/10.1007/978-3-319-66787-4_25

14. Veyrat-Charvillon, N., Gérard, B., Standaert, F.-X.: Soft analytical side-channel attacks. In: Sarkar, P., Iwata, T. (eds.) ASIACRYPT 2014. LNCS, vol. 8873, pp. 282–296. Springer, Heidelberg (2014). https://doi.org/10.1007/978-3-662-45611-8_15

Improving Side-Channel Analysis
Through Semi-supervised Learning

Stjepan Picek[1], Annelie Heuser[2], Alan Jovic[3(✉)], Karlo Knezevic[3],
and Tania Richmond[2]

[1] Delft University of Technology, Delft, The Netherlands
[2] Univ Rennes, Inria, CNRS, IRISA, Rennes, France
[3] University of Zagreb Faculty of Electrical Engineering and Computing,
Zagreb, Croatia
alan.jovic@fer.hr

Abstract. The profiled side-channel analysis represents the most powerful category of side-channel attacks. In this context, the security evaluator (i.e., attacker) gains access to a profiling device to build a precise model which is used to attack another device in the attacking phase. Mostly, it is assumed that the attacker has significant capabilities in the profiling phase, whereas the attacking phase is very restricted. We step away from this assumption and consider an attacker restricted in the profiling phase, while the attacking phase is less limited. We propose the concept of semi-supervised learning for side-channel analysis, where the attacker uses a small number of labeled measurements from the profiling phase as well as the unlabeled measurements from the attacking phase to build a more reliable model. Our results show that the semi-supervised concept significantly helps the template attack (TA) and its pooled version (TA_p). More specifically, for low noise scenario, the results for machine learning techniques and TA are often improved when only a small number of measurements is available in the profiling phase, while there is no significant difference in scenarios where the supervised set is large enough for reliable classification. For high noise scenario, TA_p and multilayer perceptron results are improved for the majority of inspected dataset sizes, while for high noise scenario with added countermeasures, we show a small improvement for TA_p, Naive Bayes and multilayer perceptron approaches for most inspected dataset sizes. Current results go in favor of using semi-supervised learning, especially self-training approach, in side-channel attacks.

1 Introduction

Side-channel analysis (SCA) consists of extracting secret data from (noisy) measurements. It is made up of a collection of miscellaneous techniques, combined in order to maximize the probability of success, for a low number of trace measurements, and as low computation complexity as possible. The most powerful attacks currently known are based on a profiling phase, where the link between

© Springer Nature Switzerland AG 2019
B. Bilgin and J.-B. Fischer (Eds.): CARDIS 2018, LNCS 11389, pp. 35–50, 2019.
https://doi.org/10.1007/978-3-030-15462-2_3

the leakage and the secret is learned under the assumption that the attacker knows the secret on a profiling device.

This knowledge is subsequently exploited to extract another secret using fresh measurements from a different device. In order to run such an attack, one has a plethora of techniques and options to choose from, where the two main types of attacks are based on (1) template attack (relying on probability estimation), and (2) machine learning (ML) techniques. When working with the typical assumption for profiled SCA that the profiling phase is not bounded, the situation actually becomes rather simple if neglecting computational costs. If the attacker is able to acquire an unlimited (or, in real-world very large) amount of traces, the template attack (TA) is proven to be optimal from an information theoretic point of view (see e.g., [1,2]). In that context of unbounded and unrestricted profiling phase, ML techniques seem not needed.

Stepping away from the assumption of an unbounded number of traces, the situation becomes much more interesting and of practical relevance. A number of results in recent years showed that in those cases, machine learning techniques can actually significantly outperform template attack (see e.g., [3–5]). Still, the aforesaid attacks work under the assumption that the attacker has a large amount of traces from which a model is learned. The opposite case would be to learn a model without any labeled examples. Machine learning approaches (mostly based on clustering) have been proposed, for instance, for public key encryption schemes where only two possible classes are present – 0 and 1 – and where the key is guessed using only a single-trace (see e.g., [6]). In the case of differential attacks (using more than one encryption) and using more than two classes, to the best of our knowledge, unsupervised machine learning techniques have not been studied yet.

In this paper, we aim to address a scenario positioned between supervised and unsupervised learning, the so-called semi-supervised learning in the context of SCA. Figure 1 illustrates the different approaches of supervised (on the left) and semi-supervised learning (on the right). Supervised learning assumes that the security evaluator first possesses a device similar to the one under attack. Having this additional device, he is then able to build a precise profiling model using a set of measurement traces and knowing the plaintext/ciphertext and the secret key of this device. In the second step, the attacker uses the obtained profiling model to reveal the secret key of the device under attack. For this, he measures a new, additional set of traces, but as the key is secret, he has no further information about the intermediate processed data and thus builds hypotheses. Accordingly, the only information which the attacker transfers between the profiling phase and the attacking phase is the profiling model he builds. We note there is a number of papers considering supervised machine learning in SCA, see e.g., [7–9].

In realistic settings, the attacker is not obliged to view the profiling phase independently from the attacking phase. He can rather combine all available resources to make the attack as effective as possible. In particular, he has at hand a set of traces for which he precisely knows the intermediate processed states (i.e., labeled data) and another set of traces with a secret unknown key and thus no information about the intermediate variable (i.e., unlabeled data). To take advantage of both sets at once, we propose a new strategy of conducting profiled side-channel analysis to build a more reliable model (see Fig. 1 on the right). This new view is of particular interest when the number of profiling traces is (very) low, and thus any additional data is helpful to improve the model estimation.

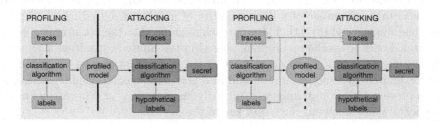

Fig. 1. Profiling side-channel scenario: traditional (left), semi-supervised (right).

To show the efficiency and applicability of semi-supervised learning for SCA, we conduct extensive experiments where semi-supervised learning outperforms supervised learning if certain assumptions are satisfied. More precisely, the results show a number of scenarios where guessing entropy on the test set is significantly lower when semi-supervised learning is used (when compared to the "classical" supervised approach). We start with the scenario that we call "extreme profiling", where the attacker has only a very limited number of traces to learn the model. From there, we increase the number of available traces, making the attacker more powerful, until we reach a setting where there is no more need for semi-supervised learning. Still, even when the supervised learning works good (i.e., succeeds in breaking an implementation), we can observe a number of scenarios where semi-supervised learning can still improve the results or at least not deteriorate them.

To the best of our knowledge, the only work up till now implementing a semi-supervised analysis in SCA is [10], where the authors conclude that the semi-supervised setting cannot compete with a supervised setting. Unfortunately, the assumed scenario is hard to justify and consequently their results are expected (but without much implication for SCA). More precisely, the authors compared the supervised attack that has more available measurements (and corresponding labels) than the semi-supervised attack. On the basis of such experiments, they concluded that the supervised attack is better, which is intuitive and straightforward. A proper comparison would be between the supervised attack that has at most the same number of labeled measurements as the semi-supervised one. Additionally, our analysis is not restricted to only one labeled class in the learning phase.

Note, we primarily focus on improving the results if the profiling phase is limited. Since we are considering extremely difficult scenarios, the improvements one can realistically expect are often not too big. Still, we consider any improvement to be relevant since it makes the attack easier, while not requiring any additional knowledge or measurements.

2 Semi-supervised Learning Types and Notation

Semi-supervised learning (denoted as SSL in the rest of the paper) is positioned in the middle between supervised and unsupervised learning. There, the basic idea is to take advantage of a large quantity of unlabeled data during a supervised learning procedure [11]. This approach assumes that the attacker is able to possess a device to conduct a profiling phase but has limited capacities. This may reflect a more realistic scenario in some practical applications, as the attacker may be limited by time, resources, and also face implemented countermeasures which prevent him from taking an arbitrarily large amount of side-channel measurements, while knowing the secret key of the device.

Let $x = (x_1, \ldots, x_n)$ be a set of n samples where each sample x_i is assumed to be drawn i.i.d. from a common distribution $\mathcal{X}$ with probability $P(x)$. This set x can be divided into three parts: the points $x_l = (x_1, \ldots, x_l)$ for which we know the labels $y_l = (y_1, \ldots, y_l)$ and the points $x_u = (x_{l+1}, \ldots, x_{l+u})$ for which we do not know the labels. Additionally, the third part is the test set $x_t = (x_{l+u+1}, \ldots, x_n)$ for which labels are also not known. We see that differing from the supervised case, where we also do not know labels in the test phase, here unknown labels appear already in the training phase. As for supervised learning, its goal is to predict a class for each sample in the test set $x_t = (x_{l+u+1}, \ldots, x_n)$. For SSL, two learning paradigms can be discussed: transductive and inductive learning [12]. In transductive learning (which is a natural setting for some SSL algorithms), predictions are performed only for the unlabeled data on a known test set. The goal is to optimize the classification performance. More formally, the algorithm makes predictions $y_t = (y_{l+u+1}, \ldots, y_n)$ on $x_t = (x_{l+u+1}, \ldots, x_n)$. In inductive learning, the goal is to find a prediction function defined on the complete space $\mathcal{X}$, i.e., to find a function $f : \mathcal{X} \to \mathcal{Y}$. This function is then used to make predictions $f(x_i)$ for each sample x_i in the test set. Obviously, transductive learning is easier, since no general rule needs to be inferred, and, consequently, we opt to conduct it. From the algorithm class perspective, we will use two approaches in order to achieve successful SSL, namely: self-training [12] (Sect. 2.1) and graph-based algorithms [12,13] (Sect. 2.2).

On an intuitive level, semi-supervised learning sounds like an extremely powerful paradigm (after all, humans learn through SSL), the results show that it is not always the case. More precisely, when comparing SSL with supervised learning, it is not always possible to obtain more accurate predictions. Consequently, we are interested in the cases where SSL can outperform supervised learning. In order for that to be possible, the following needs to hold: the knowledge on $p(x)$ one gains through unlabeled data has to carry useful information for inference of $p(y|x)$. In the case where this is not true, SSL will not be better than supervised learning and can even lead to worse results. To assume a structure about the underlying distribution of data and to have useful information in the process of inference, we use two assumptions which should hold when conducting SSL [12].

Smoothness Assumption. If two points x_1 and x_2 are close, then their corresponding labels y_1 and y_2 are close. The smoothness assumption can be generalized in order to be useful for SSL: if two points x_1 and x_2 in a high density region are close, then so should the corresponding labels y_1 and y_2 be.

Intuitively, this assumption tells us that if two samples (measurements) belong to the same cluster, then their labels (e.g., their Hamming weight or intermediate value) should be close. Note that, this assumption also implies that, if two points are separated by a low-density region, then their labels need not be close. The smoothness assumption should generally hold for SCA, as the power consumption (or electromagnetic emanation) is related to the activity of the device. For example, a low Hamming weight or a low intermediate value should result in a low side-channel measurement.

Manifold Assumption. The high-dimensional data lie on or close to a low-dimensional manifold. If the data really lie on a low-dimensional manifold, then the classifier can operate in a space of the corresponding (low) dimension. Intuitively, the manifold assumption tells us that a set of samples is connected in some way: e.g., all measurements with the Hamming weight 4 lie on their own manifold, while all measurements with the Hamming weight 5 lie on a different, but nearby, manifold. Then, we can try to develop representations for each of these manifolds using just the unlabeled data, while assuming that the different manifolds will be represented using different learned features of the data.

2.1   Self-training

In self-training (or self-learning), any classification method is selected and the classifier is trained with the labeled data. Afterward, the classifier is used to classify the unlabeled data. From the obtained predictions, one selects only those instances with the highest output probabilities (i.e., where the output probability is higher than a given threshold σ) and then adds them to the labeled data. This procedure is repeated k times.

Self-training is a well-known semi-supervised technique and one that is probably the most natural choice to start with [12]. The biggest drawback with this technique is that it depends on the choice of the underlying classifier and that possible mistakes reinforce themselves as the number of repeats increase. Naturally, one expects that the first step of self-learning will introduce errors (wrongly predicted classes). It is therefore important to retain only those instances for which the prediction probability of the class is high. Unfortunately, a very high class prediction probability (even 100%) does not guarantee that the actual class is correctly predicted. Additionally, we use adaptive threshold σ for predicted class probability, as explained in Sect. 4.

2.2   Graph-Based Learning

In graph-based learning, the data are represented as nodes in graphs, where a node is both labeled and unlabeled example. The edges are labeled with the pairwise distance of incident nodes. If an edge is not labeled, it corresponds to the infinite distance. Most of the graph-based learning methods depend on the manifold assumption and refer to the graph by utilizing the graph Laplacian. Let $G = (E, V)$ be a graph with edge weights given by $w : E \rightarrow \mathbb{R}$. The weight $w(e)$ of an edge e corresponds to the similarity of the incident nodes and a missing edge means no similarity. The similarity matrix W of graph G is defined as:

$$W_{ij} = \begin{cases} w(e) \text{ if } e = (i,j) \in E \\ 0 \text{ if } e = (i,j) \notin E \end{cases} \tag{1}$$

The diagonal matrix called the degree matrix D_{ii} is defined as $D_{ii} = \sum_j W_{ij}$. To define the graph Laplacian two well-known ways are to use:

– normalized graph Laplacian $\mathcal{L} = I - D^{-1/2}WD^{-1/2}$,
– unnormalized graph Laplacian $L = D - W$.

We use graph-based learning technique called label spreading that is based on normalized graph Laplacian. In this algorithm, node's labels propagate to neighbor nodes according to their proximity. Since the edges between the nodes have certain weights, some labels propagate easier. Consequently, nodes that are close (in the Euclidean distance) are more likely to have the same labels.

3   Experimental Setting

3.1   Classification Algorithms

In supervised learning, we use template attack (TA) and its pooled version (TA_p), random forest (RF), multilayer perceptron (MLP), and Naive Bayes (NB) algorithms. In the graph-based SSL, we use k-nearest neighbors (k-NN) (i.e., the method to assign labels) since it produces a sparse matrix that can be calculated very quickly. For self-training, we use Naive Bayes. In all the experiments, we use Python [14].

Template Attack. The template attack (TA) relies on the Bayes theorem such that the posterior probability of each class value y, given the vector of N observed attribute values x:

$$p(Y = y | X = x) = \frac{p(Y = y)p(X = x | Y = y)}{p(X = x)}, \tag{2}$$

where $X = x$ represents the event that $X_1 = x_1 \wedge X_2 = x2 \wedge \ldots \wedge X_N = x_N$.

When used as a classifier, $p(X = x)$ in Eq. (2) can be dropped as it does not depend on the class y. Accordingly, the attacker estimates in the profiling phase $p(Y = y)$ and $p(X = x | Y = y)$ which are used in the attacking phase to predict $p(Y = y | X = x)$ [15]. Note that the class variable Y is discrete while the measurement X is continuous. So, the discrete probability $p(Y = y)$ is equal to its sample frequency where $p(X_i = x_i | Y = y)$ displays a density function. Mostly in the state of the art, TA is based on a multivariate normal distribution of the noise and thus the probability density function used to compute $p(\boldsymbol{X} = \boldsymbol{x}|Y = y)$ equals:

$$p(\boldsymbol{X} = \boldsymbol{x}|Y = y) = \frac{1}{\sqrt{(2\pi)^D|\Sigma_y|}}e^{-\frac{1}{2}(\boldsymbol{x}-\boldsymbol{\mu}_y)^T\Sigma_y^{-1}(\boldsymbol{x}-\boldsymbol{\mu}_y)}, \qquad (3)$$

where $\boldsymbol{\mu}_y$ is the mean over $\boldsymbol{X}$ for $1, \ldots, D$ and Σ_y the covariance matrix for each class y. The authors of [16] propose to use only one pooled covariance matrix to cope with statistical difficulties that result into low efficiency. We will use both versions of the template attack, where we denote pooled TA attack as TA_p.

Naive Bayes. The Naive Bayes (NB) classifier [17] is also based on the Bayesian rule but is labeled "Naive" as it works under a simplifying assumption that the predictor features (measurements) are mutually independent among the D features, given the class value. The existence of highly-correlated features in a dataset can influence the learning process and reduce the number of successful predictions. Also, NB assumes a normal distribution for predictor features. NB classifier outputs posterior probabilities as a result of the classification procedure [17]. The Bayes' formula is used to compute the posterior probability of each class value y given the vector of N observed feature values x.

Multilayer Perceptron. The multilayer perceptron (MLP) classifier is a feedforward artificial neural network. MLP consists of multiple layers (at least three) of nodes in a directed graph, where each layer is fully connected to the next one and training of the network is done with the backpropagation algorithm [18].

Random Forest. Random forest (RF) is a well-known ensemble decision tree learner [19]. Decision trees choose their splitting attributes from a random subset of k attributes at each internal node. The best split is taken among these randomly chosen attributes and the trees are built without pruning. RF is a parametric algorithm with respect to the number of trees in the forest. It is also a stochastic algorithm, because of its two sources of randomness: bootstrap sampling and attribute selection at node splitting.

k-NN. k-nearest neighbors is the basic non-parametric instance-based learning method. The classifier has no training phase; it just stores the training set samples. In the test phase, the classifier assigns a class to an instance by determining the k instances that are the closest to it, with respect to Euclidean distance metric: $d(x_i, x_j) = \sqrt{\sum_{r=1}^{n}(a_r(x_i) - a_r(x_j))^2}$. Here, a_r is the r-th attribute of an instance x. The class is assigned as the most commonly occurring one among the k-nearest neighbors of the test instance. This procedure is repeated for all test set instances.

3.2   Datasets

We use three datasets in our experiments. To test across various settings, we target (1) high-SNR unprotected implementation on a smartcard [20],

(2) low-SNR unprotected implementation on FPGA, and (3) low-SNR implementation on a smartcard protected with the randomized delay countermeasure.

We do not consider the variations in the number of available points of interest (features) since in such a case, the number of scenarios would become quite large. We select 50 points of interests with the highest correlation between the class value and data set for all the analyzed data sets and investigate scenarios with a different number of classes – 9 classes and 256 classes.

Calligraphic letters (e.g., $\mathcal{X}$) denote sets, capital letters (e.g., X) denote random variables taking values in these sets, and the corresponding lowercase letters (e.g., x) denote their realizations. Let k^* be the fixed secret cryptographic key (byte) and the random variable T the plaintext or ciphertext of the cryptographic algorithm which is uniformly chosen. The measured leakage is denoted as X and we are particularly interested in multivariate leakage $\boldsymbol{X} = X_1, \ldots, X_D$, where D is the number of time samples or features (attributes) in ML terminology.

Considering a powerful attacker who has a device with knowledge about the secret key implemented, a set of N profiling traces $\boldsymbol{X}_1, \ldots, \boldsymbol{X}_N$ is used in order to estimate the leakage model beforehand. Note that this set is multi-dimensional (i.e., it has a dimension equal to $D \times N$). In the attack phase, the attacker then measures additional traces $\boldsymbol{X}_1, \ldots, \boldsymbol{X}_Q$ from the device under attack in order to break the unknown secret key k^*.

DPAcontest v4. The dataset provides measurements of a masked AES software implementation [20]. As the mask is known, one can easily turn it into an unprotected scenario. Though, as it is a software implementation, the most leaking operation is not the register writing, but the processing of the S-box operation and we attack the first round. Accordingly, the leakage model changes to

$$Y(k^*) = \mathsf{Sbox}[P_{b_1} \oplus k^*] \oplus \underbrace{M}_{\text{known mask}} , \tag{4}$$

where P_{b_1} is a plaintext byte and we choose $b_1 = 1$. Again we consider the scenario of 256 classes and 9 classes (considering $HW(Y(k^*))$). Compared to the measurements from version 2, the model-based SNR is much higher and lies between 0.1188 and 5.8577.

Unprotected AES-128 on FPGA. This dataset targets an unprotected implementation of AES-128. AES-128 core was written in VHDL in a round based architecture, which takes 11 clock cycles for each encryption. The AES-128 core is wrapped around by a UART module to enable external communication. It is designed to allow accelerated measurements to avoid any DC shift due to environmental variation over prolonged measurements. The design was implemented on Xilinx Virtex-5 FPGA of a SASEBO GII evaluation board. Side-channel traces were measured using a high sensitivity near-field EM probe, placed over a decoupling capacitor on the power line. Measurements were sampled on the Teledyne LeCroy Waverunner 610zi oscilloscope and the trace set is publicly available at https://github.com/AESHD/AES_HD_Dataset. Although the full dataset consists of 1 250 features, here we use only the 50 most important features, as selected with the Pearson correlation. A suitable and commonly used (HD) leakage model when attacking the last round of an unprotected hardware implementation is the register writing in the last round [20] These measurements are relatively noisy and the resulting model-based SNR (signal-to-noise ratio) has a maximum value of 0.0096. As this implementation leaks in HD model, we denote this implementation as AES_HD.

Random Delay Countermeasure Dataset. The third dataset uses a protected (i.e., with a countermeasure) software implementation of AES. The target smartcard is an 8-bit Atmel AVR microcontroller. The protection uses random delay countermeasure as described by Coron and Kizhvatov. The trace set is publicly available at https://github.com/ikizhvatov/randomdelays-traces [21]. Adding random delays to the normal operation of a cryptographic algorithm has an effect on the misalignment of important features, which in turns makes the attack more difficult. As a result, the overall SNR is reduced. We mounted our attacks in the Hamming weight power consumption model against the first AES key byte, targeting the first S-box operation. The dataset consists of 50 000 traces of 3 500 features each. The best 50 features were selected using Pearson correlation. For this dataset, the SNR has a maximum value of 0.0556. In the rest of the paper, we denote this dataset as the AES_RD.

3.3   Dataset Preparation

We experiment with randomly selected 50 000 measurements (profiled traces) from all three datasets. The datasets are standardized by removing the mean and scaling to unit variance. For supervised learning scenarios, the measurements are randomly divided into 1:1 ratio for training and test sets (e.g., 25 000 for training and 25 000 for testing). The training datasets are divided into 5 stratified folds and evaluated by 5-fold cross-validation procedure for appropriate parameter tuning. For semi-supervised learning scenarios, we divide the training dataset into a labeled set of size l and unlabeled set of size u, as follows:

- (100 + 24.9k): $l = 100$, $u = 24900 \rightarrow 0.4\%$ vs 99.6%
- (500 + 24.5k): $l = 500$, $u = 24500 \rightarrow 2\%$ vs 98%
- (1k + 24k): $l = 1000$, $u = 24000 \rightarrow 4\%$ vs 96%
- (10k + 15k): $l = 10000$, $u = 15000 \rightarrow 40\%$ vs 60%
- (20k + 5k): $l = 20000$, $u = 5000 \rightarrow 80\%$ vs 20%

4   Experimental Results

In side-channel analysis, an adversary is not only interested in predicting the labels $y(\cdot, k_a^*)$ in the attacking phase but he also aims at revealing the secret key k_a^*. A common measure in SCA is the guessing entropy (GE) metric. In particular, let us assume, given Q amount of samples in the attacking phase, an attack outputs a key guessing vector $\mathbf{g} = [g_1, g_2, \ldots, g_{|\mathcal{K}|}]$ in a decreasing order of probability with $|\mathcal{K}|$ being the size of the keyspace. So, g_1 is the most likely and $g_{|\mathcal{K}|}$ the least likely key candidate. The GE is the average position of k_a^* in $\mathbf{g}$. As SCA metric, we report the number of traces needed to reach a guessing entropy of 5. We use '–' in case this threshold is not reached within the test set.

In supervised learning, the classifiers are built on the labeled training sets and estimated on the unlabeled test set. When considering SSL, we first learn the classifiers on the labeled sets. Then, we learn with the labeled set and unlabeled set in a number of steps, where in each step, we augment the labeled set with the most confident predictions from the unlabeled set. Finally, we conduct the estimation phase on a different unlabeled set (test set).

For machine learning techniques that have parameters to be tuned, we conducted a tuning phase on the labeled sets and use such tuned parameters in consequent experimental phases. The best obtained tuning parameters, with respect to the accuracy of the classifiers, are: for k-NN with label spreading, we select k to be equal to 7, for random forest we use 200 trees, while for MLP, we use 4 hidden layers where the number of neurons per layer is $50, 30, 20, 50$, the 'adam' solver and the 'relu' activation function. For Naive Bayes, template attack, and its pooled version, there are no parameters to tune.

As already mentioned, for self-training, we use an adaptive threshold denoted σ. In the beginning, σ is set to the value of 0.99. The threshold value remains unchanged as long as there exists any instance in the unlabeled examples for which the probability of assignment to any class is higher than 0.99. When there are no such instances left, the σ value is decreased in the next iteration by 20% (i.e., to 79.2%) and the procedure is repeated for the remaining unlabeled examples for which a successful classification has not yet been made. The whole process is repeated 5 times, each time reducing the parameter by 20%. Thereafter, all the remaining instances are attributed to the class having the highest probability.

In Tables 1, 2 and 3, we give results on the number of traces needed to reach guessing entropy of 5 for the DPAcontest v4, AES_HD, and AES_RD datasets, respectively, for all methods and dataset sizes. In all scenarios where SSL gives better results than the supervised approach, we denote such results in bold formatting. Due to the lack of space, we do not give accuracy results but we note that, where SSL shows improvements, the accuracy increases up to 15%.

4.1   DPAcontest v4 Dataset Results

The results for DPAcontest v4, HW model, in Table 1 and in Fig. 2a clearly show the superiority of SSL approaches compared to supervised learning for a small number of traces (i.e., 100 and 500) in the training set. The only classifier not showing improvement with the introduction of SSL approaches is RF. The best results in terms of lowest GE are achieved with the MLP classifier. Another interesting observation is that TA does not reach GE = 5 for the majority of training dataset sizes for supervised learning (see also Fig. 2b), while it always reaches the goal with label spreading (LS) approach. Both for the HW model

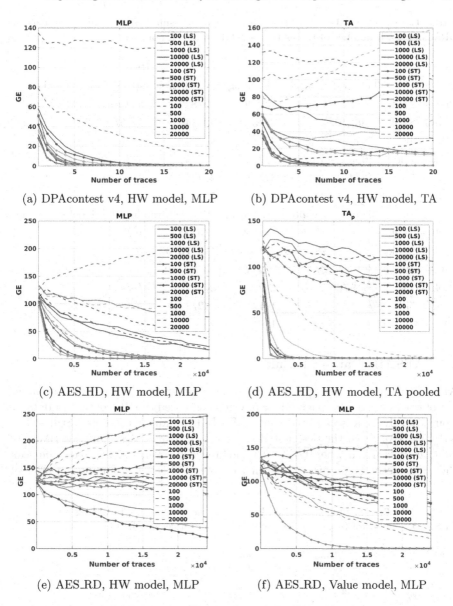

(a) DPAcontest v4, HW model, MLP   (b) DPAcontest v4, HW model, TA

(c) AES_HD, HW model, MLP   (d) AES_HD, HW model, TA pooled

(e) AES_RD, HW model, MLP   (f) AES_RD, Value model, MLP

Fig. 2. Guessing entropy results.

(9 classes) and for the intermediate value model (256 classes), LS method appears to provide better results in the majority of cases when compared to the self-training (ST) method. The NB classifier gives stable and favorable results both for HW and value models, comparable to MLP and TA_p.

Table 1. Test set results, supervised learning vs. semi-supervised learning approaches, DPAcontest v4, number of traces to reach GE = 5 (– if not reached).

Size	TA	TA_p	MLP	NB	RF
	9 classes, supervised learning/SSL:self-training/SSL:label spreading				
100 + 24.9k	–/–/**72**	9/9/**7**	–/**9**/**9**	14/**8**/**7**	17/936/47
500 + 24.5k	–/**86**/**40**	4/4/4	28/**5**/**4**	5/**6**/**4**	11/207/16
1k + 24k	–/**37**/–	4/5/4	4/6/4	4/7/5	13/375/13
10k + 15k	–/**6**/**5**	3/4/3	3/4/3	5/5/4	13/37/**12**
20k + 5k	5/**4**/**4**	3/3/3	3/3/3	4/4/4	12/17/12
25k	5	3	3	5	11
	256 classes, supervised learning/SSL:self-training/SSL:label spreading				
100 + 24.9k	–/–/–	–/–/–	–/**152**/**75**	–/**313**/**72**	–/–/–
500 + 24.5k	–/–/–	28/–/**55**	–/**10**/**17**	143/**76**/**30**	–/–/–
1k + 24k	–/–/–	5/–/**11**	–/**4**/**7**	30/**21**/**10**	–/–/–
10k + 15k	–/–/**973**	2/–/2	2/2/2	2/3/2	–/–/–
20k + 5k	–/–/**8**	2/–/2	1/1/1	2/2/2	–/–/–
25k	5	2	1	2	–

4.2   AES_HD Dataset Results

AES_HD dataset results, given in Table 2, demonstrate a highly increased number of traces needed to reach GE = 5, when compared to DPAcontest v4 dataset from Table 1. This is expected, since AES_HD contains more noise. Still, MLP, NB, and TA_p reach the designated threshold in many cases, both for HW and value models. Even when GE = 5 is not reached, from Fig. 2c, it can be seen that SSL methods are quite superior to supervised learning for the majority of

Table 2. Test set results, supervised learning vs. semi-supervised learning approaches, AES_HD, number of traces to reach GE = 5 (– if not reached).

Size	TA	TA_p	MLP	NB	RF
	9 classes, supervised learning/SSL:self-training/SSL:label spreading				
100 + 24.9k	–/–/–	–/–/–	–/**5756**/–	12777/**6091**/–	23077/–/–
500 + 24.5k	–/–/–	–/–/–	–/**12286**/–	5126/8710/22868	–/–/–
1k + 24k	–/–/–	18568/**2952**/**7015**	–/**4207**/**16070**	1913/3437/15308	15896/21812/–
10k + 15k	–/**6242**/–	2148/2397/**1615**	–/**4918**/–	1111/3010/1315	–/**16705**/–
20k + 5k	–/**5688**/–	1183/**962**/**963**	15775/**4947**/**14094**	893/1953/1034	–/**10689**/–
25k	–	1099	14693	952	–
	256 classes, supervised learning/SSL:self-training/SSL:label spreading				
100 + 24.9k	–/–/–	–/–/–	–/–/–	–/–/–	–/–/–
500 + 24.5k	–/–/–	–/–/–	–/–/–	–/–/–	–/–/–
1k + 24k	–/–/–	–/–/–	–/–/–	–/–/–	–/–/–
10k + 15k	–/–/–	–/**21470**/**17896**	–/**12385**/**14937**	6872/9270/7844	–/–/–
20k + 5k	–/–/–	–/–/**19951**	19887/**9860**/**8745**	4330/5663/4601	–/–/–
25k	–	–	–	18104	4001

input dataset sizes. This is especially pronounced for the ST approach, for which all input dataset sizes surpass even the best results for supervised learning. The results for the pooled version of TA are interesting (Fig. 2d), as they show a clear superiority of ST semi-supervised approach in all cases, and superiority of LS for larger dataset sizes in HW model. Intermediate value model results, given in the lower part of Table 2 show that it is difficult to reach the GE threshold in most cases and for most classifiers. Still, SSL methods give better results for the MLP and TA_p classifiers and slightly worse results on larger dataset sizes for the NB classifier.

4.3   AES_RD Dataset Results

AES_RD dataset is the most difficult dataset, considering its low signal-to-noise ratio and presence of a countermeasure. The results depicted in Table 3 point to an even higher number of traces needed to reach GE = 5, when compared to the AES_HD dataset. The benefit of using SSL methods for this dataset still exists, but less so when compared to the other two datasets. For example, NB classifier reaches the threshold for the dataset size of 1000 instances only for ST, then, for 10k instances, the best results are achieved with supervised learning, while for 20k instances, again ST is superior to both LS and supervised learning. From Fig. 2e, it can be seen that, in most cases, SSL methods using MLP are better than their supervised counterparts. Also, ST method for the larger number of traces appears to be superior to the other approaches. For the intermediate value model on this dataset (Table 3 below and Fig. 2f), the only clear benefit of using SSL approaches is for large dataset sizes (especially 20k for ST approach), which suggests that too much noise does not allow for efficient modeling (either for supervised or for SSL approaches), when the sample sizes are low.

Table 3. Test set results, supervised learning vs. semi-supervised learning approaches, AES_RD, number of traces to reach GE = 5 (– if not reached).

Size	TA	TA_p	MLP	NB	RF
9 classes, supervised learning/SSL:self-training/SSL:label spreading					
100 + 24.9k	–/–/–	–/–/–	–/–/–	–/–/–	–/–/–
500 + 24.5k	–/–/–	–/–/–	–/–/–	–/–/–	–/–/–
1k + 24k	–/–/–	–/–/–	–/–/–	–/**18484**/–	–/–/–
10k + 15k	–/–/–	16918/–/20325	–/–/–	14329/–/21356	–/–/–
20k + 5k	–/–/–	11735/**10846**/11475	–/–/–	15266/**12785**/15504	15539/20943/17944
25k	–	11139	–	15231	19734
256 classes, supervised learning/SSL:self-training/SSL:label spreading					
100 + 24.9k	–/–/–	–/–/–	–/–/–	–/–/–	–/–/–
500 + 24.5k	–/–/–	–/–/–	–/–/–	–/–/–	–/–/–
1k + 24k	–/–/–	–/–/–	–/–/–	–/–/–	–/–/–
10k + 15k	–/–/–	–/–/–	–/–/–	–/–/–	–/–/–
20k + 5k	–/–/–	–/–/–	–/**10210**/–	15560/**13387**/18230	–/–/–
25k	–	–	–	14860	–

5   Conclusions and Future Work

Previously, in the SCA community, profiled side-channel analysis has been considered as a strict two-step process, where only the profiled model is transferred between the two phases. Here, we explore the scenario where the attacker is more restricted in the profiling phase but can use additional available information given from the attacking measurements to build the profiled model. Two approaches to SSL have been studied in scenarios with low noise/high noise/high noise with countermeasures, 9/256 classes for prediction, and a different number of measurements in the profiling phase. As side-channel attack techniques, we use three ML methods (multilayer perceptron with four hidden layers, Naive Bayes, and random forest), template attack, and its pooled version. The obtained results show that SSL is able to help in many scenarios. Significant improvements are achieved for almost all classifiers, including template attack in the low noise scenario for the small number of samples in the learning dataset. Also, template attack was improved for the majority of dataset sizes using SSL methods. It is shown that the higher the number of samples in the profiling phase, the less influential are the added unlabeled samples from the attacking phase. When the noise level is higher, SSL methods still show superiority over supervised learning approaches for the majority of dataset sizes and when using most classifiers. The improvements are smaller since those scenarios are, in general, much more difficult to attack. For the AES_RD dataset, which has a significant amount of noise and a random delay countermeasure, a clear benefit of using SSL methods may be established only for 9-classes HW model, while for 256 classes model, both supervised learning and SSL methods perform similarly. In general, when averaged over all considered scenarios, MLP classifier demonstrates the best results, followed by TA_p, and NB. Regarding the SSL method of choice, it appears that self-training is better in the majority of cases when compared to label spreading. Still, for the low noise dataset scenario, label spreading may be used instead.

As a future work, we will concentrate on datasets with countermeasures since that setting seems to be the most problematic for SSL. A second research direction would be to consider not only those measurements with the highest probabilities but also to use the distribution of probabilities from the SSL learning. Finally, in a real-world scenario, two different devices should be considered, which may result in (slightly) different distributions (see e.g., [22, 23]).

References

1. Heuser, A., Rioul, O., Guilley, S.: Good is not good enough — deriving optimal distinguishers from communication theory. In: Batina, L., Robshaw, M. (eds.) CHES 2014. LNCS, vol. 8731, pp. 55–74. Springer, Heidelberg (2014). https://doi.org/10.1007/978-3-662-44709-3_4
2. Lerman, L., Poussier, R., Bontempi, G., Markowitch, O., Standaert, F.-X.: Template attacks vs. machine learning revisited (and the curse of dimensionality in side-channel analysis). In: Mangard, S., Poschmann, A.Y. (eds.) COSADE 2014. LNCS, vol. 9064, pp. 20–33. Springer, Cham (2015). https://doi.org/10.1007/978-3-319-21476-4_2

3. Heuser, A., Zohner, M.: Intelligent machine homicide - breaking cryptographic devices using support vector machines. In: Schindler, W., Huss, S.A. (eds.) COSADE 2012. LNCS, vol. 7275, pp. 249–264. Springer, Heidelberg (2012). https://doi.org/10.1007/978-3-642-29912-4_18
4. Picek, S., Heuser, A., Guilley, S.: Template attack versus bayes classifier. J. Cryptographic Eng. **7**(4), 343–351 (2017). https://doi.org/10.1007/s13389-017-0172-7
5. Cagli, E., Dumas, C., Prouff, E.: Convolutional neural networks with data augmentation against jitter-based countermeasures - profiling attacks without preprocessing. In: Fischer, W., Homma, N. (eds.) CHES 2017. LNCS, vol. 10529, pp. 45–68. Springer, Cham (2017). https://doi.org/10.1007/978-3-319-66787-4_3
6. Heyszl, J., Ibing, A., Mangard, S., De Santis, F., Sigl, G.: Clustering algorithms for non-profiled single-execution attacks on exponentiations. In: Francillon, A., Rohatgi, P. (eds.) CARDIS 2013. LNCS, vol. 8419, pp. 79–93. Springer, Cham (2014). https://doi.org/10.1007/978-3-319-08302-5_6
7. Maghrebi, H., Portigliatti, T., Prouff, E.: Breaking cryptographic implementations using deep learning techniques. In: Carlet, C., Hasan, M.A., Saraswat, V. (eds.) SPACE 2016. LNCS, vol. 10076, pp. 3–26. Springer, Cham (2016). https://doi.org/10.1007/978-3-319-49445-6_1
8. Picek, S., Samiotis, I.P., Kim, J., Heuser, A., Bhasin, S., Legay, A.: On the performance of convolutional neural networks for side-channel analysis. In: Chattopadhyay, A., Rebeiro, C., Yarom, Y. (eds.) SPACE 2018. LNCS, vol. 11348, pp. 157–176. Springer, Cham (2018). https://doi.org/10.1007/978-3-030-05072-6_10
9. Picek, S., Heuser, A., Jovic, A., Bhasin, S., Regazzoni, F.: The curse of class imbalance and conflicting metrics with machine learning for side-channel evaluations. IACR Trans. Cryptographic Hardware Embed. Syst. **2019**(1), 209–237 (2018). https://doi.org/10.13154/tches.v2019.i1.209-237
10. Lerman, L., Medeiros, S.F., Veshchikov, N., Meuter, C., Bontempi, G., Markowitch, O.: Semi-supervised template attack. In: Prouff, E. (ed.) COSADE 2013. LNCS, vol. 7864, pp. 184–199. Springer, Heidelberg (2013). https://doi.org/10.1007/978-3-642-40026-1_12
11. Schwenker, F., Trentin, E.: Pattern classification and clustering: a review of partially supervised learning approaches. Pattern Recogn. Lett. **37**, 4–14 (2014). https://doi.org/10.1016/j.patrec.2013.10.017
12. Chapelle, O., Schlkopf, B., Zien, A.: Semi-Supervised Learning, 1st edn. The MIT Press, Cambridge (2010)
13. Bengio, Y., Delalleau, O., Le Roux, N.: Efficient non-parametric function induction in semi-supervised learning. Technical report 1247, Département d'informatique et recherche opérationnelle, Université de Montréal (2004)
14. Pedregosa, F., et al.: Scikit-learn: machine learning in python. J. Mach. Learn. Res. **12**, 2825–2830 (2011)
15. Chari, S., Rao, J.R., Rohatgi, P.: Template attacks. In: Kaliski, B.S., Koç, K., Paar, C. (eds.) CHES 2002. LNCS, vol. 2523, pp. 13–28. Springer, Heidelberg (2003). https://doi.org/10.1007/3-540-36400-5_3
16. Choudary, O., Kuhn, M.G.: Efficient template attacks. In: Francillon, A., Rohatgi, P. (eds.) CARDIS 2013. LNCS, vol. 8419, pp. 253–270. Springer, Cham (2014). https://doi.org/10.1007/978-3-319-08302-5_17
17. Friedman, J.H., Bentley, J.L., Finkel, R.A.: An algorithm for finding best matches in logarithmic expected time. ACM Trans. Math. Softw. **3**(3), 209–226 (1977). https://doi.org/10.1145/355744.355745
18. Haykin, S.: Neural Networks: A Comprehensive Foundation, 2nd edn. Prentice Hall PTR, Upper Saddle River (1998)

19. Breiman, L.: Random forests. Mach. Learn. **45**(1), 5–32 (2001). https://doi.org/10.1023/A:1010933404324

20. TELECOM ParisTech SEN research group: DPA Contest, 4th edn. (2013–2014). http://www.DPAcontest.org/v4/

21. Coron, J.-S., Kizhvatov, I.: An efficient method for random delay generation in embedded software. In: Clavier, C., Gaj, K. (eds.) CHES 2009. LNCS, vol. 5747, pp. 156–170. Springer, Heidelberg (2009). https://doi.org/10.1007/978-3-642-04138-9_12

22. Renauld, M., Standaert, F.-X., Veyrat-Charvillon, N., Kamel, D., Flandre, D.: A formal study of power variability issues and side-channel attacks for nanoscale devices. In: Paterson, K.G. (ed.) EUROCRYPT 2011. LNCS, vol. 6632, pp. 109–128. Springer, Heidelberg (2011). https://doi.org/10.1007/978-3-642-20465-4_8

23. Choudary, O., Kuhn, M.G.: Template attacks on different devices. In: Prouff, E. (ed.) COSADE 2014. LNCS, vol. 8622, pp. 179–198. Springer, Cham (2014). https://doi.org/10.1007/978-3-319-10175-0_13

Non-profiled Mask Recovery: The Impact of Independent Component Analysis

Si Gao[1]([✉]), Elisabeth Oswald[1], Hua Chen[2], and Wei Xi[3]

[1] University of Bristol, Bristol, UK
si.gao@bristol.ac.uk
[2] Institute of Software, Chinese Academy of Sciences, Beijing, China
[3] Southern Power Grid Science Research Institute, Guangzhou, China

Abstract. As one of the most prevalent SCA countermeasures, masking schemes are designed to defeat a broad range of side channel attacks. An attack vector that is suitable for low-order masking schemes is to try and directly determine the mask(s) (for each trace) by utilising the fact that often an attacker has access to several leakage points of the respectively used mask(s). Good examples for implementations of low-order masking schemes include the table re-computation schemes as well as the masking scheme in DPAContest V4.2. We propose a novel approach based on Independent Component Analysis (ICA) to efficiently utilise the information from several leakage points to reconstruct the respective masks (for each trace) and show it is a competitive attack vector in practice.

Keywords: Side channel analysis · Masking · Independent Component Analysis

1 Introduction

Over the past decade, Side Channel Attacks (SCAs) have become a major threat for various cryptographic devices. Depending on the specific attacker model, most SCAs can be divided into two categories: profiled attacks and non-profiled attacks. In a profiled attack, the attacker (a priori) creates direct approximations of the device's leakage function, and uses these in an attack. This typically results in very efficient attacks but with the strong assumptions about the capabilities of the attacker. Non-profiled attacks only require a proportional (or weaker) approximation of the device's leakage model. The canonical example of such an attack is to approximate the device leakage with the Hamming weight of intermediate values, and utilise correlation as a distinguisher. Attacks in both categories often proceed via a divide and conquer strategy, which requires (in the divide step) to explicitly guess partial keys. Consequently (in a known plaintext setting) such attacks are limited to first and last rounds of typical block cipher constructions.

In 2017, Gao et al. proposed a new non-profiled SCA based on Independent Component Analysis (ICA) [1]. Assuming the observed leakages follow

© Springer Nature Switzerland AG 2019
B. Bilgin and J.-B. Fischer (Eds.): CARDIS 2018, LNCS 11389, pp. 51–64, 2019.
https://doi.org/10.1007/978-3-030-15462-2_4

the weighted Hamming weight model, the ICA based attack recovers the intermediate states without making any explicit key guesses. In their paper, the authors demonstrate several applications of this approach, including a new key-distinguisher, attacking the middle encryption rounds as well as reverse engineering. However, all previous discussions about ICA-based SCA focus on unprotected implementations. We are hence interested in investigating if ICA-based SCA can be useful to attack protected implementations.

For ICA-based SCA to work it is imperative to have access to several leakage points for some (targeted) intermediate value. In masked implementations, one can often observe leakages related to the manipulation of masks in the processor. Hence, ICA-based SCA could be a powerful tool for mask recovery in masked implementations, in particular optimised low-order masking schemes.

Our Contribution. In this paper, we explore the potential of ICA to compromise implementations of some (low order) masking schemes. Specifically, in table re-computation schemes, the multiple XORs in the re-computation process naturally provide multiple leakage observations for ICA. Compared with previous attacks, our ICA-based mask recovery finds the n-bit random masks with only n leakage points, whereas previous attacks take 2^n points. Experiments confirm that for smaller Sboxes ($n = 4$), ICA-based attack outperforms horizontal attacks on smart card implementations. For the Rotating Sbox Masking (RSM) scheme, which is used in the DPAContest V4, our analysis proves that if the attacker chooses the leakages wisely, the random masks can be recovered as an approximate ICA problem. Although the mask recovery becomes less accurate, the following key recovery is hardly affected.

Paper Organization. In Sect. 2, we briefly review the targeted masking schemes as well as our primary tool—ICA. Section 3 analyzes the leakage behaviour of table re-computation schemes in details. As the XORs naturally provide multiple leakage observations, ICA enables the attacker to determine both the random masks and the secret key. We present another masking scheme—the masking scheme in DPAContest V4.2—in Sect. 4. Although this scheme computes the masked tables offline, the relevant random indexes in each round provide considerable leakages for ICA-based SCA. Impacts of this approach and conclusions are further presented in Sect. 5.

2   Preliminaries

2.1   Masking Schemes

To date, masking is one of the most prevalent countermeasures for software implementations. In general, a masking scheme conceals the cryptographic intermediate states with random values. As a result, the data-dependent leakage no longer relates to the secret key. Previous studies proposed a variety of masking schemes, such as affine masking [2], polynomial masking [3] and inner product masking [4]. In this paper, we focus on Boolean masking, the most frequently implemented approach. In a Boolean masking scheme with d-shares, an intermediate state x is split into d shares $(x^{(1)}, x^{(2)}, ..., x^{(d)})$ where $x^{(1)} \oplus x^{(2)} \oplus ... \oplus x^{(d)} = x$. As each leakage point only depends on one $x^{(i)}$, the attacker cannot learn any useful information, unless they combine the leakages of all d shares.

For linear components P, implementing a Boolean masking is quite straight-forward: as $P(x^{(1)} \oplus x^{(2)} \oplus ... \oplus x^{(d)}) = P(x^{(1)}) \oplus P(x^{(2)}) \oplus ... \oplus P(x^{(d)})$, simply applying P to all d shares gives the expected outputs. For non-linear components (Sboxes), things become trickier. In order to ensure the output shares satisfy $S(x^{(1)} \oplus x^{(2)} \oplus ... \oplus x^{(d)}) = S_1(x^{(1)}) \oplus S_2(x^{(2)}) \oplus ... \oplus S_d(x^{(d)})$, at least one of the masked Sbox S_i must be related to multiple input shares. Three proposals exist in previous studies [5]:

- **Compute the Sbox arithmetically.** In 2003, Ishai, Sahai and Wagner proposed a provably secure higher-order masking scheme for bit-wise AND [6]. Alternatively, the whole Sbox can be computed as a bunch of masked ANDs and masked NOTs. Compared with the unprotected implementations, this construction significantly increases the computation cost.
- **Table Re-computation.** In many look-up table schemes, the masked Sbox is computed as a look-up table [7–9]. In the first step, these schemes often generate a masked table using all the shares from $x^{(1)}$ to $x^{(d-1)}$. Then, the output shares $(y^{(1)}, y^{(2)}, ..., y^{(d)})$ can be found by simply looking up $x^{(d)}$ in the masked table. The major drawback of this approach, is that the re-computation stage is not only costly, but also exploitable. For an n-bit Sbox, this procedure provides 2^n leakage points for each data share $x^{(i)}$. Thus, the attacker can collect all leakage points on the trace ("horizontally") and use a standard DPA style attack to recover $x^{(i)}$. For $n = 8$, this horizontal attack is actually quite efficient for software implementations [10,11].
- **Global look-up tables.** Alternatively, the masked table can also be computed offline [8]. In this case, a masked table is generated for each possible mask and stored in the data RAM/ROM. Considering the enormous memory cost, this approach is more suitable for smaller Sboxes (eg. 4-bit Sbox)[1]. For larger Sboxes, it often applies in Low-Entropy Masking Schemes (LEMS), such as the Rotating Sbox Masking (RSM) [13]. Instead of random masks, LEMS usually uses a precomputed set of constant masks, which significantly reduces the memory cost [13]. As a lightweight SCA countermeasure, it is LEMS's design philosophy to resist not all but a selection of important and powerful attacks [13]. Results from DPA Contest v4 and v4.2 are consistent with such statement: in the profiling case, the secret key can be found with only one trace [14].

2.2   Independent Component Analysis

Independent Component Analysis (ICA) [15] belongs to a class of problems called *Blind Source Separation* (BSS), which requires to separate a set of mixed

---

[1] For specific processors, such implementation is not necessarily secure [12].

signals, without the aid of information about the source signals or the mixing process. A common example is the *cocktail party problem* in which the challenge of a partygoer is to pick out a single conversation when in a noisy room.

Suppose we have n simultaneous conversations (sources) $\mathbf{S} = \{s_1, s_2, ..., s_n\}$ going on in the party room. Microphones are placed in different positions, recording m mixtures (observations) of the original sources $\mathbf{Y} = \{y_1, y_2, ..., y_m\}$. Assuming the observation y_j is a linear mixture of all sources, we have

$$y_j = a_{j,0} + a_{j,1}s_1 + a_{j,2}s_2 + ... + a_{j,n}s_n$$

where $a_{j,i}$ stands for the real-valued coefficient. The overall mixing procedure can be written as

$$\mathbf{Y} = \mathbf{AS}$$

where $\mathbf{A}$ is called the *mixing matrix*. In signal processing, such statistical model is called *Independent Component Analysis* [15]. With additional multivariate Gaussian noise $\mathbf{N}$, the noisy ICA model is defined as

$$\mathbf{Y} = \mathbf{AS} + \mathbf{N}$$

The goal of ICA, is to recover the unknown sources $\mathbf{S}$ from the observation $\mathbf{Y}$, without knowing the mixing matrix $\mathbf{A}$ or the Gaussian noise $\mathbf{N}$ in advance.

2.3 ICA in Side Channel Analysis

Assuming the target device's leakage function is linear (in the bits of the intermediate values), recovering the secret intermediate values in SCA is quite similar to an ICA problem [1]. Specifically, when operating an n-bit intermediate state x, the data-dependent leakage can be written as

$$\mathrm{L}(x) = \alpha_0 + \alpha_1 x_1 + \alpha_2 x_2 + ... + \alpha_n x_n, \ \alpha_i \in \mathbb{R} \qquad (1)$$

Here x_i represents the i-th bit[2] of x and L is a linear leakage function. This leakage function has the same form as one ICA observation (i.e. y_j in Sect. 2.2).

However, for ICA we need more than a single observation. Suppose that the device not only computes x but also computes some other intermediate state $x' = x \oplus c$ (c is a constant) at some point. Then, the attacker can also learn the leakage of $L(x')$[3]. Take $c = 00...01$ as an example, we have:

$$\begin{aligned}
L(x') &= L(x \oplus 00...01) \\
&= \alpha_0 + \alpha_1 x_1 + \alpha_2 x_2 + ... + \alpha_n(x_n \oplus 1) \\
&= \alpha_0 + \alpha_1 x_1 + \alpha_2 x_2 + ... + \alpha_n(1 - x_n) \\
&= (\alpha_0 + \alpha_n) + \alpha_1 x_1 + \alpha_2 x_2 + ... - \alpha_n x_n
\end{aligned}$$

---

[2] Throughout this paper, we always use subscript i as the i-th bit. Unlike traditional SCA, the intermediate state x here represents the random mask, which is not dependent on a key guess k.

[3] For simplicity, we assume all leakage share the same leakage function L. However, ICA does work with different L-s, as long as they are all linear combinations of x.

It is not hard to see that such leakage can be regarded as the leakage from the same intermediate state x, but with a different linear leakage function L'. Thus, if the targeted implementation has some operand like $x \oplus c$, the attacker may be able to manipulate c to get multiple "observations" for the intermediate state x. Assuming the attacker can get enough observations (the number of observations $m \geq n$), in theory, he (or she) can solve the intermediate state x as a noisy ICA problem.

In practice, considering side channel leakage usually contains high level of noise, the authors also proposed a specific ICA algorithm for SCA. Due to the space limit, we omit further details: interested readers can find this part in [1].

Unlike other traditional SCAs, recovering x with ICA does not involve any key guess. As a consequence, ICA-based SCA serves as a perfect tool for SCA in the middle rounds or SCA-based reverse engineering [1]. Indeed, the authors already provide realistic experiments to verify their results on certain software implementations. On the other hand, as stated in [1], in many realistic circumstances, finding such XOR constant c might not be an easy task. For this reason, to date, the applications of ICA-based SCA are restricted to unprotected cryptographic implementations.

3   ICA-Based Attack on a Table Re-computation Scheme

In this section, we analyse the potential application of ICA on a few masking schemes. Perhaps surprisingly, for some masking schemes, constructing multiple observations becomes much easier. The following two sections present two case studies: for each case study, we will review its mask computation, analyze its leakage and show how ICA-based SCA enables the recovery of the random masks. Comparison with previous attacks and experimental verifications are also provided in each case. We begin by studying a table re-computation scheme.

3.1   Table Re-computation Schemes

Considering the memory cost, masking schemes with global look-up table can hardly be applied to larger Sboxes (eg. the Sbox in AES). Thus, many masking schemes choose to generate the masked table online. In a d-shares table re-computation scheme, $(x^{(1)}, x^{(2)}, ..., x^{(d-1)})$ is taken to the computation to create a masked table T. In the last step, the implementation simply looks up $x^{(d)}$ in T and returns $T(x^{(d)})$ as the output shares. To ensure its security against SCA, designers may also add some other procedures, such as refreshing T with fresh randomness after each table look-up [9]. Meanwhile, most masked table re-computations are rather similar: for clarity, we present a d-shares table re-computation procedure in Algorithm 1.

3.2   Previous Attacks

Note that in Algorithm 1, line 3 always produces 2^n leakages for each share. More specifically, assuming the leakage function is L, the attacker learns the leakages

---

Algorithm 1. A d-shares table re-computation for an n-bit Sbox

---

Input: $x^{(1)},...,x^{(d)}$ such that $x = x^{(1)} \oplus x^{(2)} \oplus ... \oplus x^{(d)}$
    Shared table T such that $\underset{i}{\oplus} T(u)^{(i)} = S(u)$

Output: Shared table T such that $\underset{i}{\oplus} T\left(x^{(d)}\right)^{(i)} = S(x)$

1: **for** $i = 1$ **to** $d - 1$ **do**
2:     **for all** $u \in \{0,1\}^n$ **do**
3:         $T'(u) = T\left(u \oplus x^{(i)}\right)$
4:     **end for**
5:     $T = T'$
6: **end for**

---

of $(L(x^{(i)}), L(x^{(i)} \oplus 1), ..., L(x^{(i)} \oplus (2^n - 1)))$. As all these leakages depend on the same share $x^{(i)}$, the attacker can take a guess about $x^{(i)}$ and verify this guess with Correlation Power Analysis (CPA) [16]. Unlike traditional CPA which utilises a specific leakage point across many traces (i.e. a "vertical" attack), this attack utilizes all the 2^n leakages on the same trace (i.e. it is a "horizontal" attack). Having recovered the masks, key recovery is trivial: since all $d - 1$ input shares (random masks) are already known, a traditional vertical CPA on the leakage of $x^{(d)}$ reveals the secret key. Previous studies proved that, for 8-bit Sboxes ($n = 8$), such "horizontal" attack is a serious threat for table re-computation schemes [10].

A common countermeasure for the horizontal attacks is to randomly shuffle the constant u in line 3. Since the computation follows some random order $(\varphi(0), \varphi(1), ..., \varphi(2^n - 1))$, $x^{(i)}$ alone can no longer determine all the 2^n leakages. However, for many smart card applications, generating and storing an n-bit random permutation φ in memory is far too expensive. Instead, they prefer to use some pseudo-random function φ that can be computed online. However, the computation of φ provides new leakages for the attacker. Tunstall et al. showed that the attacker can easily explore such leakages and recover the entire permutation φ [11]. Moreover, Bruneau et al. proposed a multi-variate attack which combines all 2^n leakages on one trace into a statistic that depends on $x^{(i)}$ [5]. As the combination is unordered, random shuffling does not affect the final statistic. Although $x^{(i)}$ cannot be recovered, the attacker finds the secret key through higher-order attacks, with the leakage of $x^{(i)}$ as well as this statistic.

3.3   ICA-Based Attack

Mask Recovery. The leakages that occur in table re-computation schemes are a perfect match for ICA. Specifically, each bit of the intermediate state x now becomes an independent binary source. Assuming the leakage function is linear, the attacker can always use the leakage of x as one observation for ICA. As stated previously, the leakage of $L(x \oplus c)$ can also be regarded as the leakages of x with a different leakage function. In other words, for table re-computation schemes, the attacker can always find 2^n independent observations through 2^n

XOR constants. In fact, ICA only needs n observations for a successful recovery. Taking noise into consideration, the formal model can be written as:

$$l = L(x^{(i)}) + \mathbf{N}$$

where $\mathbf{N}$ represents the random noise. As stated in Sect. 2.3, ICA-based SCA helps to recover the secret share $x^{(i)}$.

Key Recovery. Since all $d - 1$ secret shares are already recovered, the following key recovery becomes trivial. Take the last round attack of AES for instance, assuming the corresponding ciphertext byte is c and related round key byte is k, we have

$$x^{(d)} = S^{-1}(c \oplus k) \oplus x^{(1)} \oplus x^{(2)} \oplus ... \oplus x^{(d-1)}$$

Since the attacker has the leakage of $x^{(d)}$, traditional CPA helps to determine the correct key guess for k, as long as the value of $x^{(1)} \oplus x^{(2)} \oplus ... \oplus x^{(d-1)}$ is given.

Comparison with Previous Attacks. Compared with horizontal CPAs, our ICA-based mask recovery uses only n leakage samples. Since horizontal CPA takes guesses about $x^{(i)}$, it only applies to one certain trace. In other words, the sample size for horizontal CPA on table re-computation schemes is always 2^n. Previous studies showed that for $n = 8$, horizontal CPA works quite well with software implementations [10,11]. However, for smaller Sboxes (eg. $n = 4$), horizontal CPA becomes less effective [11]. This is not surprising though: as a non-profiled attack, CPA requires several traces to achieve a stable recovery. For our ICA-based mask recovery, smaller Sbox is hardly a problem. Since our approach uses only n leakage points, it works well even if $n = 2$. Meanwhile, the mask recovery in horizontal CPA is basically a one-dimensional attack: since each trace has different input shares (random masks), horizontal CPA only works on the horizontal axis. The following key recovery, on the other hand, only collects information on the vertical axis. In Bruneau et al.'s work [5], since the horizontal leakages are packed into one statistic, their attack mainly works on the vertical axis. On the contrary, our approach is essentially a two-dimensional attack. Both the multiple leakages on one trace ("horizontal") and the leakage model shared by all traces ("vertical") are taken into consideration. In some cases, this two-dimensional property becomes a limitation: if the target implementation uses random shuffling as a countermeasure, the frequently changing random order φ completely defeats our attack. Since the 2^n horizontal leakages in our attack are not packed together (like Bruneau et al.'s attack), this random order prevents our attack to explore the vertical information. However, such protection only works if the designers use a new φ for each encryption. If the random φ is fixed, our attack works exactly the same way: as ICA does not require to know the mixing matrix, we can recover $x^{(i)}$ without knowing φ. For easy comparison, we list the attacks mentioned above with 2-shares table re-computation schemes in Table 1[4].

---

[4] A v-variate attack means it takes v leakage samples in total.

Table 1. Comparison of attacks with 2-shares table re-computation schemes

	Variate	Fix shuffle	Random shuffle
horizontal CPA	$2^n + 1$		
Bruneau's attack	$2^{n+1} + 1$	✓	✓
Our approach	$n + 1$	✓	

3.4   Experimental Validation

To show that our ICA-based attack works, we have implemented a 2-shares version of Coron's masking scheme [9] on an IC card with 8-bit microprocessor (Atmega163). The power consumption was measured with a PicoScope 3206D oscilloscope at a sampling rate of 1 GSa/s. The target cipher uses the 4-bit Sbox of PRESENT [17]. Since the previous studies already proved that horizontal CPA works well with 8-bit Sboxes, here we aim to test whether it still gives satisfying recovery with smaller Sboxes. Our entire trace set contains 200 traces, with 2 000 000 samples covering the Sbox computation in the last round. Results from both horizontal CPA and our ICA-based attack are presented in Fig. 1.

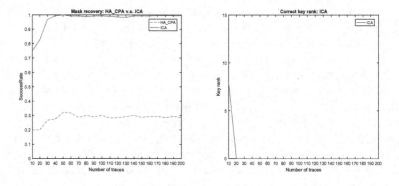

Fig. 1. Mask and key recovery: horizontal CPA v.s. ICA

Clearly the small 4-bit Sbox is an issue for horizontal CPA: as there are only 16 leakage samples on each trace, mask recovery becomes less reliable. In our experiments, only 30% of the random masks are successfully recovered. As most recovered masks are incorrect, further key recovery becomes less effective. On the other hand, our ICA-based mask recovery finds over 90% of the random masks correctly with only 40 traces. Figure 1 shows such attack is quite efficient: the key recovery becomes stable after only 20 traces.

4   ICA-Based Attack on DPAContest v4.2

As table re-computation schemes produce the leakages of $(x^{(i)}, x^{(i)} \oplus 1, ..., x^{(i)} \oplus 2^n - 1)$, recovering the random masks with ICA seems quite straightforward.

In the following, let us consider a more subtle example: the masking scheme in DPAContest v4.2.

4.1   The Rotating Sbox Masking Scheme

Unlike typical table re-computation schemes, the masking scheme in DPAContest v4 uses global look-up tables, where the masked tables are pre-computed offline. As stated previously, for larger Sboxes (like AES), storing all possible masked tables is impossible for many commonly used encryption devices. Instead, DPA-Contest v4 uses Rotating Sbox Masking (RSM) [13], which uses a set of constant masks rather than completely random masks. More specifically, in the latest version (DPAContest v4.2) [18], the implementation uses the following mask set:

$$M[0:15] = \{0x03, 0x0c, 0x35, 0x3a, 0x50, 0x5f, 0x66, 0x69,$$
$$0x96, 0x99, 0xa0, 0xaf, 0xc5, 0xca, 0xf3, 0xfc\}$$

Before any encryption, 16 masked tables (MS_i) are pre-computed and stored in memory:
$$MS_i(x) = S(x \oplus M[i]) \oplus M[(i+1) \bmod 16]$$

In each encryption, the encryption device randomly picks a 16 elements offset array $O[0:15]$, where each $O[i]$ is a 4-bit random offset. According to the mask set, the initial 128 bit mask is

$$\text{Mask}(0) = \{M[O[0]], M[O[1]], ..., M[O[15]]\}$$

At the end of one encryption round, each mask byte is "rotated" right for one position in the masking set. Thus, in the $(r+1)$-th round, the input mask is:

$$\text{Mask}(r) = \{M[(O[0]+r)\bmod16], M[(O[1]+r)\bmod16], ..., M[(O[15]+r)\bmod16]\}$$

Algorithm 2 describes the masked round function of AES-128 in detail.

Algorithm 2. Masked round function of AES-128 in DPAContest v4.2

Input: masked input state $X = \{X[0], X[1], ..., X[15]\}$
         random mask index array $O = \{O[0], O[1], ..., O[15]\}$
         subkey $RK = \{RK[0], RK[1], ..., RK[15]\}$
         masked output state $X = \{X[0], X[1], ..., X[15]\}$
1: $X = X \oplus RK$ ▷ AddRoundKey
2: **for** $i = 0$ **to** 15 **do**
3:   $X_i = MS_{(O[i]+r)\bmod 16}(X[i])$ ▷ Masked Sbox
4: **end for**
5: $X = \text{ShiftRow}(X)$
6: $X = \text{MixColumn}(X)$
7: $X = X \oplus \text{MixColumn}(\text{ShiftRow}(\text{Mask}(r+1))) \oplus \text{Mask}(r+1)$ ▷
   Mask Compensation

In addition, considering the threat of higher-order SCA, random shuffling is applied to the first/last round. Since the Sbox computation order is not given, the attacker can hardly combine leakages from multiple traces and learn the secret key from conventional vertical SCA.

4.2 Previous Attacks

Although there are many attacks in the hall of fame of DPAContest V4.2, fewer participants give detailed descriptions of their attacks. As a result, we can only present a brief overview of the current results. Apparently, profiling attacks work well with DPAContest v4.2. Most profiling attack recovers the secret key with a few traces, whereas the best one works with only one trace. On the other hand, most non-profiled attacks use much more traces. To date, the best non-profiled attack existed is due to Zeyi Liu et al. [14]. According to the hall of fame, their attack takes only 14 traces, whereas all other non-profiled attacks need a few hundred traces.

In theory, horizontal CPA still works for this scheme. Denote the 4-bit $O[0]$ as x, in each Sbox computation, the processor needs x to decide which masked table should be used. Algorithm 3 presents the assembly codes of the Sbox computation in DPAContest v4.2.

Algorithm 3. ASM codes of the masked Sbox computation in DPAContest v4.2

```
 1: ldi YH,hi8(__offset__)        ▷ point to the offset array location
 2: ldi YL,0x00
 3: ld offset, Y                   ▷ load offset x
 4: ldi ZH, hi8(aes_sbox0)
 5: add offset,I2                  ▷ x = x + r
 6: andi offset,0x0F               ▷ x = x mod 16
 7: add ZH, offset                 ▷ Determine the masked table
 8: clr ZL
 9: mov ZL, ST11                   ▷ Table look up
10: clr ST11
11: lpm ST11, Z
```

As we can see in line 5–6, in the table look-up procedure, the attacker finds the leakage of $(x + r) \bmod 16$. Although the first/last round Sbox computation is shuffled, the rest 8 rounds in the middle still provide exploitable leakages. Specifically, the data-dependant leakages for round 2–9 can be written as $\{L((x + 1) \bmod 16), L((x + 2) \bmod 16), ..., L((x + 8) \bmod 16)\}$. In this case, the attacker can guess x and verify his guess with horizontal CPA. Nonetheless, considering there are only 8 leakage samples available, recovering the random masks with horizontal CPA seems to be a difficult task.

4.3   ICA-Based Attack

Apparently, applying ICA in this scheme is not as straightforward as table re-computation schemes. Following the previous construction, the random mask index x can be regarded as 4-bit binary sources. However, as the leakages here depend on $(x + r) \mod 16$, the "XOR-constant" method [1] no longer provides multiple observations. Nonetheless, in round 9, we have

$$(x + 8) \mod 16 = x \oplus 8$$

As a result, the leakage of round 9 forms a valid ICA observation. Similarly, the Boolean function of $y = (x + 4) \mod 16$ can be written as:

$$y_1 = x_1 \oplus x_2$$
$$y_2 = x_2 \oplus 1$$
$$y_3 = x_3$$
$$y_4 = x_4$$

Clearly, the least significant 3 bits have the same expressions as $x \oplus 4$. The only difference lies in the most significant bit y_1. Since ICA is a linear[5] procedure, the linear mixture of x can never express $x_1 \oplus x_2$. As a consequence, in ICA, the leakage of y_1 can be regarded as random noise. More specifically, in round 5,

$$l = L(y) + \mathbf{N}$$
$$= \alpha_0 + \alpha_1 y_1 + \alpha_2 y_2 + \alpha_3 y_3 + \alpha_4 y_4 + \mathbf{N}$$
$$= \alpha_0 + \alpha_2 - \alpha_2 x_2 + \alpha_3 x_3 + \alpha_4 x_4 + \mathbf{N} + \alpha_1 (x_1 \oplus x_2)$$
$$= L'(x) + \mathbf{N}'$$

In other words, the leakages in round 5 can be regarded as a noisier obser-vation of x with an equivalent leakage function where $\alpha_1 = 0$. Similar property holds for the leakages of $(x + 2) \mod 16$ and $(x + 1) \mod 16$, although the signal-to-noise-ratio (SNR) will be further reduced. As a result, attackers can recover the offset $O[0]$ with the leakages from round $(2, 3, 5, 9)$. With the random masks recovered, the following key recovery becomes much easier. Unlike the Sbox, the MixColumn computations in the first round are not shuffled. Therefore, attack-ers can explore the leakages of MixColumn and learn the secret key through conventional vertical SCA.

4.4   Experimental Validation

We show how our ICA-based attack can be applied here with the EM traces provided by DPAContest [14]. In our experiments, the leakage of offset $O[0]$ appears not only in the Sbox computations, but also in the MixColumn compu-tations. For better recovery, in each round, our ICA-based analysis takes both

---

[5] Here linear means linear on real values, rather than GF_{2^n}.

observations as its inputs. As a result, in the mask recovery stage, our analysis uses 8 observations to retrieve 4 sources. Even with these extra leakages, our mask recovery is not as good as the previous section. As we can see in Fig. 2, the success rate for our ICA-based mask recovery is around 80%. Nonetheless, the following key-recovery proves that 80% accuracy is still good enough for key recovery: the correct key is almost determined after only 30 traces. On the other hand, in our experiment, 8 leakages can hardly support a horizontal CPA: only 10% of the recovered masks are correct and thus key recovery becomes infeasible.

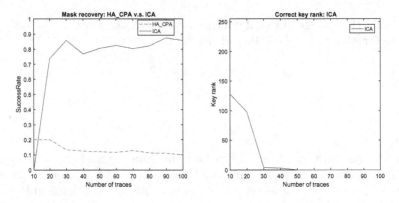

Fig. 2. Mask and key recovery: horizontal CPA v.s. ICA

5   Conclusion

In 2017, Gao et al. have proposed a novel side channel analysis based on independent component analysis (ICA) [1]. As this ICA-based SCA does not take a "guess-and-determine" procedure, this approach is quite useful for attacking the middle rounds or reverse engineering. However, previous work only studied unprotected implementations.

In this paper, we demonstrated the potential of ICA to defeat some masking schemes: table re-computation and the RSM masking scheme in DPAContest V4.2. Our analysis shows that, assuming the attacker can choose the leakage samples wisely, the random masks in both schemes can be effectively recovered. Compared with the previous attacks, our mask recovery requires fewer leakages. For masking scheme designers, our attack is another warning: horizontal attacks are indeed serious practical threats. If the same (or relevant) mask appears multiple times during the computation, the attacker may learn considerable information about the mask, even if it never mixes with any masked intermediate state.

Acknowledgements. This work has been funded in part by the National Key R&D Program of China(2018YFB0904900, 2018YFB0904901) and EPSRC under grant agreement EP/N011635/1 (LADA).

References

1. Gao, S., Chen, H., Wu, W., Fan, L., Cao, W., Ma, X.: My traces learn what you did in the dark: recovering secret signals without key guesses. In: Handschuh, H. (ed.) CT-RSA 2017. LNCS, vol. 10159, pp. 363–378. Springer, Cham (2017). https://doi.org/10.1007/978-3-319-52153-4_21

2. von Willich, M.: A technique with an information-theoretic basis for protecting secret data from differential power attacks. In: Honary, B. (ed.) Cryptography and Coding 2001. LNCS, vol. 2260, pp. 44–62. Springer, Heidelberg (2001). https://doi.org/10.1007/3-540-45325-3_6

3. Roche, T., Prouff, E.: Higher-order glitch free implementation of the AES using secure multi-party computation protocols. J. Cryptogr. Eng. **2**, 111–127 (2012)

4. Balasch, J., Faust, S., Gierlichs, B., Verbauwhede, I.: Theory and practice of a leakage resilient masking scheme. In: Wang, X., Sako, K. (eds.) ASIACRYPT 2012. LNCS, vol. 7658, pp. 758–775. Springer, Heidelberg (2012). https://doi.org/10.1007/978-3-642-34961-4_45

5. Bruneau, N., Guilley, S., Najm, Z., Teglia, Y.: Multi-variate high-order attacks of shuffled tables recomputation. In: Güneysu, T., Handschuh, H. (eds.) CHES 2015. LNCS, vol. 9293, pp. 475–494. Springer, Heidelberg (2015). https://doi.org/10.1007/978-3-662-48324-4_24

6. Ishai, Y., Sahai, A., Wagner, D.: Private circuits: securing hardware against probing attacks. In: Boneh, D. (ed.) CRYPTO 2003. LNCS, vol. 2729, pp. 463–481. Springer, Heidelberg (2003). https://doi.org/10.1007/978-3-540-45146-4_27

7. Messerges, T.S.: Securing the AES finalists against power analysis attacks. In: Goos, G., Hartmanis, J., van Leeuwen, J., Schneier, B. (eds.) FSE 2000. LNCS, vol. 1978, pp. 150–164. Springer, Heidelberg (2001). https://doi.org/10.1007/3-540-44706-7_11

8. Prouff, E., Rivain, M.: A generic method for secure SBox implementation. In: Kim, S., Yung, M., Lee, H.-W. (eds.) WISA 2007. LNCS, vol. 4867, pp. 227–244. Springer, Heidelberg (2007). https://doi.org/10.1007/978-3-540-77535-5_17

9. Coron, J.-S.: Higher order masking of look-up tables. In: Nguyen, P.Q., Oswald, E. (eds.) EUROCRYPT 2014. LNCS, vol. 8441, pp. 441–458. Springer, Heidelberg (2014). https://doi.org/10.1007/978-3-642-55220-5_25

10. Pan, J., den Hartog, J.I., Lu, J.: You cannot hide behind the mask: power analysis on a provably secure S-Box implementation. In: Youm, H.Y., Yung, M. (eds.) WISA 2009. LNCS, vol. 5932, pp. 178–192. Springer, Heidelberg (2009). https://doi.org/10.1007/978-3-642-10838-9_14

11. Tunstall, M., Whitnall, C., Oswald, E.: Masking tables—an underestimated security risk. In: Moriai, S. (ed.) FSE 2013. LNCS, vol. 8424, pp. 425–444. Springer, Heidelberg (2014). https://doi.org/10.1007/978-3-662-43933-3_22

12. Kutzner, S., Nguyen, P.H., Poschmann, A., Wang, H.: On 3-share threshold implementations for 4-bit S-boxes. In: Prouff, E. (ed.) COSADE 2013. LNCS, vol. 7864, pp. 99–113. Springer, Heidelberg (2013). https://doi.org/10.1007/978-3-642-40026-1_7

13. Nassar, M., Souissi, Y., Guilley, S., Danger, J.L.: RSM: A small and fast countermeasure for AES, secure against 1st and 2nd-order zero-offset SCAs. In: 2012 Design, Automation & Test in Europe Conference & Exhibition (DATE), pp. 1173–1178 (2012)

14. TELECOM ParisTech SEN research group: DPA contest v4. http://www.dpacontest.org/v4/

15. Hyvärinen, A., Oja, E.: Independent component analysis: algorithms and applications. Neural Netw. **13**, 411–430 (2000)
16. Brier, E., Clavier, C., Olivier, F.: Correlation power analysis with a leakage model. In: Joye, M., Quisquater, J.-J. (eds.) CHES 2004. LNCS, vol. 3156, pp. 16–29. Springer, Heidelberg (2004). https://doi.org/10.1007/978-3-540-28632-5_2
17. Bogdanov, A., Knudsen, L.R., Leander, G., Paar, C., Poschmann, A., Robshaw, M.J.B., Seurin, Y., Vikkelsoe, C.: PRESENT: an ultra-lightweight block cipher. In: Paillier, P., Verbauwhede, I. (eds.) CHES 2007. LNCS, vol. 4727, pp. 450–466. Springer, Heidelberg (2007). https://doi.org/10.1007/978-3-540-74735-2_31
18. Bhasin, S., Bruneau, N., Danger, J.-L., Guilley, S., Najm, Z.: Analysis and improvements of the DPA contest v4 implementation. In: Chakraborty, R.S., Matyas, V., Schaumont, P. (eds.) SPACE 2014. LNCS, vol. 8804, pp. 201–218. Springer, Cham (2014). https://doi.org/10.1007/978-3-319-12060-7_14

How (Not) to Use Welch's T-Test
in Side-Channel Security Evaluations

François-Xavier Standaert[(⊠)]

ICTEAM/ELEN/Crypto Group, Université catholique de Louvain,
Ottignies-Louvain-la-Neuve, Belgium
`fstandae@uclouvain.be`

Abstract. The Test Vector Leakage Assessment (TVLA) methodology
is a qualitative tool relying on Welch's T-test to assess the security
of cryptographic implementations against side-channel attacks. Despite
known limitations (e.g., risks of false negatives and positives), it is sometimes considered as a pass-fail test to determine whether such implementations are "safe" or not (without clear definition of what is "safe").
In this note, we clarify the limited quantitative meaning of this test
when used as a standalone tool. For this purpose, we first show that
the straightforward application of this approach to assess the security
of a masked implementation is not sufficient. More precisely, we show
that even in a simple (more precisely, univariate) case study that seems
best suited for the TVLA methodology, detection (or lack thereof) with
Welch's T-test can be totally disconnected from the actual security level
of an implementation. For this purpose, we put forward the case of a
realistic masking scheme that looks very safe from the TVLA point-
of-view and is nevertheless easy to break. We then discuss this result
in more general terms and argue that this limitation is shared by all
"moment-based" security evaluations. We conclude the note positively,
by describing how to use moment-based analyses as a useful ingredient
of side-channel security evaluations, to determine a "security order".

1 Introduction

Leakage detection tests have recently emerged as a convenient solution to perform preliminary (black box) evaluations of resistance against side-channel analysis. Cryptography Research (CRI)'s non-specific (fixed vs. random) T-test is
a popular example of this trend [8,13]. It works by comparing the leakages of
a cryptographic (e.g., block cipher) implementation with fixed plaintexts (and
key) to the leakages of the same implementation with random plaintexts (and
fixed key)[1], thanks to Welch's T-test [31]. Besides its conceptual simplicity, the
main advantage of such a test, that was carefully discussed in [11,19,27], is its

---

[1] The Test Vector Leakage Assessment methodology in [8,13] includes other options
such as non-specific semi-fixed vs. random tests and specific tests – we focus on the
non-specific fixed vs. random test that is the most popular in the literature.

© Springer Nature Switzerland AG 2019
B. Bilgin and J.-B. Fischer (Eds.): CARDIS 2018, LNCS 11389, pp. 65–79, 2019.
https://doi.org/10.1007/978-3-030-15462-2_5

low sampling complexity. That is, by comparing only two (fixed vs. random) classes of leakages, one reduces the detection problem to a simpler estimation task. And since these tests are generally applied independently to many leakage samples (e.g., corresponding to a full block cipher execution), they generally take advantage of the larger signal (i.e., the larger difference of means between the fixed and random classes) that occur for some samples with high probability.

Limitations and Improvements. The counterpart to this lower sampling complexity is a risk of false negatives and positives. Regarding false negatives, it may for example happen that for some informative samples, the mean values of the fixed and random classes are identical (resp., very similar), which makes detection impossible (resp., measurement-intensive). Yet, by applying the TVLA methodology to large enough traces (possibly with a few different fixed classes), the risk that significant leakages remain unnoticed for a complete (e.g., block cipher) implementation is usually expected to remain negligible. Regarding false positives, they rather relate to the fact that a (non-specific) T-test spots informative samples independent of their exploitability with standard Differential Power Analysis (DPA) attacks [18]. For example, the latter attacks typically target an enumerable part of the key that is manipulated in the first block cipher rounds, while the real and random classes differ in all the cipher rounds. More specific (and informative) detections can however be obtained by computing more specific metrics (i.e., targeting specific computations of the implementation), at the cost of a more expensive estimation. So in summary, the state-of-the-art typically views the TVLA methodology as a tradeoff between the sampling complexity and the informativeness of the leakage detection. Note that as discussed in [11], the sampling complexity of non-specific T-tests can be further reduced by considering two fixed classes (rather than a fixed and a random one).

A Tempting Shortcoming. In view of these advantages and limitations, it is sometimes considered that the TVLA methodology is *"a pass-fail test which determines whether the crypto implementation is safe or not"* [26]. But this naturally raises the question of what is precisely meant by "safe". For example, it is tempting (and as will be shown, incorrect) to expect that a device successively passing a non-specific T-test with Q traces is secure against side-channel attacks with up to Q traces. Clearly, this cannot hold in general. Indeed, and even assuming that the aforementioned false positives and negatives do not occur, another limitation of the original TVLA methodology is that it is inherently univariate. This implies that whenever multivariate attacks are more powerful than univariate ones, a leaking device can pass a non-specific T-test despite being weak in the general sense (i.e., breakable with less traces than used by the TVLA methodology). Concrete examples of this situation include the exploitation of static leakages [20, 24], and serial implementations of masking schemes for which the number of exploitable leakage samples grows quadratically in the number of shares, which implies that univariate attacks become less and less relevant to evaluate their security level as this number of shares increases [3]. Note that the work of Schneider and Moradi in [27] mitigates this limitation by integrating the possibility to estimate mixed statistical moments in their leakage detection. Yet, even in that case the resulting evaluation remains insufficient since corresponding to the exploitation of one tuple of leaking samples, while the optimal attack should take advantage of all the informative tuples in the leakage traces [14].

Note also that this kind of limitation was already mentioned from the introduction of the TVLA methodology. In particular, [16] (Section 5) clearly points out that blinded RSA implementations suffering from SPA leakages (which are one more example of highly multivariate attacks) may pass the T-test despite being vulnerable to other attacks, and therefore require additional analyses.

The Case of Parallel Masked (e.g., Threshold) Implementations. In practice, non-specific T-tests have been the method of choice for the security evaluation of higher-order threshold implementations manipulating their shares in parallel, such as discussed in [4,6,7]. Based on this state-of-the-art, our goal in this note is to further clarify what is learned (and what is missed) by the standalone application of the TVLA methodology in this case. Admittedly, our results do not contradict the published literature. (Precisely: the previous papers did not claim that the application of this methodology was correlated with a quantitative security level). We only recall that performing univariate T-tests is only an ingredient of a sound side-channel security evaluation that has to be combined with other ones, and that the gap between the standalone application of this methodology and a sound security evaluation increases with the security levels. More precisely, in the case of masking the TVLA methodology is good to detect a "security order" (i.e., the lowest key-dependent statistical moment of the leakage distribution). But in general a high security order is not sufficient to guarantee a high security level (e.g., number of traces for key recovery): one also needs to ensure a sufficient noise. So in order to claim quantitative results for masked/threshold implementations, the TVLA methodology has to be combined with a noise analysis and/or information theoretic evaluation.

In order to make our discussion concrete, we next consider side-channel attacks exploiting a single leakage sample corresponding to the parallel manipulation of several shares in a masked/threshold implementation. Based on this example, we compare the number of samples needed to detect fixed and random (or fixed) classes with a non-specific T-test and the DPA security of the implementation. None of our conclusions are new from the theoretical point-of-view. We only use this example to make explicit that even ignoring the issue of highly multivariate attacks, the standalone application of the TVLA methodology can be highly misleading regarding the actual security level of an implementation (i.e., the number of traces needed for key recovery). In this respect, the main concern of this note is not the use of the TVLA methodology for research purposes, but its potential misuse in the security evaluation of real products.

Cautionary Remarks. Despite the goal of this note is to prevent the misuse of the TVLA methodology when evaluating real products, we are not claiming that it is currently misused by any evaluation laboratory. We wrote it as a complement to several informal discussions that we had over the last months with researchers and engineers unconvinced that applying the TVLA methodology is not sufficient to state quantitative conclusions on the physical security of a cryptographic implementation, which is now clarified by the next example. Conceptually, this example in fact falls under the general (and known) observation that the TVLA methodology is unable to detect SPA leakages (e.g., mentioned in [16]). So it should be viewed as a reminder that such SPA leakages can happen even in the case of univariate attacks against parallel masking schemes. In this respect, the note is also of (mostly) prospective nature, since the limitation it points out relates to (very) high order masking schemes, while the TVLA methodology has mostly been used for low order masked implementations so far. Besides, and as will be clear in Sect. 3, our results do not contradict the value of the TVLA methodology, as an ingredient to detect the security order of a masked implementation, or as a useful first step before more advanced analyses.

2   Case Study: How Not to Use the T-Test

2.1   Setup and Metrics

Our following discussions will be based on the parallel implementation of a simple masking scheme such as described in [2]. More precisely, we will consider the simplest example where all the shares are in $\mathsf{GF}(2)$ (generalizations to larger fields follow naturally). In this setting, we have a sensitive variable x that is split into m shares such that $x = x_1 \oplus x_2 \oplus \ldots \oplus x_m$, with $\oplus$ the bitwise XOR. The first $m - 1$ shares are picked up uniformly at random: $(x_1, x_2, \ldots, x_{m-1}) \xleftarrow{\text{R}} \{0, 1\}$, and the last one is computed as $x_m = x \oplus x_1 \oplus x_2 \oplus \ldots \oplus x_{m-1}$.

Denoting the vector of shares $(x_1, x_2, \ldots, x_m)$ as $\bar{x}$, we will consider an adversary who observes a single leakage sample corresponding to the parallel manipulation of these shares. A simple model for this setting is to assume this sample to be a linear combination of the shares, namely:

$$\mathsf{L}_1(\bar{x}) = \left(\sum_{i=1}^{m} \alpha_i \cdot x_i \right) + N,$$

where $+, \cdot$ are the addition and multiplication in $\mathbb{R}$, the α_i's are coefficients in $\mathbb{R}$ and N is a noise random variable that we will assume Gaussian distributed with variance σ_n^2. The case with all α_i's equal to one corresponds to the popular Hamming weight leakage function. A slightly more sophisticated model would additionally consider quadratic terms, leading to:

$$\mathsf{L}_2(\bar{x}) = \left(\sum_{i=1}^{m} \alpha_i \cdot x_i \right) + \left(\sum_{i,j=1}^{m} \beta_{i,j} \cdot (x_i \wedge x_j) \right) + N,$$

with $\wedge$ the bitwise AND. The algebraic degree of this function can be extended similarly up to $d \leq m$, capturing increasingly complex leakages.

A standard (worst-case) metric to capture the informativeness of these leakages is the mutual information [29] that can be computed as follows:

$$\mathrm{MI}(X; \mathsf{L}_d(\bar{X})) = \mathsf{H}[X] + \sum_{x \in \mathcal{X}} \Pr[x] \cdot \sum_{l \in \mathcal{L}} \mathsf{f}(l|x) \cdot \log_2 \Pr[x|l].$$

In this equation, $f(l|x)$ is the conditional Probability Density Function (PDF) of the leakages $L(\bar{X})$ given the secret X, which (assuming Gaussian noise) can be written as the following Gaussian mixture model:

$$f(l|x) = \sum_{\bar{x} \in \mathcal{X}^{d-1}} \mathcal{N}\left(l|(x,\bar{x}), \sigma_n^2\right),$$

and the conditional probability $\Pr[x|l]$ is computed thanks to Bayes' theorem as:

$$\Pr[x|l] = \frac{f(l|x)}{\sum_{x^* \in \mathcal{X}} f(l|x^*)}.$$

We recall that this mutual information metric is correlated with the measurement complexity of a worst-case template attack, as demonstrated in [10], which we next use as a relevant (quantitative) metric to capture side-channel security.

In our simple (single-bit secret) case, the TVLA methodology works by collecting Q_0 (resp. Q_1) traces corresponding to the secret value $X = 0$ (resp. $X = 1$) and stores them in vectors $\bar{L}_0$ (resp. $\bar{L}_1$). In order to capture higher-order security, and following what was done in [4,6,7,27], we then process these vectors by removing their mean (so that we next estimate central moments) and raise them to a power o, that we will denote as the attack order. This leads to vectors $\bar{L}_0'$ (resp. $\bar{L}_1'$) of which the samples equal (e.g., for $\bar{L}_0'$):

$$\bar{L}_0'(i) = \left(\bar{L}_0(i) - \hat{\mathsf{E}}(\bar{L}_0)\right)^o,$$

with $\hat{\mathsf{E}}$ the sample mean operator and for $1 \le i \le Q_0$. Based on these leakage vectors, the TVLA methodology computes Welch's T statistic as follows:

$$\Delta = \frac{\hat{\mathsf{E}}(\bar{L}_0') - \hat{\mathsf{E}}(\bar{L}_1')}{\sqrt{\frac{\hat{\mathrm{var}}(\bar{L}_0')}{Q_0} + \frac{\hat{\mathrm{var}}(\bar{L}_1')}{Q_1}}},$$

with $\hat{\mathrm{var}}$ the sample variance operator. The side-channel literature usually assumes this T statistic to be significant when a threshold of 5 is passed.[2]

2.2   Experimental Results

Based on the setup in the previous section, we started by performing an information theoretic evaluation of our parallel implementation of a Boolean encoding, which is reported in Fig. 1. In order to allow an easier interpretation of the results, we use the Signal-to-Noise Ratio (SNR) as X axis, defined as the variance of the noise-free traces (e.g., m/4 for a Hamming weight model) divided by the variance of the noise. It better reflects the fact that the impact of the noise depends on the scaling of the signal. The figure carries the usual intuitions:

---

[2] In general, this threshold has to be set in function of the number of samples in the traces, to reflect the probability that a high Δ is observed by chance [9].

Boolean masking provides limited security for low noise levels; the slope of the IT curve reveals the security order of the implementation (i.e., relates to the smallest key-dependent moment of the leakage distribution) for high noise levels; and a leakage function mixing the shares in a non-linear manner (e.g., a quadratic one for the dotted curve) reduces the security order according to its algebraic degree.[3] For our discussions, it is mostly the first observation that matters.

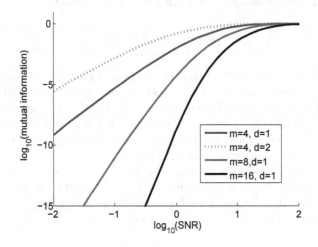

Fig. 1. Information theoretic evaluation of the (parallel) Boolean encoding. (Color figure online)

Note that in the case of the degree 1 leakage function with all α_i's equal to 1, it is easy to see that the high information observed for low noise levels corresponds to a powerful and concrete attack. Namely, without noise the adversary just has to check whether the leakage sample he obtains is odd or even.

As a complement to this information theoretic evaluation, we launched the TVLA methodology. For this purpose, we started with the case of an $m = 4$-share masking, leaking according to a linear leakage function (i.e., $d = 1$) and for a very low noise level ($\sigma_n^2 = 10^{-2}$). It corresponds to the rightmost point of the plain blue curve of Fig. 1 and therefore to an insecure implementation. Since the security order in this 4-share case study is expected to be four, we carried out Welch's T-test with traces raised to powers $o = 3$ and $o = 4$ and reported the results of ten independent experiments in Fig. 2. As expected, the third-order test does not succeed while the fourth-order one does. However, it already requires a couple of hundreds traces to detect with confidence, which seems a lot compared to the (large) information leaked by this sample.

---

[3] A higher-degree leakage function manipulating shares in parallel is in fact the natural mathematical model to capture the independence issues discussed in [2], which can be caused in practice by glitches, transition-based leakages or couplings.

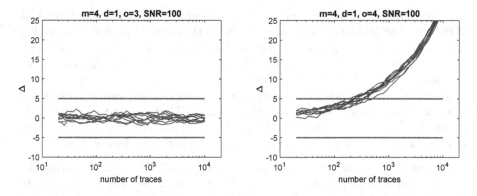

Fig. 2. Results of the TVLA methodology for 4-share (parallel) masking.

In order to confirm this first impression, we then launched the TVLA methodology for the cases of of an $m = 8$-share and $m = 12$-share masking (same leakage function, same noise level). As expected again, the lowest successful detection orders were respectively 8 and 12. But as reported in Fig. 3, the complexity of the detection task increases significantly (in fact, exponentially) with the number of shares, which clearly contradicts the information theoretic analysis of the Boolean encoding for low noise levels. Hence, this case study highlights an issue with the (tempting shortcoming of the) TVLA methodology, since the number of traces needed to detect with it can be made arbitrarily larger than the one needed to recover the secret (by increasing the number of shares m).

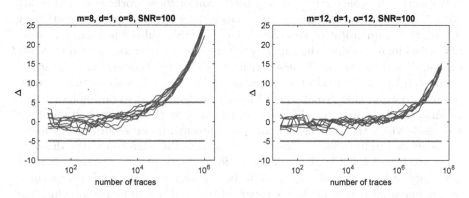

Fig. 3. Results of the TVLA methodology for 8- and 12-share parallel masking.

2.3 Interpretation

What Went Wrong? In short, the main issue of TVLA methodology as applied in the previous subsection is that *it assumes an adversarial strategy*, which relies on estimating the statistical moments of the leakage distribution. In theory this is a risky approach since security arguments generally aim at being independent of the adversarial strategy. Our example shows that even in practice, estimating statistical moments is in fact not the best strategy to attack a masked implementation with low noise levels (which naturally follows from the hypotheses in masking proofs [10]). Furthermore, the gap between this strategy and the optimal one increases with the security order. Note that our previous examples focus on parallel implementations (which are a more natural target for the application of Welch's T-test since mitigating the dimensionality issue discussed in introduction), but the same observation holds for serial implementations.[4]

An Analogy. A similar situation was observed in [15,17] when comparing the Gaussian mixture and Gaussian adversaries: the latter one does in fact exactly the same "mistake" as the TVLA methodology since "summarizing" a mixture into a statistical moment, namely the (co)variance. So for low noise levels, the Gaussian adversary will generally overstate the security level of a protected implementation, by interpreting mask (or supply voltage) variations as a single Gaussian with larger (co)variance. As in our previous example, this amounts to implicitly assume the existence of a large enough noise without testing it.

Impact for Threshold Implementations. These results illustrate that testing a masked/threshold implementation with the TVLA methodology *only* is not sufficient to gain accurate insights on its security level, especially as the security order increases. However, our observations do not contradict the results in [4,6,7] where the authors only claimed a security order (which is exactly what the TVLA methodology is good for – see next). Reading these papers, it is also clear that their authors are well aware that noise is needed for their countermeasure to provide security. So concretely, the only limitation of these works is that they are not quantitative. In this respect, our results come with the important cautionary remark that a quantitative approach is increasingly needed when masking security orders increase, since the gap between the number of traces needed to detect fixed and random (or fixed) classes with the TVLA methodology and the actual (worst-case) security level of an implementation also increases in this context. In order to avoid this caveat, the TVLA methodology has to be combined with an analysis of the noise (and ideally, an information theoretic evaluation of the leakages), which then enables a quantified implementation security assessment. As mentioned in introduction, we again insist that the main concern in this note is not the use of the TVLA methodology for research purposes (where claiming a security order and assuming noise to be a security parameter is acceptable), but its potential misuse in the security evaluation of real products for which the noise is fixed (i.e., not a security parameter) and the most relevant metric is the number of traces needed to perform a successful key recovery.

We note also that we would obtain similar conclusions with more complex (i.e., not only linear) leakages since noise is in general a necessary condition for the security of the masking countermeasure. Yet, trivial examples (e.g., checking

---

[4] In a trivial manner: an adversary getting d noise-free leakages corresponding to the d shares of a secret x will not estimate moments but simply XOR them together.

whether the leakage is odd or even in the parallel case and XORing leakage samples in the serial cas) would not work anymore in this case.

Impact for Other Security Evaluation Tools. Quite naturally, the TVLA methodology is not the only side-channel distinguisher focusing on the estimation of statistical moments. In fact, the higher-order DPAs described in [25,30] or higher-order variations of the Correlation Power Analysis (CPA) described in [21] suffer from the same drawback. Namely, they are only indicative of the actual security level of an implementation *if* the best adversarial strategy is to estimate statistical moments of the leakage distribution. Yet, not sufficient does not mean not necessary. In the next section, we will show that moment-based evaluations remain a useful ingredient for sound side-channel security evaluations.

3 Clarification: How to Use the T-Test

3.1 Separation of Duties

First recall that the only thing our previous experiments showed is that launching a T-test cannot be sufficient for the side-channel security evaluation of a masked/threshold implementation (even in univariate case studies that seem the most suitable context for such tests). In fact, this observation again derives from masking security proofs (e.g., in [10]) where it is explicitly mentioned that such a countermeasure provides security under two hypotheses: sufficient noise and independence. So recast positively from this more theoretical viewpoint, the take home message of this note becomes that the TVLA methodology is useful to determine the security order of an implementation, and that the noise level (which also depends on the number of exploitable leakage samples [14]) has to be tested independently. Interestingly, looking back at the information theoretic plot of Fig. 1 allows putting these observations together, since it shows that when the noise is sufficiently large, the slope of the IT curves reflects the security order, suggesting that the best adversarial strategy is indeed to estimate higher-order statistical moments in this case (e.g., as discussed in [10,21]).

3.2 Beyond the TVLA Methodology

Given that we restrict the goal of the TVLA methodology to the detection of the security order of a masked/threshold implementation, the remaining question is to know whether it is an efficient solution for this purpose. In this respect, one can notice that the main drawback of the processing described in Sect. 2.1 is that it directly raises the leakage samples to a certain power o. This implies that as the noise increases, the number of samples needed to detect will increase exponentially with the number of shares (because the noise is amplified), just as expected from secure masking. But this also implies that this approach is inherently limited if one wants to claim very high security levels. So as for other security evaluation tasks (e.g., key enumeration vs. rank estimation [23]), one can wonder whether an evaluator can benefit from some shortcut to determine the security order, thanks to additional knowledge he may have access to?

A natural option for this purpose is to take advantage of mask knowledge (if available). That is, say the evaluator has access to the shares' vector $\bar{x}$ for each of his leakage samples. Then, he will be able to identify repeated samples for each of the 2^{m-1} possible sharings of the sensitive variable x. Further say that the number of samples per sharing is N_a for simplicity, then the evaluator can pre-process his leakage samples by averaging them (for each sharing). As a result of this pre-processing, the vectors $\bar{L}_0$ and $\bar{L}_1$ of Sect. 2.1 now have $\tilde{Q}_0 = \tilde{Q}_1 = 2^{m-1}$ values (rather than $N_a \cdot 2^{m-1}$ ones without this pre-processing). But the noise of these pre-processed samples has been reduced *before* raising them to the power o, which mitigates the "noise amplification" of the masking scheme. Concretely, it then remains to determine the averaging parameter N_a which naturally depends on the SNR. Typically, one can choose it so that $\text{SNR} \cdot N_a = 10$ (which means that the pre-processed measurements have $\text{SNR} = 10$).

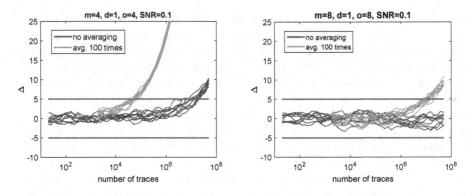

Fig. 4. Comparison between the TVLA and TVLA^2 methodologies.

For illustration, the results of such a "TVLA + averaging" methodology (next denoted as TVLA^2) for a smaller SNR of 0.1, with $m = 4$ and $m = 8$ shares, are represented in Fig. 4. Note that the value of the X axis corresponds to $Q_0 + Q_1$ for the standard TVLA methodology, and to $N_a \cdot 2^m$ for the TVLA^2 one. In other words, it represents the total number of leakage samples used to detect in both cases (which explains why the TVLA^2 curves are shifted by a factor N_a). Several interesting observations can be highlighted. First, the TVLA methodology starts detecting with confidence after 10^7 leakage samples for the $m = 4$ case. This value is nicely related to the MI value of Fig. 1 for the same case ($m = 4$, $\text{SNR} = 10^{-1}$), which is worth $\approx 10^{-6}$ and implies that the number of samples to perform a key recovery should be larger than 10^6 [10]. Similarly, we see that the TVLA methodology does not detect anything for the $m = 8$ case, which is expected since the the MI is then below 10^{-10} for a $\text{SNR} = 10^{-1}$. Second, the average pre-processing of the TVLA^2 methodology significantly improves the complexity of the detection task. This is due to the previously mentioned noise reduction before amplification. In order to make this gain more explicit, Fig. 5 additionally compares the results of the $TVLA^2$ methodology for SNRs of 10^{-1} and 10^{-2}. It confirms that the reduction of the SNR by a factor 10 causes an increase of the number of traces needed to detect by a similar factor 10 (and not a factor 10^m as would be observed with the TVLA methodology).

Note that when applying the $TVLA^2$ methodology, the number of traces needed to detect is even less correlated with the security level of the target implementation than with the TVLA methodology (since concrete adversaries do not know mask values and are not able to perform an average pre-processing). Yet, in view of the limited quantitative meaning of the TVLA methodology in general, and if the $TVLA^2$ methodology is only used to detect a security order, this drawback is not very critical (when mask knowledge is accessible!).

Eventually, and more negatively, we see from Fig. 4 that the complexity of the $TVLA^2$ detection still (inevitably) increases exponentially in the number of shares m (since the left and right plots of the have the same SNR). This is in fact exactly the cause of our negative examples in Sect. 2.2. So the average pre-processing is only useful to mitigate the exponential increase of the noise.

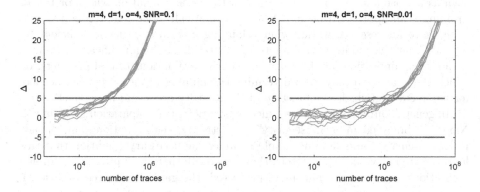

Fig. 5. Results of the $TVLA^2$ methodology for different noise levels.

Quite naturally, the improvement in this last section can be combined similarly with other statistical tools such as the previously mentioned higher-order DPAs (in [25, 30]) or higher-order variations of the CPA (in [21]). In those cases as well, the trick is to take advantage of the masks knowledge in order to pre-process the traces by averaging before estimating higher-order statistical moments. And of course, there as well, the effectiveness of the distinguisher will then only reflect the security order, and be uncorrelated with the attack complexity.

4   Conclusions

Evaluating the security of a leaking device is a challenging problem (see [28] for a recent survey). For the masking countermeasure, it implies to test whether the hypotheses required to deliver its security promises are fulfilled.

The first hypothesis is that the leakage of the shares are independent of each other. Concretely this can be tested by computing a security order, which is the lowest statistical moment of the leakage PDF that depends on the target secret. The TVLA methodology is good for this purpose. Yet, as the security order increases, the exponential amplification of the noise provided by masking renders the sampling complexity of such an approach unreachable. In case the evaluator can access the masks during a profiling phase, it is possible to mitigate this noise amplification, by averaging the leakage traces before computing the security order (i.e., before raising the samples to some power).

Independent of the security order, the second hypothesis is that the leakages are sufficiently noisy. In this respect, the main observation of this note is that launching the TVLA methodology does not allow to guarantee a sufficient noise (since it in fact only tests the security order). This implies that claiming concrete security levels for masked/threshold implementations requires an additional step such as a noise analysis or an information theoretic evaluation with worst-case profiling – an approach that is not yet systematically followed. While it is not a big issue for research works, where claiming a security order is sufficient to indicate that the countermeasure has a potential for noise amplification, it may be a serious limitation for the concrete security evaluations of real products, of which the goal eventually is to determine the number of measurements needed for key recovery (which is a function of the security order and noise level).

In general, our results provide a nice illustration of the separation given in [2]. Namely, "bounded moment security" is a strictly weaker notion than "noisy leakage security", and can only imply it under the necessary condition that the leakages are noisy. More concretely, they also recall that as cryptographic implementations become more and more protected, the gap between (cost-efficient) "conformance/validation-style" testing and (more expensive) "evaluation-style" testing is likely to increase. In this respect, combining conformance/validation-style testing for checking simple properties that implementations have to fulfill "locally" (e.g., a security order and a noise level in the case of masking, or their combination via an information theoretic metric) with more formal approaches to analyze security "globally", such as proposed in [1], seems promising.

As a closing note, we mention that the detection of a security order discussed in this paper is based on univariate statistics. While one may (intuitively) expect that reductions of the security order via glitches, transitions or coupling (as mentioned in Footnote 2) happen mostly at this univariate level, and that increasing the number of dimensions exploited by the adversary will be more prejudicial to the noise level of the implementations, this is certainly something that requires further practical investigations (e.g., by analyzing security order reductions via mixed statistical moments for serial masked implementations – a task for which the tools of Schneider and Moradi in [27] are a good starting point). In this respect, it is worth observing that most tools used to extend the T-test to multiple samples rely on an independence assumption. Investigating the impact of this assumption is yet another interesting open problem.

Acknowledgments. The author is grateful to Carolyn Whitnall for useful feedback. The author is is an associate researcher of the Belgian Fund for Scientific Research (FNRS-F.R.S.). This work was funded in parts by the ERC project 724725 (acronym SWORD) and by the H2020 project REASSURE.

References

1. Barthe, G., Belaïd, S., Dupressoir, F., Fouque, P.-A., Grégoire, B., Strub, P.-Y.: Verified proofs of higher-order masking. In: Oswald and Fischlin [22], pp. 457–485
2. Barthe, G., Dupressoir, F., Faust, S., Grégoire, B., Standaert, F.-X., Strub, P.-Y.: Parallel implementations of masking schemes and the bounded moment leakage model. In: Coron, J.-S., Nielsen, J.B. (eds.) EUROCRYPT 2017, Part I. LNCS, vol. 10210, pp. 535–566. Springer, Cham (2017). https://doi.org/10.1007/978-3-319-56620-7_19
3. Battistello, A., Coron, J.-S., Prouff, E., Zeitoun, R.: Horizontal side-channel attacks and countermeasures on the ISW masking scheme. In: Gierlichs and Poschmann [12], pp. 23–39
4. Bilgin, B., Gierlichs, B., Nikova, S., Nikov, V., Rijmen, V.: Higher-order threshold implementations. In: Sarkar, P., Iwata, T. (eds.) ASIACRYPT 2014, Part II. LNCS, vol. 8874, pp. 326–343. Springer, Heidelberg (2014). https://doi.org/10.1007/978-3-662-45608-8_18
5. Carlet, C., Hasan, M.A., Saraswat, V. (eds.): SPACE 2016. LNCS, vol. 10076. Springer, Cham (2016). https://doi.org/10.1007/978-3-319-49445-6
6. De Cnudde, T., Bilgin, B., Reparaz, O., Nikov, V., Nikova, S.: Higher-order threshold implementation of the AES S-Box. In: Homma, N., Medwed, M. (eds.) CARDIS 2015. LNCS, vol. 9514, pp. 259–272. Springer, Cham (2016). https://doi.org/10.1007/978-3-319-31271-2_16
7. De Cnudde, T., Reparaz, O., Bilgin, B., Nikova, S., Nikov, V., Rijmen, V.: Masking AES with d+1 shares in hardware. In: Gierlichs and Poschmann [12], pp. 194–212
8. Cooper, J., De Mulder, E., Goodwill, G., Jaffe, J., Kenworthy, G., Rohatgi, P.: Test vector leakage assessment (TVLA) methodology in practice (extended abstract). In: ICMC 2013 (2013). http://icmc-2013.org/wp/wp-content/uploads/2013/09/goodwillkenworthtestvector.pdf
9. Ding, A.A., Zhang, L., Durvaux, F., Standaert, F.-X., Fei, Y.: Towards sound and optimal leakage detection procedure. In: Eisenbarth, T., Teglia, Y. (eds.) CARDIS 2017. LNCS, vol. 10728, pp. 105–122. Springer, Cham (2018). https://doi.org/10.1007/978-3-319-75208-2_7
10. Duc, A., Faust, S., Standaert, F.-X.: Making masking security proofs concrete - or how to evaluate the security of any leaking device. In: Oswald and Fischlin [22], pp. 401–429
11. Durvaux, F., Standaert, F.-X.: From improved leakage detection to the detection of points of interests in leakage traces. In: Fischlin, M., Coron, J.-S. (eds.) EUROCRYPT 2016, Part I. LNCS, vol. 9665, pp. 240–262. Springer, Heidelberg (2016). https://doi.org/10.1007/978-3-662-49890-3_10

12. Gierlichs, B., Poschmann, A.Y. (eds.): CHES 2016. LNCS, vol. 9813. Springer, Heidelberg (2016). https://doi.org/10.1007/978-3-662-53140-2
13. Goodwill, G., Jun, B., Jaffe, J., Rohatgi, P.: A testing methodology for side channel resistance validation. In: NIST Non-invasive Attack Testing Workshop (2011). http://csrc.nist.gov/news_events/non-invasive-attack-testing-workshop/papers/08_Goodwill.pdf
14. Grosso, V., Standaert, F.-X.: Masking proofs are tight and how to exploit it in security evaluations. In: Nielsen, J.B., Rijmen, V. (eds.) EUROCRYPT 2018, Part II. LNCS, vol. 10821, pp. 385–412. Springer, Cham (2018). https://doi.org/10.1007/978-3-319-78375-8_13
15. Grosso, V., Standaert, F.-X., Prouff, E.: Low entropy masking schemes, revisited. In: Francillon, A., Rohatgi, P. (eds.) CARDIS 2013. LNCS, vol. 8419, pp. 33–43. Springer, Cham (2014). https://doi.org/10.1007/978-3-319-08302-5_3
16. Jaffe, J., Rohatgi, P., Witteman, M.: Efficient side-channel testing for public key algorithms: RSA case study. In: NIST Non-invasive Attack Testing Workshop (2011). http://csrc.nist.gov/news_events/non-invasive-attack-testing-workshop/papers/09_Jaffe.pdf
17. Kamel, D., et al.: Towards securing low-power digital circuits with ultra-low-voltage Vdd randomizers. In: Carlet et al. [5], pp. 233–248
18. Mangard, S., Oswald, E., Standaert, F.-X.: One for all - all for one: unifying standard differential power analysis attacks. IET Inf. Secur. 5(2), 100–110 (2011)
19. Mather, L., Oswald, E., Bandenburg, J., Wójcik, M.: Does my device leak information? An a priori statistical power analysis of leakage detection tests. In: Sako, K., Sarkar, P. (eds.) ASIACRYPT 2013, Part I. LNCS, vol. 8269, pp. 486–505. Springer, Heidelberg (2013). https://doi.org/10.1007/978-3-642-42033-7_25
20. Moradi, A.: Side-channel leakage through static power - should we care about in practice? In: Batina, L., Robshaw, M. (eds.) CHES 2014. LNCS, vol. 8731, pp. 562–579. Springer, Heidelberg (2014). https://doi.org/10.1007/978-3-662-44709-3_31
21. Moradi, A., Standaert, F.-X.: Moments-correlating DPA. In: Proceedings of the 2016 ACM Workshop on Theory of Implementation Security, TIS 2016, pp. 5–15. ACM, New York (2016)
22. Oswald, E., Fischlin, M. (eds.): EUROCRYPT 2015, Part I. LNCS, vol. 9056. Springer, Heidelberg (2015). https://doi.org/10.1007/978-3-662-46800-5
23. Poussier, R., Standaert, F.-X., Grosso, V.: Simple key enumeration (and rank estimation) using histograms: an integrated approach. In: Gierlichs and Poschmann [12], pp. 61–81
24. Del Pozo, S.M., Standaert, F.-X., Kamel, D., Moradi, A.: Side-channel attacks from static power: when should we care? In: Nebel, W., Atienza, D. (eds.) Proceedings of the 2015 Design, Automation & Test in Europe Conference & Exhibition, DATE 2015, Grenoble, France, 9–13 March 2015, pp. 145–150. ACM (2015)
25. Prouff, E., Rivain, M., Bevan, R.: Statistical analysis of second order differential power analysis. IEEE Trans. Comput. 58(6), 799–811 (2009)
26. Roy, D.B., Bhasin, S., Patranabis, S., Mukhopadhyay, D., Guilley, S.: What lies ahead: extending TVLA testing methodology towards success rate. Cryptology ePrint Archive, Report 2016/1152 (2016). http://eprint.iacr.org/2016/1152
27. Schneider, T., Moradi, A.: Leakage assessment methodology - extended version. J. Cryptogr. Eng. 6(2), 85–99 (2016)
28. Standaert, F.-X.: Towards fair and efficient evaluations of leaking cryptographic devices - overview of the ERC project CRASH, part I (invited talk). In: Carlet et al. [5], pp. 353–362

29. Standaert, F.-X., Malkin, T.G., Yung, M.: A unified framework for the analysis of side-channel key recovery attacks. In: Joux, A. (ed.) EUROCRYPT 2009. LNCS, vol. 5479, pp. 443–461. Springer, Heidelberg (2009). https://doi.org/10.1007/978-3-642-01001-9_26

30. Waddle, J., Wagner, D.: Towards efficient second-order power analysis. In: Joye, M., Quisquater, J.-J. (eds.) CHES 2004. LNCS, vol. 3156, pp. 1–15. Springer, Heidelberg (2004). https://doi.org/10.1007/978-3-540-28632-5_1

31. Welch, B.L.: The generalization of student's problem when several different population variances are involved. Biometrika **34**, 28–35 (1947)

Scalable Key Rank Estimation (and Key Enumeration) Algorithm for Large Keys

Vincent Grosso[(✉)]

Univ Lyon, UJM-Saint-Etienne, CNRS, Laboratoire Hubert Curien UMR 5516,
Saint-Etienne, France
vincent.grosso@univ-st-etienne.fr

Abstract. Evaluation of security margins after a side-channel attack is an important step of side-channel resistance evaluation. The security margin indicates the brute force effort needed to recover the key given the leakages. In the recent years, several solutions for key rank estimation algorithms have been proposed. All these solutions give an interesting trade-off between the tightness of the result and the time complexity for symmetric key. Unfortunately, none of them has a linear complexity in the number of subkeys, hence these solutions are slow for large (asymmetric) keys. In this paper, we present a solution to obtain a key rank estimation algorithm with a reasonable trade-off between the efficiency and the tightness that is suitable for large keys. Moreover, by applying backtracking we obtain a parallel key enumeration algorithm.

1 Introduction

Side-channel attacks are powerful attacks against cryptographic implementations. To perform a side-channel attack, an attacker needs to be able to measure some physical properties (e.g. power consumption, electromagnetic radiation) of the device while it computes some key dependent operations. With this additional information, some attacks can be performed against cryptographic implementations. Hence, cryptographic algorithms required secure implementations.

To evaluate the security margin, evaluation labs generally launch some popular attacks to evaluate if an adversary can break an implementation by performing, for example, a key recovery attack. This approach is adapted since the leakage of an implementation dependents on the device. Thus, the security obtained by an implementation is highly dependent on the underlying device.

Most of state of the art side-channel attacks follow a divide-and-conquer strategy, where the master key is split into several pieces, called subkeys. The attacker/evaluator mounts an independent attack for each of these subkeys. He then needs to combine the different results of the attacks. A security evaluation only based on a success or failure of a key recovery attack is limited by the

V. Grosso—Part of this work was done while the author was at Radboud University Nijmegen, Digital Security Group, The Netherlands.

computational power of the evaluator. To get rid of this limitation a solution is to compute the rank of the key instead of performing a key recovery attack. The rank corresponds to the number of keys needed to be tested before recovering the actual key. Recently, several papers studied how to evaluate the security by evaluating the computational power required after a side-channel attack [1, 8, 11, 15]. These papers compute an estimation of the rank of the key after a side-channel attack, without being limited by the evaluator computational power. All these papers focus on symmetric key size. In [8] the authors managed to evaluate ranks for 1024-bit keys, but for larger keys, this solution could have some limitations.

Our Contributions. We study the cost of the solution of Glowacz et al. for large keys. Next, we present a variation of this key rank estimation algorithm. This variation allows us to obtain a linear complexity of the algorithm in the number of subkeys. We then derive some tighter bound for our construction. These tight bounds allow us to have an efficient and tight solution for key rank estimation for large keys (size greater than 1024 bits). Finally, by applying a similar idea as Poussier et al. [13], we propose a new key enumeration algorithm.

2 Background

2.1 Side-Channel Attacks and Notations

For the rank estimation/key enumeration problems, the details on the divide-and-conquer attack are not necessary. We just need to specify the output of the attack. Let us assume that the attacker targets a η-bit **master key**. An adversary using a divide-and-conquer strategy will split this key into ν **sub-keys** of (for simplicity equally sized) κ **bits of subkey**. For each subkey k_i the attacker will obtain a list of probability for each possible value of the key $\mathcal{L}_i = \{\Pr[k_i = 0|\text{SCI}], \ldots, \Pr[k_i = 2^\kappa - 1|\text{SCI}]\}$, where SCI stands for the side-channel information the adversary obtained. Divide-and-conquer strategy is useful as $\nu \times 2^\kappa$ is smaller than 2^η. Note that if the adversary scores instead of probability he could either use a Bayesian extension [14] or use direct results [4].

2.2 Key Enumeration Algorithms

From the result of an attack, either all the correct subkeys have the highest probability of the list of the candidate subkeys or the attacker need to test the most likely keys. Some solution exists to recombine this information in a smart way [2,6,10,11,13,14]. All these algorithms have been tested in a symmetric key setting and provide efficient solution.

The algorithms proposed in [2,11,13] can be separate in two phases: a construction phase (that is similar to key rank estimation) and a backtracking part that enumerates the keys. For symmetric keys setting, the first part (construction) is negligible in comparison to the second (backtracking).

2.3   Rank Estimation Algorithms

A rank estimation algorithm is a tool that allows an evaluator to estimate the brute force an attacker need to perform a successful attack, i.e. how many keys the attacker needs to test in the recombination phase before she recovers the actual key (the key is known by the evaluator). As we want to evaluate security against a smart adversary we should assume that she can enumerate the keys from the most probable one to the least probable one (but still in its computational power limits).

Definition 1 (Rank of the key). *The rank of the key k after a side-channel attack is defined as the number of keys that have a higher probability than k.*

$$rank(k) = \#\{k^* | \Pr[k^*|\text{SCI}] \geq \Pr[k|\text{SCI}]\}.$$

Where $\#$ stands for the cardinality of the set.

Definition 2 (Tightness). *The tightness of an estimation is the logarithm of the ratio between the upper and lower bound $\log_2 \left(\dfrac{rank\_upper\_bound}{rank\_lower\_bound} \right).$*

In the rest of this paper, the probability of a key is equal to the product of the probabilities of its subkeys. Hence, we suppose that the subkeys probabilities are independent, and so the different attacks.

The main advantage of using a key rank estimation algorithm is that an evaluator does not need to perform the brute force search to estimate the costs of such a search. In the past few years, several solutions have been proposed to solve this problem [1,8,11,15]. Efficient rank estimation algorithms [1,8,11] share the same step that introduces error: they map the probabilities to integers (see [12] for a discussion on the errors introduced by algorithms that calculate security margins). Using this simplification they can estimate the rank of the key quite efficiently, with bounded error due to some truncation that appears during the conversion from real (float) to integer. Hence, these algorithms cannot compute the rank, but an upper bound (*rank_upper_bound*) and a lower bound (*rank_lower_bound*) of the rank. These rank estimation algorithms are based on samples, i.e.they use result of an attack and calculate bounds on the rank. To obtain some indication of the security level of the device several experiments attacks are launched and results could be displayed in a security graph as proposed in [15].

Some other solutions exist to evaluate the security of a device that can be faster and adaptable for large keys [7,16]. These solutions are based on metrics, i.e. do not use directly result of an attack, but use results of several attacks to compute a metric e.g. the success rate. However, solutions based on metric could misestimate the actual computational power of an attack, as pointed out in [12].

2.4   The Histogram Solution

Since our solution is based on the Glowacz et al. solution [8], we give some more highlight on this solution. In the rest of the paper, we refer to this solution as FSE'15. The different steps of this algorithm can be summarized as follow:

1. *from multiplicative relation to additive relation*: since the subkeys are independent we have $\Pr[k_1, k_2|SCI] = \Pr[k_1|SCI] \times \Pr[k_2|SCI]$. By using logarithm, we have $\log(\Pr[k_1, k_2|SCI]) = \log(\Pr[k_1|SCI]) + \log(\Pr[k_2|SCI])$.
2. *from reals to integers*: in the FSE'15 solution, this step is done by casting the results of the side-channel attacks into histograms. For each subkey a histogram is built, the histograms should have the same bin size. The bin height corresponds to the number of candidate subkeys that have a log probability included between the limits of the bin.
3. *convolution of histograms*: the convolution of histograms gives us the distribution of the combination of the probabilities of different combination of subkeys. Remark the height of i-th bin of H_3 that is the result of the convolution of H_1 and H_2 is $H_3(i) = \sum_j H_1(j) \times H_2(i - j)$. This is the number of couples of subkey candidates that have the sum of the estimated sum of log probabilities that correspond to the center of the bin i.
4. *calculate bound*: This is done by summing the bins that represent a higher log probability than the bin of the key's log probability ($\pm$ the error bounds). Hence, having tight error bounds allow obtaining tighter results.

In Listing 1 we give a simplified version of the code of the two last steps.

Listing 1. Matlab implementation of FSE'15 solution.

```
function [mini,maxi] = rank(hi,b)                              1
% Inputs:                                                      2
%hi: list of histogram score for each subkey (hi(subkey,:))    3
%b: bin index of the log probability of the actual key         4
%Outputs    Mini the minimum rank of the key                   5
%           Maxi the maximum rank of the key                   6
[dim,~]=size(hi);                                              7
H=conv(hi(1,:),hi(2,:));                                       8
for i=3:dim                                                    9
    H=conv(H,hi(i,:));                                         10
end                                                            11
mini=sum(H(b+(dim/2)+1:length(H)));                            12
maxi=sum(H(b-dim/2:length(H)));                                13
end                                                            14
```

Since the histograms put every log probabilities in the bin center some error could appear. In [8] the authors show that the maximum distance in numbers of bin between a bin of a sum of log probabilities and the bin where the FSE algorithm could put it is $\frac{\nu}{2}$. That is why the minimum and maximum are shifted by such a value.

Example 1. Let us assume we have two subkeys k_1, k_2 of 3 bits. With the probabilities given in Table 1. As our histograms will use the logarithm of the probabilities (to have an additive relation), we also provide the logarithm values and also the key candidates' bin.

We construct the histograms as follows. The bin 1 corresponds to the number of keys with logarithm probabilities between -16 and -12, the bin 2 corresponds to the number of keys with logarithm probabilities between -12 and -8, the bin 3 corresponds to the number of keys with logarithm probabilities between -8 and -4 and the bin 4 corresponds to the number of key with logarithm probabilities between -4 and 0. The histograms are displayed in Fig. 1. H_1 is the histogram for the subkey candidates of k_1. The sum of the bins gives us 8 that is the number of subkey candidates. H_2 is the histogram for the subkey candidates of k_2.

Then by performing the convolution we have the distribution of all possible couple for the subkeys (k_1, k_2). In the histogram of Fig. 1, the bin 1 should correspond to the number of couples of candidate keys with logarithm probabilities between -30 and -26, since we only look at the center of the bin some error could appear here.

Table 1. Probabilities of subkeys candidates and their logarithm and bin values.

Candidate	k_1			k_2		
	Pr	log	bin	Pr	log	bin
0	0.6643	-0.5901	1	0.0012	-9.7027	3
1	0.2588	-1.9501	1	0.0011	-9.8283	3
2	0.0313	-4.9977	2	0.3588	-1.4787	1
3	0.0412	-4.6012	2	0.0713	-3.8100	1
4	0.0001	-13.2877	4	0.5643	-0.8255	1
5	0.0020	-8.9658	3	0.0012	-9.7027	3
6	0.0013	-9.5873	3	0.00005	-14.2877	4
7	0.0010	-9.9658	3	0.00205	-8.9302	3

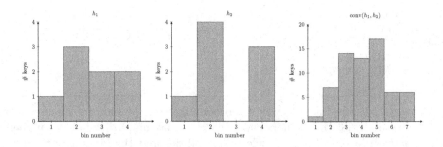

Fig. 1. The histograms for the two subkeys and the convolution result.

Part 3 (for loop line 9 in Listing 1) of such an algorithm is the most expensive part. We need to perform $nb\_subkeys - 1$ convolution, each convolution having a cost in $nlog(n)$ when FFT is used. Remark this n is the size of the outputted histogram (and thus on the number of convolutions already performed), that means the cost of convolution became more and more expensive as the size of the histogram H grows. It comes out that the cost of the rank estimation of

Glowacz et al. grows not linearly with the number of subkeys. This observation is validated by experiments in Sect. 4.

During the computation, we need to use large numbers (a bin can contain a number between 0 and 2^η). Hence, to avoid precision error due to large number we need to use large integer library and/or the Chinese remainder theorem as proposed in Appendix B of [8].

Another limitation for large keys is the size of the histogram that will grow linearly in the number of subkeys. After the convolution i-th the size of the histogram H is of size $(i - 1) \times dim$, the value stored in that table could go up to 2^η. This could be expensive for large key and high precision. The FSE'15 solution needs to store the last histogram.

Example 2. That means for histograms with 2^{16} bins and for a key of 256 subkeys, we need to store a table of $\simeq 2^{24}$ values. These values are integers of at most 2048 bits (if subkeys are bytes). That means around 4 GB.

If the size of the key doubles the memory required double. Remark for the enumeration all intermediate histograms need to be stored to apply the backtracking solution this could require some large amount of memory.

3   Scalable Rank Estimation Algorithm

The main idea of our solution is to keep histogram with a constant number of bins. This is achieved by batching two by two the bins of the convolution's result histograms (line 15 in Listing 2).

Listing 2. Matlab implementation of our solution.

```
function [mini,maxi] = rank(hi,b)                                    1
% Inputs/output same as Listing 1                                    2
[dim,~]=size(hi);                                                    3
H2=cell(log2(dim),dim/2);                                            4
for i=2:2:dim                                                        5
    H=conv(hi(i-1,:),hi(i,:));                                       6
    H2{1,i/2}=[H(2:2:length(H)),0]+H(1:2:length(H));                 7
end                                                                  8
dim=dim/2;                                                           9
j=1;                                                                10
while dim>1                                                         11
    j=j+1;                                                          12
    for i=2:2:dim                                                   13
        H=conv(H2{j-1,i-1},H2{j-1,i});                              14
        H2{j,i/2}=[H(2:2:length(H)),0]+H(1:2:length(H));            15
    end                                                             16
    dim=dim/2;                                                      17
end                                                                18
mini=sum(H2{j,1}(b+error(dim)+1:length(H2{j,1})));                  19
maxi=sum(H2{j,1}(b+error(dim):length(H2{j,1})));                    20
end                                                                21
```

Where the error function is a function that gives the approximation error due to our casting and batching. This function and the values outputted are discussed in Subsect. 3.3.

As for the FSE'15 solution we perform convolution on histograms and obtain the histogram H, but after this step we batch bins in pairs and obtain the histogram H_2. The i-th bin of H_2 is equal to the sum of the $2i$-th and the $2i+1$-th bins of H, $H_2(i) = H(2i) + H(2i+1)$. Doing so H_2 has the same number of bins as the initial histogram. But then the bin size of the histogram after the batching is twice as large as the bin size of the loop input histograms.

For rank estimation, we need to perform convolution between histogram with equally sized bins. By performing the batching we increase the width of the bins. To solve the problem we use a recursive approach, we do convolutions of histograms two by two, batch and start a new level of convolutions. Hence we perform convolution in a tree like structure, see the right part of Fig. 2. The tree like structure can be used without batching to have similar result as FSE'15.

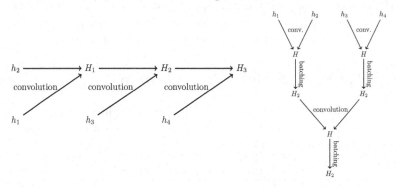

Fig. 2. Representation of the FSE'15 solution (left) and ours (right).

Example 3. In our Example 1, the batching step outputs the histogram in Fig. 3. The batching step merge bin 2 by 2. That means the first bin in the new histogram corresponds to the sum of the bins 1 and 2 from the result of the convolution histogram of Fig. 1.

3.1 On the Time Complexity

Our algorithm performs the same number of convolutions as FSE'15. But in our solution, the size (i.e. the number of bins) of the histogram stays the same, the bin size increase.

While for the FSE'15 solution the size of H_i histograms grows, $size(H_i) = ((i+1) \times nb\_bin\_init) - i$, the size of the H_2 histograms in our solution stay the same as the initial histograms, i.e. $size(H_2) = nb\_bin\_init$. That means that convolution in level 1 of the tree (right part of Fig. 2) should require similar computation as the convolution in the last level. Thus, we expect for our solution to have a time that grows linearly with the number of subkeys. This is verified by experiments in Subsect. 4.1.

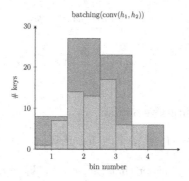

Fig. 3. The batched result.

3.2   On Memory Complexity

As we can see on the Fig. 2 our method is a tree exploration. That means we can explore it in breadth first or in depth first search.

In the case of a breadth first search, the most expensive step we have to store is the batched histograms after the first step of convolutions, in that case, we need to store $\frac{\nu}{2}$ tables of nb_bin_init values. If the size of the key doubles the memory required double.

Example 4. For the same values as Example 2, 2^{16} bins and 256 subkeys, we need to store 2^{23} values. That is around 2 GB.

In the case of depth first search, we need to store at most one batched histogram per level ($\log_2 \nu$). If the size of the key doubles the memory required increase by one histogram.

Example 5. For the same values as Example 2, we need to store 2^{19} values. That is around 128 MB.

For simplicity we describe in Listing 2 the breadth first search. Both breadth and deep first technique have similar time, the choice of one over the other is then based on memory available.

3.3   Bounded Error

The tight bounds we obtain for our method lead to efficient tight results. The error is introduced when we cast real numbers into integers as for FSE'15. Our solution also introduces error when the batching step is performed.

For the rounding error that appears when we transform real numbers into integers. For every log probability of a subkey candidate $k = i$ and for histogram of bin width 2ϵ there exist a bin b_i of center c_i such that $c_i - \epsilon \leq \log(\Pr[k = i]) \leq c_i + \epsilon$.

If we look at the combined candidate $(k_1 = i, k_2 = j)$ we know that for the initial histogram we have:

$$c_i - \epsilon \leq \log(\Pr[k_1 = i]) \leq c_i + \epsilon$$
$$c_j - \epsilon \leq \log(\Pr[k_2 = j]) \leq c_j + \epsilon.$$

By summing the inequalities we obtain:

$$c_i + c_j - 2\epsilon \leq \log(\Pr[k_1 = i]) + \log(\Pr[k_2 = j]) \leq c_i + c_j + 2\epsilon.$$

The convolution will consider that the couple $(k_1 = i, k_2 = j)$ has log probability $c_i + c_j$. Hence the distance between the real log probability and the log probability considered by the convolution is 2ϵ. If we add ν of such inequalities the distance between the real log probability and its bin is bounded by $\nu\epsilon$. That is the bound of the FSE'15 method.

In our case we have also to consider the batching step. Remark when we batch the bins of width w center c_i, c_{i+1} (resp. c_{i-1}, c_i), the new center is $\dfrac{c_i + c_{i+1}}{2} = c_i + \dfrac{w}{2}$ (resp. $\dfrac{c_{i-1} + c_i}{2} = c_i - +\dfrac{w}{2}$). That means we have the inequality:

$$c_i - \frac{w}{2} \leq batch(c_i) \leq c_i - \frac{w}{2}.$$

Putting the two errors for each level in our tree we double the error of the histograms inputs and add an error of half bin width of histogram inputs. For the first level, we will have:

$$batch(c_i + c_j) - 3\epsilon \leq c_i + c_j - 2\epsilon \leq \log(\Pr[k_1 = i]) + \log(\Pr[k_2 = j])$$
$$\leq c_i + c_j + 2\epsilon \leq batch(c_i + c_j) + 3\epsilon.$$

By iterating the error propagation we obtain error for our method. Remark the error can be, more efficiently, computed by the following formula if the input histograms at the first level have bin width 2ϵ:

$$error = \nu\epsilon + \lceil \log_2(\nu) \rceil \frac{\nu}{2}\epsilon.$$

Remark that the final histogram has bin width of $2^{\nu+1}\epsilon$

In FSE'15 the error was given as a number of bin, in our case doing so we will have overestimated margins. Calculate the lower and upper bins from the log probability of the key $\pm$ error give tighter margins.

As for FSE'15 if we double the number of bins we reduce by two the error.

3.4 Non Power of 2 Cases

If the number of subkeys is not a power of two our first convolution step (line 5 in Listing 2) should be adapted.

During the first step of convolutions, we perform a reduced number of convolutions such that at the end of this step the number of histograms is a power of 2. To keep the histograms with the same bin size we need to perform batching on all histograms, even the ones that do not go to the first convolution loop. We refer to longer version of this paper for more details.[1]

4   Experiments

We compare the efficiency of different approaches of key ranking based on histograms (i.e. FSE'15 and our method) in terms of time efficiency and precision.

In all our experiment we consider simulations. We target the memory loading of the key (or subkeys). The memory load target seems to fit the assumption of independence of subkeys for large keys. Note that such attacks have been used for attacks against AVR XMEGA [5]. These attacks do not use the structure of the cipher so can be adapted to asymmetric key implementations at a cost of more computation (linear in the key size). We assume that the attacker was able to perfectly recovered the leakage function.

For our experiments, we have a set of parameters that we modify that we detailed hereafter.

- *The number of subkeys.* The number of subkeys is the principal parameters we want to compare.
- *The precision.* The precision is an important point of comparison for rank estimation algorithms. In our case, we compare histogram based solution the precision is the number of bins.
- *The leakage function.* As we target the memory load of a subkey we can observe only one output of the leakage function $\mathcal{L}$. The only observation we get is $\mathcal{L}(k) + \mathcal{N}$, where k is the subkey and $\mathcal{N}$ is some noise. If we perform several measurements for the same subkey we will observe the same deterministic part of the leakage. Hence, if $\mathcal{L}(k_1) = \mathcal{L}(k_2)$, we will obtain the same probability for k_1 and k_2. Such a property will impact the tightness result of any key rank algorithm that targets such values.
- *The noise.* We consider white Gaussian noise with different variance noise.
- *The size of the subkeys.* For our experiments, we target 8-bit subkeys.

4.1   Same Precision

We compare in term of efficiency our method versus the FSE method. In this experiment we look at the tightness and time of our method with 2^{16} bins per histogram at the beginning, FSE'15 with the same amount of bins and FSE'15 with less bins $\left(\dfrac{2^{16}}{\nu} \right)$ such that the final histogram have a similar amount of bins as our method. The choice of 2^{16} bins per histogram at the beginning is motivated by the fact this gives quite tight bound in an efficient manner for FSE'15 [8].

---

[1] https://eprint.iacr.org/2018/175.

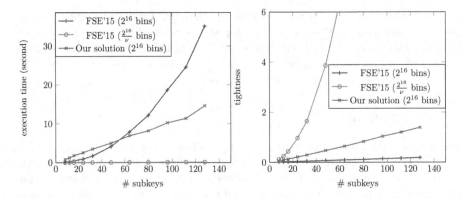

Fig. 4. Execution time (left) and tightness of the bound (right) of Matlab implementations of the FSE'15 solution and ours for different sizes of keys (16 bits of precision) and an SNR of 8.

On the graph, we can see that the FSE'15 solution with a constant number of bins (2^{16}) have an execution time that grows faster than linearly, but it is the solution that offers the tightest bound. However, if we use FSE'15 with the same number of bins for the final histogram the solution is quite efficient but the tightness explodes for large keys. Our method seems to have a linear time complexity and a linear increase of the tightness in the size of the key.

4.2 Similar Tightness

We compare our method to the FSE'15 method to obtain similar tightness. We look at two levels of tightness 1 bit and 0.3 bit. To obtain similar tightness when the size of the key increase we need to increase the number of bins of the initial histograms. The results are plotted in Fig. 5.

The first observation we can make is that the tighter we want the rank estimation, the smallest is the ratio between the time gap between our method and FSE'15. Secondly, since we need to increase the number of bins of the initial histograms the time complexity grows faster than linearly even for our method. However, for a large number of subkeys our solution more efficient than the FSE'15 solution.

4.3 NTL Implementation

Matlab implementation of the solution has some limitations mainly due to the fact that large integers are stored in doubles. That means that bins cannot be higher than 2^{1024}. Thus for large keys (>1024-bit), the implementation could lead to an incorrect result. To solve this problem Glowacz et al. [8] suggest to use Chinese remainder theorem.

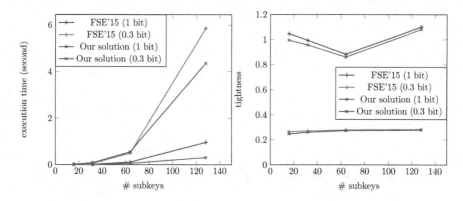

Fig. 5. Execution time (left) and tightness of the bound (right) of Matlab implementations of the FSE'15 solution and ours for similar tightness.

To override these issues we implement our solution using a big integer library: the NTL library. We look at histograms starting with 2^{12} and perform the convolution of: 16, 32, 64, 128, 256, 512 and 1024 histograms. For the classical FSE'15 method for the 128 convolutions and an initial number of bins 2^{12} we get an error message saying that histograms where too large (the number of bins) to perform the convolution. Our C implementation allows to obtain rank for very large keys (up to 1024 subkeys in less than 15 s).

4.4 Comparison with CHES 2017

At CHES 2017 Choudary and Popescu present an "impressively fast, scalable and tight security evaluation tools" [3]. Note that their tool does not calculate the rank of the key but the expected value of the rank. As pointed out in [9] it is not clear how to evaluate the power computation required to recover the key from the expected value of the rank. This is mainly due to the distribution of the rank that is not easy to model. However, we want to compare our method, the FSE'15 method and the CHES 2017 method in terms of efficiency/tightness. As the CHES 2017 do not offer parameters to tighten the bounds we play with the number of bins for FSE and our method to have similar tightness. The results are plotted in Fig. 6.

We can see that indeed the CHES'17 solution is quite efficient. In the same time, for such a tightness all solutions run in less than 100 ms for 128 subkeys. For such bounds, it seems that the rank computation's time is not the bottleneck of an evaluation.

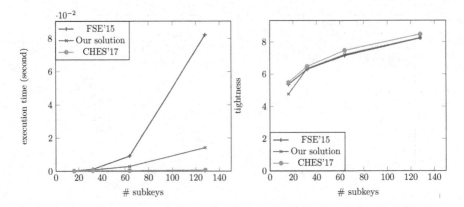

Fig. 6. Execution time (left) and tightness of the bound (right) of Matlab implementations of the FSE'15 solution and ours for similar tightness as CHES'17.

5   Key Enumeration

We can apply similar idea as the backtracking used in [13]. Our technique speed up the construction phase of a solution like [13]. In general, this step is negligible for key enumeration algorithm. We refer to longer version of this paper for more details.[2] However, our enumeration algorithm has an advantage when memory needed to store histograms is too large.

6   Conclusion

We present a trick to reduce the cost of rank estimation for a large number of subkeys based on the rank estimation of [8]. It can be applied to evaluate security against side-channel of cryptographic implementation that uses large keys. Our solution has the advantage to have a linear complexity in the number of subkeys. Our method allows to estimate efficiently rank of the key thanks to the tight bounds we manage to evaluate. Finally, our algorithm could be used as a construction phase for an enumeration algorithm. This algorithm could be useful when the number of subkeys if large and thus classical enumeration algorithm required a large amount of memory. Finally, our error bound estimation could be applied to other cases, in particular we can look at not equally sized histograms.

Acknowledgments. I thank the anonymous reviewers and Mathieu Carbone, Romain Poussier and François-Xavier Standaert for the improvements pointed out.

---

[2] https://eprint.iacr.org/2018/175.

References

1. Bernstein, D.J., Lange, T., van Vredendaal, C.: Tighter, faster, simpler side-channel security evaluations beyond computing power. IACR Cryptology ePrint Archive 2015, 221 (2015). http://eprint.iacr.org/2015/221
2. Bogdanov, A., Kizhvatov, I., Manzoor, K., Tischhauser, E., Witteman, M.: Fast and memory-efficient key recovery in side-channel attacks. In: Dunkelman, O., Keliher, L. (eds.) SAC 2015. LNCS, vol. 9566, pp. 310–327. Springer, Cham (2016). https://doi.org/10.1007/978-3-319-31301-6_19
3. Choudary, M.O., Popescu, P.G.: Back to massey: impressively fast, scalable and tight security evaluation tools. In: Fischer, W., Homma, N. (eds.) CHES 2017. LNCS, vol. 10529, pp. 367–386. Springer, Cham (2017). https://doi.org/10.1007/978-3-319-66787-4_18
4. Choudary, M.O., Poussier, R., Standaert, F.-X.: Score-based vs. probability-based enumeration – a cautionary note. In: Dunkelman, O., Sanadhya, S.K. (eds.) INDOCRYPT 2016. LNCS, vol. 10095, pp. 137–152. Springer, Cham (2016). https://doi.org/10.1007/978-3-319-49890-4_8
5. Choudary, O., Kuhn, M.G.: Efficient template attacks. In: Francillon, A., Rohatgi, P. (eds.) CARDIS 2013. LNCS, vol. 8419, pp. 253–270. Springer, Cham (2014). https://doi.org/10.1007/978-3-319-08302-5_17
6. David, L., Wool, A.: A bounded-space near-optimal key enumeration algorithm for multi-subkey side-channel attacks. In: Handschuh, H. (ed.) CT-RSA 2017. LNCS, vol. 10159, pp. 311–327. Springer, Cham (2017). https://doi.org/10.1007/978-3-319-52153-4_18
7. Duc, A., Faust, S., Standaert, F.-X.: Making masking security proofs concrete: or how to evaluate the security of any leaking device. In: Oswald, E., Fischlin, M. (eds.) EUROCRYPT 2015. LNCS, vol. 9056, pp. 401–429. Springer, Heidelberg (2015). https://doi.org/10.1007/978-3-662-46800-5_16
8. Glowacz, C., Grosso, V., Poussier, R., Schüth, J., Standaert, F.-X.: Simpler and more efficient rank estimation for side-channel security assessment. In: Leander, G. (ed.) FSE 2015. LNCS, vol. 9054, pp. 117–129. Springer, Heidelberg (2015). https://doi.org/10.1007/978-3-662-48116-5_6
9. Martin, D.P., Mather, L., Oswald, E., Stam, M.: Characterisation and estimation of the key rank distribution in the context of side channel evaluations. In: Cheon, J.H., Takagi, T. (eds.) ASIACRYPT 2016. LNCS, vol. 10031, pp. 548–572. Springer, Heidelberg (2016). https://doi.org/10.1007/978-3-662-53887-6_20
10. Martin, D.P., Montanaro, A., Oswald, E., Shepherd, D.J.: Quantum key search with side channel advice. IACR Cryptology ePrint Archive 2017, 171 (2017). http://eprint.iacr.org/2017/171
11. Martin, D.P., O'Connell, J.F., Oswald, E., Stam, M.: Counting keys in parallel after a side channel attack. In: Iwata, T., Cheon, J.H. (eds.) ASIACRYPT 2015. LNCS, vol. 9453, pp. 313–337. Springer, Heidelberg (2015). https://doi.org/10.1007/978-3-662-48800-3_13
12. Poussier, R., Grosso, V., Standaert, F.-X.: Comparing approaches to rank estimation for side-channel security evaluations. In: Homma, N., Medwed, M. (eds.) CARDIS 2015. LNCS, vol. 9514, pp. 125–142. Springer, Cham (2016). https://doi.org/10.1007/978-3-319-31271-2_8
13. Poussier, R., Standaert, F.-X., Grosso, V.: Simple key enumeration (and rank estimation) using histograms: an integrated approach. In: Gierlichs, B., Poschmann, A.Y. (eds.) CHES 2016. LNCS, vol. 9813, pp. 61–81. Springer, Heidelberg (2016). https://doi.org/10.1007/978-3-662-53140-2_4

14. Veyrat-Charvillon, N., Gérard, B., Renauld, M., Standaert, F.-X.: An optimal key enumeration algorithm and its application to side-channel attacks. In: Knudsen, L.R., Wu, H. (eds.) SAC 2012. LNCS, vol. 7707, pp. 390–406. Springer, Heidelberg (2013). https://doi.org/10.1007/978-3-642-35999-6_25
15. Veyrat-Charvillon, N., Gérard, B., Standaert, F.-X.: Security evaluations beyond computing power. In: Johansson, T., Nguyen, P.Q. (eds.) EUROCRYPT 2013. LNCS, vol. 7881, pp. 126–141. Springer, Heidelberg (2013). https://doi.org/10.1007/978-3-642-38348-9_8
16. Ye, X., Eisenbarth, T., Martin, W.: Bounded, yet sufficient? How to determine whether limited side channel information enables key recovery. In: Joye, M., Moradi, A. (eds.) CARDIS 2014. LNCS, vol. 8968, pp. 215–232. Springer, Cham (2015). https://doi.org/10.1007/978-3-319-16763-3_13

Shorter Messages and Faster Post-Quantum Encryption with Round5 on Cortex M

Markku-Juhani O. Saarinen[1]([⊠]), Sauvik Bhattacharya[2],
Oscar Garcia-Morchon[2], Ronald Rietman[2], Ludo Tolhuizen[2],
and Zhenfei Zhang[3]

[1] PQShield Ltd., Oxford, UK
mjos@pqshield.com
[2] Philips, Eindhoven, The Netherlands
{sauvik.bhattacharya,oscar.garcia-morchon,ronald.rietman,ludo.tolhuizen}
@philips.com
[3] OnBoard Security, Wilmington, USA
zzhang@onboardsecurity.com

Abstract. Round5 is a Public Key Encryption and Key Encapsulation Mechanism (KEM) based on General Learning with Rounding (GLWR), a lattice problem. We argue that the ring variant of GLWR is better suited for embedded targets than the more common RLWE (Ring Learning With Errors) due to significantly shorter keys and messages. Round5 incorporates GLWR with error correction, building on design features from NIST Post-Quantum Standardization candidates Round2 and Hila5. The proposal avoids Number Theoretic Transforms (NTT), allowing more flexibility in parameter selection and making it simpler to implement. We discuss implementation techniques of Round5 ring variants and compare them to other NIST PQC candidates on lightweight Cortex M4 platform. We show that the current development version of Round5 offers not only the shortest key and ciphertext sizes among Lattice-based candidates, but also has leading performance and implementation size characteristics.

Keywords: Post-Quantum Cryptography · Lattice cryptography · GLWR · Embedded implementation · Cortex M4

1 Introduction

There is well-founded speculation that the estimated time required for development of quantum computers capable of breaking RSA and Elliptic Curve Cryptography (ECC) [25,30] is shorter than the long term confidentiality requirements of some current highly sensitive communications and data. Such risk analysis prompted the National Security Agency (NSA) to revise its cryptographic algorithm recommendations in 2015 and to announce a "transition period" until quantum resistant replacement algorithms can be fielded [6,23].

© Springer Nature Switzerland AG 2019
B. Bilgin and J.-B. Fischer (Eds.): CARDIS 2018, LNCS 11389, pp. 95–110, 2019.
https://doi.org/10.1007/978-3-030-15462-2_7

The algorithm identification and standardization task fell largely to National Institute of Standards and Technology (NIST), who specified evaluation criteria and organized a public call for Post-Quantum Cryptography (PQC) algorithms in 2016 [20,21]. A total of 69 public key encryption, key encapsulation, and digital signature algorithm submissions were made by the November 2017 deadline [22].

The new proposals rely on a wide variety of quantum-resistant hard problems from areas such as lattices, coding theory, isogenies of supersingular curves, and multivariate equations. A set of selected PQC algorithms is expected to eventually fulfill all of the tasks that have up to now been assigned to classically secure (RSA and ECC) public key algorithm standards. This includes cryptography in lightweight embedded applications and smart cards.

2 Round5 Ring-Switching Variants R5ND "b"

Round5 is an amalgam of two lattice-based first-round candidates in the NIST Post-Quantum cryptography project, Round2 [14] and Hila5 [29]. Like its two parent proposals, Round5 can be used for both public key encryption and key encapsulation, and it inherits the use of a rounding problem from Round2 (GLWR, Sect. 2.1) and error correction from Hila5 (XEf, Sect. 3.1).

The use of a rounding problem together with error correction lends Round5 unique bandwidth efficiency properties. A full description of Round5, its design, classical and quantum security analysis, and parameter selection can be found in [5] and our upcoming NIST submission documents. Details of that analysis are outside the scope of this work but we note that the new parameter selection addresses the potential issues regarding classical attack bounds in the original Round2 submission. This work offers a technically simpler but functionally equivalent description of the algorithm when compared to those specifications.

We further note that the Round5 "b" parameter sets discussed in this paper are not final or "official" since both the NIST standardization effort and Round5 algorithm development are still ongoing at the time of writing.

2.1 Generalized Learning with Rounding

There is a relatively large set of interrelated hard problems used in lattice cryptography. One of the most common ones is Learning With Errors (LWE), which has a security reduction to worst-case quantum hardness of shortest vector problems GAPSVP and SIVP [26,27]. Learning With Rounding (LWR) was introduced in [3], where it was shown to have a security reduction from LWE. Round2 utilizes a version called General Learning With Rounding (GLWR).

A key feature of Round5 is the use of *rounding* in the form of a lossy compression function, Round. It maps $x \in \mathbb{Z}_a$ to $\mathbb{Z}_b$ with rounding constant h:

$$\mathsf{Round}_{a \to b}(x, h) = \left\lfloor \frac{b}{a} \cdot x + h \right\rfloor \bmod b. \tag{1}$$

This is equivalent to rounding of bx/a to closest integer when $h = 1/2$. Each coefficient is operated on separately when Round or modular reduction ("mod") is applied to polynomials, vectors, or matrices.

Definition 1 (General LWR (GLWR)). *Let d, n, p, q be positive integers such that $q \geq p \geq 2$, and $n \in \{ 1, d \}$. Let $\mathcal{R}_{n,q}$ be a polynomial ring, and let D_s be a probability distribution on $\mathcal{R}_n^{d/n}$.*

- *The search version of the GLWR problem $sGLWR_{d,n,m,q,p}(D_s)$ is as follows: given m samples of the form $(\mathbf{a}_i, b_i = \mathsf{Round}_{q \to p}(\mathbf{a}_i^T\mathbf{s} \bmod q, 1/2))$ with $\mathbf{a}_i \in \mathcal{R}_{n,q}^{d/n}$ and a fixed $\mathbf{s} \leftarrow D_s$, recover $\mathbf{s}$.*
- *The decision version of the GLWR problem $dGLWR_{d,n,m,q,p}(D_s)$ is to distinguish between the uniform distribution on $\mathcal{R}_{n,q}^{d/n} \times \mathcal{R}_{n,p}$ and the distribution $(\mathbf{a}_i, b_i = \mathsf{Round}_{q \to p}(\mathbf{a}_i^T\mathbf{s}_i \bmod q, 1/2))$ with $\mathbf{a}_i \leftarrow \mathcal{R}_{n,q}^{d/n}$ and a fixed $s \leftarrow D_s$.*

2.2 Highly Flexible Parameters: Embedded Use Case

The $n = 1$ case of GLWR corresponds to the original LWR problem of [3]. In this work we restrict ourselves to the $n = d$ case, which corresponds to the Ring-LWR (RLWR) problem and offers shorter public keys and ciphertext messages. See [5] for a full list of parameter sets.

Round5 has both chosen ciphertext (CCA) and chosen plaintext (CPA) secure versions. The CPA versions are faster and are configured to have smaller keys at the price of a slightly higher failure rate, making them better suited for ephemeral key establishment. On the other hand, parameter selection leading to a negligible error rate and the added security of CCA Fujisaki-Okamoto Transform [13,15] is needed in public key encryption applications, where messages and public keys have long lifetimes. Therefore the CCA variant is referred to as "Round5.PKE", while the CPA version is called "Round5.KEM". They both internally rely on the same building lock, an IND-CPA encryption scheme. Since both key establishment and public key encryption use cases are relevant to embedded applications, we consider them both.

In addition to the LWR/RLWR and CCA/CPA distinctions, Round5 defines parameter sets for each NIST encryption security category NIST1, NIST3, and NIST5. These correspond to the security level of AES with 128, 192, and 256 - bit key length, respectively, against a quantum or classical adversary [21].

However all applications clearly don't need to implement all variants. We adopt the strategy taken in NSA's Commercial National Security Algorithm (CNSA) suite [23] which standardizes only a single set of parameters and algorithms at 192-bit (classical) security level. This facilitates interoperability and parameter-specific implementation optimizations, leading to smaller implementation footprint. CNSA is approved up to TOP SECRET in United States.

Round5 Designators. This work focuses on variants with designators R5ND_3KEMb and R5ND_3PKEb. One can read the designators aloud as "Round 5" (R5), "ring variant" (ND for $n = d$), "post-quantum security category 3" (3), "CPA security for ephemeral keys" (KEM) or "CCA security for public key encryption" (PKE). The last lower case letter signifies the chronological order in which the particular parameter set was investigated. Letter "b" simply means that we are discussing the second publicly proposed variant of Round5. A higher letter does not necessarily indicate that the particular parameter set ends up being the best one.

Table 1. Internal parameters and external attributes for the R5ND_3 "b" variants of Round5 discussed in this paper. The security estimates are made with very conservative assumptions and correspond to NIST3 security level. See also Tables 4 and 5.

Parameter	R5ND_3KEMb	R5ND_3PKEb
Dimension	$n = 756$	$n = 756$
Degree ($n = d$ for ring variants)	$d = 756$	$d = 756$
Nonzero elements in ternary secrets	$h = 242$	$h = 242$
Large (main) modulus	$q = 2^{12}$	$q = 2^{12}$
Rounding modulus	$p = 2^8$	$p = 2^8$
Compression modulus	$t = 2^2$	$t = 2^3$
Encrypted secret size (bits)	$|K| = 192$	$|K| = 192$
Error correction code size (bits)	$l = 103$	$l = 103$
Transmitted secret (bits $\mu = |K| + l$)	$\mu = 295$	$\mu = 295$
Random bit flips corrected (by XEf)	$f = 3$	$f = 3$
Public key size (bytes)	780	810
Secret key size (bytes)	24	828
Ciphertext expansion (bytes)	830	891
Shared secret size (bytes)	24	24
Quantum security	2^{176}	2^{176}
Classical security	2^{193}	2^{193}
Decryption failure rate	2^{-78}	2^{-171}

2.3 High-Level Algorithm Overview

Table 1 summarizes the internal and external parameters of our implementation.

Round5 uses two polynomial rings[1]; $x^{n+1} - 1$, with $n+1$ prime, and its subring $\Phi_{n+1} = (x^{n+1} - 1)/(x - 1) = x^n + \cdots + x + 1$. We observe that $x^n \bmod \Phi_{n+1} = -\sum_0^{n-1} x^i$. Therefore one can utilize a trick for reducing modulo Φ_{n+1}, first reducing a result modulo cyclic $x^{n+1} - 1$ where $x^{i+n+1} \equiv x^i$, and then subtracting the x^n coefficient from the rest of coefficients (and itself).

---

[1] Originally only one ring was used. As pointed out by Mike Hamburg, use of two rings yields better error analysis, and works much better with error correction.

The small-norm secrets have special structure: sparse ternary polynomial set $D \subset \{-1,0,1\}^n$ has $\frac{h}{2}$ coefficients set to $+1$, $\frac{h}{2}$ coefficients set to -1, and $n - h$ coefficients being zero.

Algorithm 1. KeyGenCPA(σ, γ): Key generation for CPA case.

Input: Random seeds σ, γ.

1: $\mathbf{a} \xleftarrow{\$\sigma} \mathbb{Z}_q^n$ *Uniform polynomial, seed σ.*

2: $\mathbf{s} \xleftarrow{\$\gamma} D$ *Sparse ternary polynomial, seed γ.*

3: $\mathbf{b} \leftarrow \mathsf{Round}_{q \to p}(\mathbf{a} * \mathbf{s} \bmod \Phi_{n+1}, 1/2)$ *Compress product to range $0 \leq b_i < p$.*

4: $\mathsf{sk} = \mathbf{s}$ **s**: *Random seed γ is sufficient.*

5: $\mathsf{pk} = (\mathbf{a}, \mathbf{b})$ **a**: *Random seed σ,* **b**: $n \log_2 p$ *bits.*

Output: Public key $\mathsf{pk} = (\mathbf{a}, \mathbf{b})$ and secret key $\mathsf{sk} = \mathbf{s}$.

Ignoring a lot of detail, the basic key generation procedure KeyGenCPA() is given by Algorithm 1 while Algorithms 2 and 3 describe the basic encryption and decryption operations EncryptCPA() and DecryptCPA(), respectively. The function Sample_μ takes μ lowest-order coefficients of input. Note that the rounding constant for Round is actually not always $1/2$ – we refer to the submission documents and [5] for a full technical definition of Round5.

Algorithm 2. EncryptCPA($\mathbf{m}, \mathsf{pk}, \rho$): Public key encryption (CPA).

Input: Message $\mathbf{m} = \{0,1\}^m$, public key $\mathsf{pk} = (\mathbf{a}, \mathbf{b})$, random seed ρ.

1: $\mathbf{r} \xleftarrow{\$\rho} D$ *Sparse ternary polynomial, seed ρ*

2: $\mathbf{u} \leftarrow \mathsf{Round}_{q \to p}(\mathbf{a} * \mathbf{r} \bmod \Phi_{n+1}, 1/2)$ *Compress product to range $0 \leq u_i < p$.*

3: $\mathbf{t} \leftarrow \mathsf{Sample}_\mu(\mathbf{b} * \mathbf{r} \bmod x^{n+1} - 1)$ *Noisy shared secret, truncate to $\mathbb{Z}_p^\mu$.*

4: $\mathbf{v} \leftarrow \mathsf{Round}_{p \to t}(\mathbf{t} + \frac{p}{2}\mathbf{m}, 1/2)$ *Add message + error correction $\mathbf{m} \in \mathbb{Z}_2^\mu$.*

5: $\mathsf{ct} = (\mathbf{u}, \mathbf{v})$ **u**: $n \log_2 p$ *bits,* **v**: $\mu \log_2 t$ *bits.*

Output: Ciphertext $\mathsf{ct} = (\mathbf{u}, \mathbf{v})$.

Algorithm 3. DecryptCPA(ct, sk): Decryption (CPA).

Input: Ciphertext $\mathsf{ct} = (\mathbf{u}, \mathbf{v})$, secret key $\mathsf{sk} = \mathbf{s}$.

1: $\mathbf{t}' \leftarrow \mathsf{Sample}_\mu(\mathbf{u} * \mathbf{s} \bmod x^{n+1} - 1)$ *Noisy shared secret, truncate to $\mathbb{Z}_p^\mu$.*

2: $\mathbf{m} \leftarrow \mathsf{Round}_{p \to 2}(\frac{p}{t}\mathbf{v} - \mathbf{t}', 1/2)$ *Remove noise, correct errors in $\mathbf{m} \in \mathbb{Z}_2^\mu$.*

Output: Plaintext $\mathsf{pt} = \mathbf{m}$.

To see why the algorithm works, note that the shared secrets in Algorithms 2 and 3 satisfy approximately $\mathbf{t} \approx \mathbf{t}' \approx \mathbf{a} * \mathbf{s} * \mathbf{r}$. Even though the two multiplications are in a different rings, the second ring is a subring of the first. Since $\mathbf{s}$ and $\mathbf{r}$ are "balanced", their coefficients sum to zero and they are divisible by $(x - 1)$. High bits of $\mathbf{t}$ are used as a "one time pad" to transport the message payload.

CPA-KEM. The chosen-plaintext secure (IND-CPA) key encapsulation mode is constructed from EncryptCPA() and DecryptCPA() in straightforward fashion by randomizing seed ρ and composing the message $\mathbf{m} \in \{0,1\}^{\mu}$ from random key $\mathbf{k} \overset{\$}{\leftarrow} \{0,1\}^{|K|}$ and an error correction code (Sect. 3.1). Both parties compute the shared secret as $\mathbf{ss} = h(\mathbf{k}, \mathbf{ct})$ (after error correction in decapsulation.)

CCA-KEM. The CPA scheme is transformed into a chosen ciphertext (IND-CCA2) secure one (in R5ND_3PKEb) using the Fujisaki-Okamoto Transform [13, 15]:

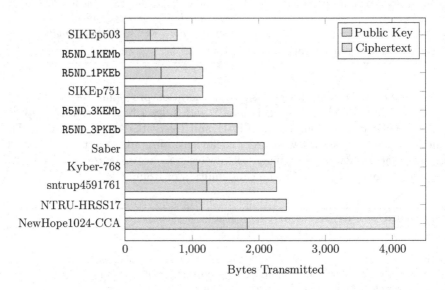

Fig. 1. Bandwidth usage in key establishment. In addition to other relatively bandwidth-efficient lattice schemes, we include SIKEp503 (Category 1) and SIKEp751 (Category 3), which are the only candidates with shorter messages. However their performance is several orders of magnitude slower than that of Round5 – see Table 2.

- **Key generation** requires storing secret coins $\mathbf{z} \overset{\$}{\leftarrow} \{0,1\}^{|K|}$ and the public key from KeyGenCPA with the secret key: $\mathtt{CCAsk} = (\mathbf{sk}, \mathbf{z}, \mathbf{pk})$.
- **Encapsulation.** We hash $\mathbf{m} \in \{0,1\}^{\mu}$ consisting of a random message and error correction with the public key to create a triplet of $|K|$-bit quantities $(\mathbf{l}, \mathbf{g}, \rho) = h(\mathbf{m}, \mathbf{pk})$. Then compute $\mathbf{c} = (\mathsf{EncryptCPA}(\mathbf{m}, \mathbf{pk}, \rho)$ and set ciphertext as $\mathbf{ct} = (\mathbf{c}, \mathbf{g})$. The shared secret is $\mathbf{ss} = h(\mathbf{l}, \mathbf{ct})$.
- **Decapsulation** computes $\mathbf{m'} = \mathsf{DecryptCPA}(\mathbf{c}, \mathbf{sk})$ from the first part of ciphertext and uses that to create its version of triplet $(\mathbf{l'}, \mathbf{g'}, \rho') = h(\mathbf{m'}, \mathbf{pk})$. This is then used in simulated encryption $\mathbf{c'} = \mathsf{EncryptCPA}(\mathbf{m'}, \mathbf{pk}, \rho')$. If there is a match $\mathbf{ct} = (\mathbf{c'}, \mathbf{g'})$, we set $\mathbf{ss} = h(\mathbf{l'}, \mathbf{ct})$. In case of mismatch $\mathbf{ct} \neq (\mathbf{c'}, \mathbf{g'})$ we use our stored coins $\mathbf{z}$ for deterministic output $\mathbf{ss} = h(\mathbf{z}, \mathbf{ct})$.

KEMs and Public Key Encryption. While R5ND_3KEMb (CPA) is sufficient for purely ephemeral key establishment, we suggest R5ND_3PKEb (CCA) for public key encryption [7]. One of course needs to further define a Data Encapsulation Mechanism (DEM) in order to transmit actual messages rather than just keys.

3 Implementation Tweaks and Optimizations

The operation of Round5 in a ring is analogous to "LP11" [19] encryption, but using rounding instead of synthetic random error. Our lightweight implementation in particular shares some similarity with "half-truncated" lightweight Ring-LWE scheme TRUNC8 [28], but uses a sparse ternary vector instead of a binary secret. Here we highlight some key factors the embedded implementation to be faster and more compact than the reference implementation (and Round2).

Simplifications. There are a number of practical simplifications related to our specific parameter choices. Since p and q are powers of two, there is a lot of masking by $p - 1$ and $q - 1$. However much of this is unnecessary since carry bits do not flow from higher bits towards lower bits in addition and subtraction. Therefore all intermediate values can be kept at full word length. Most of the arithmetic operates internally on 16-bit words, well suited for lightweight targets.

SHAKE-256. We use SHAKE-256 [11] consistently for hashing and random byte sequence generation. Round2 used SHA3-512 for "short-output hashing", usually truncating the result to 32 bytes. SHA3-512 with its 1024-bit internal state and slow speed is clearly an overkill. Round2 furthermore specified a "DRBG" based on AES-256 [10] in counter mode [9]. SHAKE-256 is designed as a extendable output function (XOF) and takes over the functions of DRBG.

There were instances of double hashing within the algorithm, such as hashing input to get a fixed-length DRBG seed – which is of course unnecessary in case of an arbitrary-input XOF. Another case was the three-output G function which was previously implemented with three iterations of hashing rather than cutting a longer XOF output into three shorter pieces.

Faster Generation of Sparse Ternary Vectors. We use a rejection sampling method rather than the sorting method originally used in Round2. This faster method allows us to store a random seed instead of a full ternary vector as the secret key. See Sect. 3.3 and Algorithm 4 for more details. The original method was chosen to have constant time execution (even though it didn't always have that in practice). We note that even though rejection sampling has variable execution time, it does not leak secrets if the distribution is not secret, the original secret values are statistically independent, and a non-rejected result itself does not cause a timing variation (e.g. via memory accesses).

3.1 Error Correcting Code XEf

A 3-error correcting block code is used to decrease the failure rate. The code is built using the same strategy as codes used by TRUNC8 [28] (2-bit correction) and HILA5 [29] (5-bit correction).

Our linear parity code consists of $2f = 6$ "registers" R_i of size $|R_i| = l_i$. We view the payload block m as a binary polynomial $m_{|K|-1}x^{|K|-1} + \cdots + m_1 x + m_0$ of length equivalent to shared secret K. Registers are defined via cyclic reduction

$$R_i = m \bmod x^{l_i} - 1, \tag{2}$$

or equivalently by

$$r_{(i,j)} = \sum_{k \equiv j \bmod l_i} m_k \tag{3}$$

where $r_{(i,j)}$ is bit j of register R_i. A transmitted message consists of the payload m concatenated with register set r (a total of $|K| + \sum l_i$ bits).

Upon receiving a message $(m' \mid r)$ one computes code r' corresponding to m' and compares it to the received code r – that may also have errors. Errors are in coefficients m'_j where there is parity disagreements $r_{(i,j \bmod l_i)} \neq r'_{(i,j \bmod l_i)}$ for multitude of registers R_i. We use a majority rule and flip bit m'_j if

$$\sum_{i=1}^{2f} \left(\left(r_{(i,j \bmod l_i)} - r'_{(i,j \bmod l_i)} \right) \bmod 2 \right) \geq f + 1 \tag{4}$$

where the sum is taken as the number of disagreeing register parity bits at j.

It is easy to show that if all length pairs satisfy $\operatorname{lcm}(l_i, l_j) \geq |K|$ when $i \neq j$ then this code always corrects at least f errors. Typically one chooses coprime lengths $l_1 < l_2 < \cdots < l_{2f}$ so that $l_1 l_2 \geq |K|$.

Our R5ND_3 variants have $f = 3$ and $(l_1, l_2, \cdots, l_6) = (13, 15, 16, 17, 19, 23)$. The code adds $\sum_i l_i = l = 103$ bits to the message, bringing the total to $192 + 103 = 295$ bits. We have verified that our implementation always fixes 3 bit flips anywhere in the 295-bit block and 4 bit flips with $P = 44785504/309177995 \approx 14.5\%$. Its main advantage over other error-correcting codes is that it can be implemented without table look-ups and conditional cases and it is therefore resistant to timing attacks. See Tables 1 and 3 for overall failure rate estimates.

3.2 Arithmetic of Sparse Ternary Polynomials

Unlike many other fast lattice-based schemes, our R5ND_3 variants do not use the (Nussbaumer) Number Theoretic Transform (NTT) for its ring arithmetic [24]. This allows more flexibility for selection of n and greater variance in implementation techniques leading to substantial reduction in implementation footprint.

Multiplication of a ring element with $\{-1, 0, +1\}$ coefficients requires only additions and subtractions. Furthermore the use of power-of-2 moduli q, p, t means that no modular reduction is required. This greatly simplifies implementation, especially on hardware targets, but also on microcontrollers without a multiplier (where performance gains are likely to be more significant than on Cortex M).

Implementation of sparse ternary multiplication required special attention as that is the workhorse of Round2 and a large portion of its execution time is spent performing this operation. Clearly its complexity is $O(hn)$ but even though this is asymptotically worse than $O(n \log n)$ of NTT, our findings indicate that it is significantly better in practice with the parameters of R5ND_3KEMb and R5ND_3PKEb.

The lowest level loops in multiplication are simple vector additions and subtractions. Since there is an equivalent number $(h/2)$ of $+1$ and -1 terms in the ternary polynomials, the computation is organized in a way that allows an addition and an subtraction to be paired in a each loop.

Similar techniques are highly effective on SIMD targets such as AVX2 as well, but require special cache attack countermeasures. Cache attacks are not a concern with Cortex M SoCs (since all memory is internal to the chip and there is no RAM cache[2]) We note that our cache-resistant portable implementation runs at about half of the speed of normal version.

Algorithm 4. SparseTernary(s): A ternary vector with weight h from seed s.

Input: Seed value s, dimension and degree n, scaling factor $k = \lfloor 2^{16}/n \rfloor$.

1:	$\mathbf{z} \leftarrow \mathsf{SHAKE256}(s)$	*Absorb the seed s into Keccak state.*
2:	$\mathbf{v} \leftarrow 0^n$	*Initialize as zero.*
3:	**for** $i = 0, 1, \ldots h - 1$ **do**	
4:	**repeat**	
5:	**repeat**	
6:	$t' \leftarrow$ two bytes from z	*z represents the (endless) output of XOF.*
7:	**until** $t' < kn$	*Rejection step with the unscaled value.*
8:	$t \leftarrow \lfloor t'/k \rfloor$	*Remove the integer scaling factor k.*
9:	**until** $v_t = 0$	*Another rejection. Vector is sparse.*
10:	$v_t \leftarrow (-1)^i$	*Alternating $+1, -1, +1, \cdots$.*
11:	**end for**	

Output: A vector $\mathbf{v}$ which has $\frac{h}{2}$ elements set to $+1$, $\frac{h}{2}$ set to -1 and $n - h$ zeros.

3.3   Sparse Ternary Vector Generation

Algorithm 4 describes our deterministic method for creating sparse ternary vectors of weight h. It uses rejection sampling to obtain uniformly random index $0 \le t < n$. This is clearly not a constant time operation – however we can see that a rejection sampler does not leak information about t since bytes in $\mathbf{z}$ are statistically independent. This has caused some false positives when automated tools are used to detect timing leaks.

---

[2] http://infocenter.arm.com/help/index.jsp?topic=/com.arm.doc.dai0321a.

Even though Algorithm 4 produces correct results, in practice the vector $\mathbf{v}$ is only used to store only an "occupancy table" of free slots, while the actual indices t are stored in two lists of $+1$ and -1 coefficient offsets (which correspond to coefficient of degree $n + 1 - t$ in ring polynomial representation). These lists of length $h/2$ are used in multiplication rather than scanning $\mathbf{v}$. There is no reason to sort the lists – a randomized pattern may even work as a free cache attack countermeasure on targets where that may be a problem.

The use of scaling factor k greatly lowers the rejection rate of the inner sampler. With R5ND_3KEMb and R5ND_3PKEb we have $n = 756$ and $k = \lfloor 2^{16}/n \rfloor = 86$, leading to rejection rate of just $1 - kn/2^{16} = 0.007935$.

There is a secondary rejection when finding non-empty slots in the $\mathbf{v}$ vector, which might make an algorithm of this sort run in essentially quadratic time if h is close to n. However in our case the density is bound by $h/n \leq 1/3$.

A simple implementation of secondary rejection should be timing attack resistant on the Cortex M4, which has no data cache. However we also have a "countermeasure" version that stores the occupancy of v_i in list of a dozen 64-bit words (the sign doesn't matter, so a single bit is enough). This version scans the entire list with constant-time Boolean logic for every probe.

Table 2. Communication parameters and cycle count breakdown of the optimized C implementation on Cortex-M4 for some NIST PQC candidate KEMs. First columns give the size of public key, secret key, and ciphertext in bytes. The following columns give the number of cycles required for key generation, encapsulation, and decapsulation.

Algorithm	Size in Bytes			Cycles (k = 1000, M = 10^6)		
	PK	SK	CT	KeyGen	Encaps	Decaps
R5ND_1KEMb	445	16	539	527 k	758 k	294 k
R5ND_3KEMb	780	24	830	1,029 k	1,429 k	492 k
R5ND_5KEMb	972	32	1082	2,037 k	2,798 k	924 k
R5ND_1PKEb	538	570	621	658 k	984 k	1,265 k
R5ND_3PKEb	780	828	891	1,032 k	1,510 k	1,913 k
R5ND_5PKEb	972	1036	1161	2,003 k	2,849 k	3,639 k
Kyber-768 [2]	1088	2400	1152	1,333 k	1,765 k	1,935 k
NewHope1024CCA [1]	1824	3680	2208	1,505 k	2,326 k	2,493 k
Saber (Assembler) [8]	992	2304	1088	7,156 k	9,492 k	11,612 k
sntrup4591761 [4]	1218	1600	1047	166,215 k	11,274 k	31,733 k
NTRU-HRSS17 [16]	1138	1418	1278	187,525 k	5,429 k	15,405 k
SIKEp751 [17]	564	644	596	3,775 M	6,114 M	6,572 M

4   Performance on Cortex M4

We benchmarked a group of comparable NIST First Round KEM and PKE proposals on Cortex-M4. A NIST Category 3 variant ("192 quantum bit security") was used if available. We used an optimized C version in our tests, linked with an efficient assembler-language SHA3 implementation (excluded from code size). Our results are summarized in Table 2 and Figs. 1 and 2. We are also including assembler optimized Cortex M4 numbers for Saber from [18] for completeness. Source code is available at https://github.com/mjosaarinen/r5nd_tiny.

Test Setup. We wanted a fair comparison that eliminates bias caused by poor testing setup. For example the initial NIST tests of Hila5 indicated poor performance, but this was caused by extremely poor implementation of `randombytes()` in the NIST test suite. This function (i.e. the test suite itself) was consuming 80 % of cycles. Some other submitters were aware of this pitfall and created a faster layer of random number generation *inside* their implementation. Our test code consistently uses a fast implementation of SHAKE for random numbers.

Gnu C compiler `arm-none-eabi-gcc` was used with optimization flags set to `-Ofast -mthumb`. Our testing was performed on NXP MK20DX256 Microcontroller on a Teensy[3] board, which we ran at 24 MHz. Cycle counts at higher speeds are slightly less accurate due to interference by the memory controller.

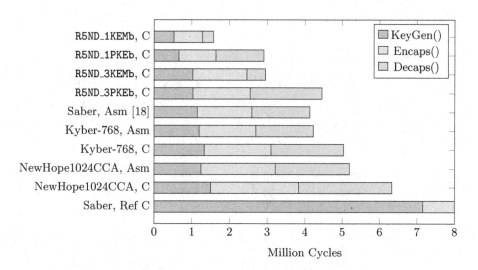

Fig. 2. Visualization of relative speed of key establishment, including assembler versions from [18] and PQM4. We have excluded algorithms that require more than 200 M cycles (several seconds). Round5 implementations are in written in C, yet highly competitive in terms of speed.

---

[3] Teensy 3.2 is an inexpensive (under $20) miniature (18 × 36 mm or 0.7 × 1.4") Cortex-M4 development board: https://www.pjrc.com/store/teensy32.html.

For comparison, a highly optimized X25519 scalar multiplication requires 907 k cycles on Cortex M4 [12] – but has only 128-bit classical security. Four scalar multiplications are needed for Diffie-Hellman, so our plain C implementations of R5ND_1KEMb, R5ND_1PKEb, and even higher-security R5ND_3KEMb are faster.

Table 3. Engineering and security comparison for key establishment use case with Cortex M4 at NIST Security Level 3. Xfer: Total data transferred (public key + ciphertext). Time: Time required for KeyGen() + Encaps() + Decaps() on Cortex-M4 at 24 MHz. Code: Size of implementation in bytes, excluding hash function and other common parts. Fail: Decryption failure bound. PQ Sec: Claimed quantum complexity. Classic: Claimed classical complexity.

Algorithm	Xfer	Time	Code	Fail	PQ Sec	Classic
R5ND_3KEMb	1610	0.123s	4464	2^{-78}	2^{176}	2^{193}
R5ND_3PKEb	1671	0.185s	5232	2^{-171}	2^{176}	2^{193}
Saber (Assembler) [8,18]	2080	0.172s	?	2^{-136}	2^{180}	2^{198}
Kyber-768 [2]	2240	0.210s	7016	2^{-142}	2^{161}	2^{178}
sntrup4591761 [4]	2265	8.718s	71024	0	?	2^{248}
NTRU-HRSS17 [16]	2416	7.814s	11956	0	2^{123}	2^{136}
NewHope1024-CCA [1]	4032	0.264s	12912	2^{-216}	2^{233}	?
SIKEp751 [17]	1160	685.9s	19112	0	2^{124}	2^{186}

Table 4. Round5 "b" ring variant parameter sets for key establishment.

	Parameters	CPA NIST1	CPA NIST3	CPA NIST5
Round5.KEM	d, n, h	490, 490, 162	756, 756, 242	940, 940, 414
	q, p, t	$2^{10}, 2^7, 2^4$	$2^{12}, 2^8, 2^2$	$2^{12}, 2^8, 2^3$
	$B, \bar{n}, \bar{m}, f$	1, 1, 1, 3	1, 1, 1, 3	1, 1, 1, 3
	μ	$128 + 91$	$192 + 103$	$256 + 121$
	Public key	445 B	780 B	972 B
	Ciphertext	539 B	830 B	1082 B
	PQ Security	2^{118}	2^{176}	2^{232}
	Classical	2^{128}	2^{193}	2^{256}
	Failure rate	2^{-78}	2^{-78}	2^{-95}
	Version $(f_{d,d}^{(0)})$	R5ND_1KEMb	R5ND_3KEMb	R5ND_5KEMb

Dominance of Hashing in KEM Speed Measurement. Our measurement results on other candidates are consistent with those produced by the PQCRYPTO group in "PQM4: Post-quantum crypto library for the ARM

Table 5. Round5 "b" ring variant parameter sets for public key encryption.

	Parameters	CCA NIST1	CCA NIST3	CCA NIST5
Round5.PKE	d, n, h	522, 522, 208	756, 756, 242	940, 940, 406
	q, p, t	$2^{13}, 2^8, 2^3$	$2^{12}, 2^8, 2^3$	$2^{12}, 2^8, 2^4$
	$B, \bar{n}, \bar{m}, f$	1, 1, 1, 3	1, 1, 1, 3	1, 1, 1, 3
	μ	$128 + 91$	$192 + 103$	$256 + 121$
	Public key	538 B	780 B	972 B
	Ciphertext	621 B	891 B	1161 B
	PQ Security	2^{117}	2^{176}	2^{232}
	Classical	2^{128}	2^{193}	2^{256}
	Failure rate	2^{-202}	2^{-171}	2^{-131}
	Version $(f_{d,d}^{(0)})$	R5ND_1PKEb	R5ND_3PKEb	R5ND_5PKEb

Cortex-M4" project[4]. However we didn't use their testing script system as it is targeted to a board using different flashing and communication mechanisms.

The reason for initial performance measurement divergence was that PQM4 experiments used a hand-crafted assembler implementation of the SHA3 core. This optimized permutation takes 11,785 cycles, while its optimized C language equivalent takes 32,639 cycles. This emphasizes the fact that benchmarks of fast lattice KEMs are also benchmarks of symmetric primitive implementations used.

5 Conclusions

In this work we have examined the suitability of Round5 post-quantum key establishment and public key encryption algorithm for embedded and other limited-resource use cases. We focused on R5ND_3KEMb and R5ND_3PKEb variants on Cortex M4 platform and compared them to some other compact NIST PQC proposals at the same security level.

Round5 combines the design features of two candidates in the NIST Post-Quantum Cryptography project, Round2 and Hila5. Round5 has new parameter selection, addressing various NIST PQC security levels and use cases. Optimization of parameters was performed primarily for bandwidth at given security level; the public key and ciphertext sizes of the new variant are smaller than those of other lattice candidates and second smallest only to SIKE (which is not practical on embedded targets due to its very high computational requirements).

Round5 relies on an error correcting code (based on that of Hila5) to further reduce failure probability, and thus allow parameters to be adjusted for even better bandwidth efficiency. There are many other new features and changes in relation to Round2, such as use of SHAKE-256 for deterministic pseudorandom sequence generation, and a new method for creating sparse ternary polynomials.

---

[4] PQM4 source code and results are available at https://github.com/mupq/pqm4.

The avoidance of Number Theoretic Transform in multiplication helps to bring the implementation size down, but has raised questions about performance. We benchmarked the Round5 ring variants on a Cortex M4 microcontroller and found them to have equivalent, or significantly better performance characteristics than other comparable candidates. Table 3 offers an "engineering" comparison for a key establishment use case at NIST Category 3 security level, and shows why we see Round5 as a leading candidate, at least on embedded targets.

References

1. Alkim, E., et al.: NewHope: algorithm specifcations and supporting documentation. First Round NIST PQC Project Submission Document, November 2017. https:// csrc.nist.gov/Projects/Post-Quantum-Cryptography/Round-1-Submissions
2. Avanzi, R., et al.: CRYSTALS-Kyber: algorithm specifications and supporting documentation. Fist Round NIST PQC Project Submission Document, November 2017. https://csrc.nist.gov/Projects/Post-Quantum-Cryptography/Round-1-Submissions
3. Banerjee, A., Peikert, C., Rosen, A.: Pseudorandom functions and lattices. In: Pointcheval, D., Johansson, T. (eds.) EUROCRYPT 2012. LNCS, vol. 7237, pp. 719–737. Springer, Heidelberg (2012). https://doi.org/10.1007/978-3-642-29011-4_42
4. Bernstein, D.J., Chuengsatiansup, C., Lange, T., van Vredendaal, C.: Ntru prime 20171130. Fist Round NIST PQC Project Submission Document, November 2017. https://csrc.nist.gov/Projects/Post-Quantum-Cryptography/Round-1-Submissions
5. Bhattacharya, S., et al.: Round5: Compact and fast post-quantum public-key encryption. Submitted for publication, August 2018. https://eprint.iacr.org/2018/725
6. CNSS. Use of public standards for the secure sharing of information among national security systems. Committee on National Security Systems: CNSS Advisory Memorandum, Information Assurance 02–15 July 2015
7. Cramer, R., Shoup, V.: Design and analysis of practical public-key encryption schemes secure against adaptive chosen ciphertext attack. SIAM J. Comput. 33(1), 167–226 (2003). http://www.shoup.net/papers/cca2.pdf
8. D'Anvers, J.-P., Karmakar, A., Roy, S.S., Vercauteren, F.: SABER: Mod-LWR based KEM. Fist Round NIST PQC Project Submission Document, November 2017. https://csrc.nist.gov/Projects/Post-Quantum-Cryptography/Round-1-Submissions
9. Dworkin, M.: Recommendation for block cipher modes of operation: Methods and techniques. NIST Special Publication 800–38A, December 2001
10. FIPS. Specification for the Advanced Encryption Standard (AES). Federal Information Processing Standards Publication 197, November 2001. http://csrc.nist.gov/publications/fips/fips197/fips-197.pdf
11. FIPS. SHA-3 standard: Permutation-based hash and extendable-output functions. Federal Information Processing Standards Publication 202, August 2015
12. Fujii, H., Aranha, D.F.: Curve25519 for the Cortex-M4 and beyond. In: LATIN-CRYPT 2017 (2017). http://www.cs.haifa.ac.il/~orrd/LC17/paper39.pdf

13. Fujisaki, E., Okamoto, T.: Secure Integration of asymmetric and symmetric encryption schemes. In: Wiener, M. (ed.) CRYPTO 1999. LNCS, vol. 1666, pp. 537–554. Springer, Heidelberg (1999). https://doi.org/10.1007/3-540-48405-1_34
14. Garcia-Morchon, A.: Round2: KEM and PKE based on GLWE. First Round NIST PQC Project Submission Document, November 2017. https://csrc.nist.gov/Projects/Post-Quantum-Cryptography/Round-1-Submissions
15. Hofheinz, D., Hövelmanns, K., Kiltz, E.: A modular analysis of the Fujisaki-Okamoto transformation. In: Kalai, Y., Reyzin, L. (eds.) TCC 2017. LNCS, vol. 10677, pp. 341–371. Springer, Cham (2017). https://doi.org/10.1007/978-3-319-70500-2_12
16. Hülsing, A., Rijneveld, J., Schanck, J.M., Schwabe, P.: NTRU-HRSS-KEM: Algorithm specifications and supporting documentation. Fist Round NIST PQC Project Submission Document, November 2017. https://csrc.nist.gov/Projects/Post-Quantum-Cryptography/Round-1-Submissions
17. Jao, D., et al.: Supersingular isogeny key encapsulation. First Round NIST PQC Project Submission Document, November 2017. https://csrc.nist.gov/Projects/Post-Quantum-Cryptography/Round-1-Submissions
18. Karmakar, A., Mera, J.M.B., Roy, S.S., Verbauwhede, I.: Saber on ARM: CCA-secure module lattice-based key encapsulation on ARM. In: CHES 2018 (2018). https://eprint.iacr.org/2018/682
19. Lindner, R., Peikert, C.: Better key sizes (and attacks) for LWE-based encryption. In: Kiayias, A. (ed.) CT-RSA 2011. LNCS, vol. 6558, pp. 319–339. Springer, Heidelberg (2011). https://doi.org/10.1007/978-3-642-19074-2_21
20. Moody, D.: Post-quantum cryptography: NIST's plan for the future. Talk given at PQCrypto 2016 Conference, 23–26 February 2016, Fukuoka, Japan, February 2016. https://pqcrypto2016.jp/data/pqc2016_nist_announcement.pdf
21. NIST. Submission requirements and evaluation criteria for the post-quantum cryptography standardization process. Official Call for Proposals, National Institute for Standards and Technology, December 2016. http://csrc.nist.gov/groups/ST/post-quantum-crypto/documents/call-for-proposals-final-dec-2016.pdf
22. NIST. Post-quantum cryptography - round 1 submissions. National Institute for Standards and Technology, December 2017. https://csrc.nist.gov/Projects/Post-Quantum-Cryptography/Round-1-Submissions
23. NSA/CSS. Information assurance directorate: Commercial national security algorithm suite and quantum computing FAQ, January 2016. https://apps.nsa.gov/iaarchive/library/ia-guidance/ia-solutions-for-classified/algorithm-guidance/cnsa-suite-and-quantum-computing-faq.cfm
24. Nussbaumer, H.J.: Fast polynomial transform algorithms for digital convolution. IEEE Trans. Acoust. Speech Signal Process. **28**, 205–215 (1980)
25. Proos, J., Zalka, C.: Shor's discrete logarithm quantum algorithm for elliptic curves. Quantum Inf. Comput. **3**(4), 317–344 (2003). arXiv. https://arxiv.org/abs/quant-ph/9508027
26. Regev, O.: On lattices, learning with errors, random linear codes, and cryptography. In: STOC 2005, pp. 84–93. ACM, May 2005
27. Regev, O.: On lattices, learning with errors, random linear codes, and cryptography. J. ACM **56**(6), 1–34 (2009)
28. Saarinen, M.-J.O.: Ring-LWE ciphertext compression and error correction: tools for lightweight post-quantum cryptography. In: Proceedings of the 3rd ACM International Workshop on IoT Privacy, Trust, and Security, IoTPTS 2017, pp. 15–22. ACM, April 2017. https://eprint.iacr.org/2016/1058

29. Saarinen, M.-J.O.: HILA5: on reliability, reconciliation, and error correction for Ring-LWE encryption. In: Adams, C., Camenisch, J. (eds.) SAC 2017. LNCS, vol. 10719, pp. 192–212. Springer, Cham (2018). https://doi.org/10.1007/978-3-319-72565-9_10

30. Shor, P.W.: Algorithms for quantum computation: discrete logarithms and factoring. In: Proceedings of the FOCS 1994, pp. 124–134. IEEE (1994). arXiv https://arxiv.org/abs/quant-ph/9508027

Yet Another Size Record for AES: A First-Order SCA Secure AES S-Box Based on $GF(2^8)$ Multiplication

Felix Wegener[✉] and Amir Moradi

Horst Görtz Institute for IT Security, Ruhr University Bochum, Bochum, Germany
{felix.wegener,amir.moradi}@rub.de

Abstract. It is well known that Canright's tower field construction leads to a very small, unprotected AES S-box circuit by recursively embedding Galois Field operations into smaller fields. The current size record for the AES S-box by Boyar, Matthews and Peralta improves the original design with optimal subcomponents, while maintaining the overall tower-field structure. Similarly, all small state-of-the-art first-order SCA-secure AES S-box constructions are based on a tower field structure.

We demonstrate that a smaller first-order secure AES S-box is achievable by representing the field inversion as a multiplication chain of length 4. Based on this representation, we showcase a very compact S-box circuit with only one $GF(2^8)$-multiplier instance. Thereby, we introduce a new high-level representation of the AES S-box and set a new record for the smallest first-order secure implementation.

1 Introduction

The increasing pervasiveness of electronics leads to ever smaller devices in demand of strong cryptography and resistance against side-channel analysis (SCA). Hence, the need to find area-optimal implementations of SCA-protected implementations of strong cryptographic primitives persists. The Advanced Encryption Standard (AES) is a cryptographically sound primitive that is notoriously difficult to protect against side-channels with low area-overhead due to the high algebraic degree of its S-box. While the size for unprotected implementations of the AES S-box has steadily decreased from 195 gates for Canright's S-box [4] to 115 gates for the S-box of Boyar *et al.* [3], masked implementations do not exhibit such a clear trend. Instead, they provide some trade-off between area, latency and fresh randomness. Interestingly, most current state-of-the-art first-order secure implementations follow the tower-field construction [2,6,10,17]. In contrast, our aim is to achieve the lowest possible circuit size by extending our former approach [18] and decomposing the S-box even further into multiplications in $GF(2^8)$.

Our Contribution. We present two designs for a first-order secure AES S-box based on a multiplication chain with four multiplications in $GF(2^8)$ to realize the

© Springer Nature Switzerland AG 2019
B. Bilgin and J.-B. Fischer (Eds.): CARDIS 2018, LNCS 11389, pp. 111–124, 2019.
https://doi.org/10.1007/978-3-030-15462-2_8

inversion: First, we achieve a new size record for the AES S-box and demonstrate the suitability of our design for low-area and low-power applications. Second, we show an area-latency trade-off that is practical whenever the implementation speed is limited by the number of random bits per cycle.

Outline. In Sect. 2 we introduce the underlying concepts of our contribution and define our notation for the rest of the paper. In Sect. 3 we present our main contribution. We compare implementation results in Sect. 4 and provide a side-channel evaluation in Sect. 5.

2 Preliminaries

In the following we introduce an exponentiation based representation of the AES S-box, the concept of multiplication chains and Domain-oriented Masking.

2.1 AES S-Box Representations

The AES S-box consists of an inversion in $GF(2^8)$ followed by an affine mapping. While the affine part is simple to mask, the inversion has algebraic degree seven and can be represented in many different ways. Here, we represent inversion as exponentiation according to the relation

$$x^{-1} = x^{254}$$

in $GF(2^8)$. Given only this representation it is unclear how many multiplications are necessary to obtain the end result. An upper bound can be determined by considering the exponent's binary representation $(11111110)_b$. Its Hamming weight minus one describes the number of multiplications in a square-and-multiply algorithm. Hence, The inversion can be computed with six multiplications and several squaring operations. Note that minimizing the number of squaring operations is of little interest as it is a linear operation over $GF(2^8)$ and hence easy to mask with a low area overhead.

2.2 Multiplication and Addition Chains

Given a monomial x^n over $GF(2^8)$, we aim to find a program that, starting from the identity function x^1 over $GF(2^8)$, computes x^n with the fewest multiplications and an arbitrary number of squaring operations. This can be formalized as finding a sequence of monomials $(v_0, \ldots, v_s)$ with the following conditions

$$v_0(x) = x^1,$$
$$v_i(x) = v_j^{2^{e_1}}(x) \circ v_k^{2^{e_2}}(x), \quad j, k < i, \; e_1, e_2 \in \mathbb{N}$$
$$v_s(x) = x^n$$

and minimal length. As there is a straightforward homomorphism between the group of natural numbers and exponentiation in a finite field

$$\phi : \mathbb{N} \to \mathcal{F}(\mathrm{GF}(2^8)), \quad \phi(k) = x^k$$

we can transform the problem into the realm of natural numbers:

Let n be a natural number, we call $v = (v_0, \ldots, v_s)$ an addition chain for n of length s, if the below expression holds.

$$v_0 = 1,$$
$$v_i = v_j \cdot 2^{e_1} + v_k \cdot 2^{e_2}, \ j, k < i, \ e_1, e_2 \in \mathbb{N}$$
$$v_s = n$$

From this representation it is straightforward to implement an exhaustive search algorithm to find the smallest length s for a given number n.

2.3   Domain-Oriented Masking

In 2016 Gross *et al.* [10] introduced Domain-oriented Masking (DOM), a masking scheme for multiplications over finite fields that extends classical Threshold Implementations by applying the non-completeness property to each input-bit individually, thereby enabling d-th order secure designs with only $d + 1$ input shares. In the following, we recall the construction of a first-order secure DOM-*indep* $\mathrm{GF}(2^n)$-multiplier.

To achieve first-order security of a multiplication operation $Z = X \cdot Y$, inputs are independently separated into two domains X_A, Y_A and X_B, Y_B with Boolean masking, such that $X = X_A \oplus X_B$ and $Y = Y_A \oplus Y_B$ hold. The multiplication itself can then be executed with four insecure $\mathrm{GF}(2^n)$-multipliers, which may not combine both domains of the same input variable (cf. Fig. 1). Further, the cross domain products $X_A Y_B$ and $X_B Y_A$ are refreshed with n-bits of randomness (R) before being reintroduced to either domain. To prevent the propagation of glitches a register stage is placed directly after the multipliers, respectively after the refreshing stage. Finally, each share of Z can be computed with an XOR-operation between the two registers in each domain. The correctness $Z = Z_A \oplus Z_B$ is easy to verify.

While a generalization of DOM for arbitrary non-linear blocks exists [15], we do not introduce it here, as our focus remains a $\mathrm{GF}(2^8)$-multiplier forming the core element of our secure implementation.

3   Implementation

In this section we describe our methodology to derive a mathematical description of the AES S-box based on $\mathrm{GF}(2^8)$-multiplication and subsequently present two variations of circuits based on it.

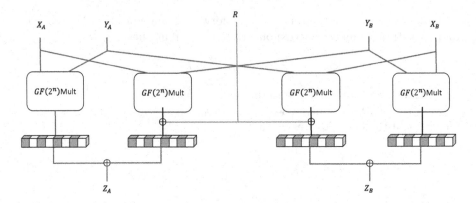

Fig. 1. Domain-oriented Masking: First-order secure DOM-*indep* GF(2^n)-multiplier

3.1 Methodology

Our aim is to realize the AES S-box based on GF(2^8)-multiplications in the smallest possible hardware area. As the inversion x^{-1} in GF(2^8) can be represented as an exponentiation x^{254} the challenge is to find a shortest multiplication chain. As shown in Sect. 2.2 this corresponds to finding a minimal addition chain for 254.

Chain Length. As noted in [11,14,18] the inversion in GF(2^8) can be decomposed into two cubic functions (x^k, x^l) with Hamming weights $wt(k) = wt(l) = 3$. This directly yields a realization with four multiplications as each function x^k, $wt(k) = m$ can be implemented with $m-1$ multiplications, e.g., naively with the square-and-multiply algorithm. Further, exhaustive computations to determine a length three addition chain for 254 do not yield a result. Hence, we chose to realize the inversion with four multiplications in GF(2^8).

As a secondary goal for circuit minimization, we aim to reduce the overhead in linear operations and delay registers to facilitate the multiplication-based architecture.

Minimal Overhead. Multiplication chains of length four may still differ in their overhead for linear operations (x^{2^k}) and for delay registers which are necessary when an intermediate result is not directly processed, which occurs in a multiplication chain whenever v_i depends on v_j with $j < i - 1$. To determine which multiplication chain leads to the smallest area, we determine the size of linear components based on squaring x^{2^k} alone and in composition with the AES affine function Aff. Further, we determine the size reduction through integration of multiple exponentiations into one hardware circuit. More specifically, we synthesized each 8-to-8-bit component

$$x^{2^k}, \quad k = 1, \ldots 7$$
$$\text{Aff} \circ x^{2^k}, \quad k = 1, \ldots 7$$

and the pairs

$$(x^{2^k}, x^{2^l}), \quad k, l = 1, \ldots 7$$

as 8-to-16-bit components to determine their sizes in the UMC $0.18\,\mu\text{m}$ library (cf. Table 1).

Table 1. Size of all linear functions x^{2^i} and Aff $\circ$ x^{2^i} individually (left) and combined in pairs (right).

Function	Size (GE)
x^{128}	23.7
x^{16}	33.3
x^2	22.7
x^{32}	33.3
x^4	31.7
x^{64}	29.7
x^8	32.0
Aff $\circ$ x^1	41.7
Aff $\circ$ x^{128}	40.7
Aff $\circ$ x^{16}	36.3
Aff $\circ$ x^2	40.3
Aff $\circ$ x^{32}	36.7
Aff $\circ$ x^4	36.3
Aff $\circ$ x^{64}	29.7
Aff $\circ$ x^8	34.0

Function	Size (GE)
$x^{128} \| x^{16}$	52.3
$x^{128} \| x^2$	41.3
$x^{128} \| x^{32}$	49.0
$x^{128} \| x^4$	50.7
$x^{128} \| x^{64}$	43.7
$x^{128} \| x^8$	47.0
$x^{16} \| x^2$	44.7
$x^{16} \| x^4$	54.3
$x^{16} \| x^8$	54.3
$x^{32} \| x^{16}$	49.7
$x^{32} \| x^2$	45.0
$x^{32} \| x^4$	52.3
$x^{32} \| x^8$	53.0
$x^4 \| x^2$	45.7
$x^{64} \| x^{16}$	53.7
$x^{64} \| x^2$	48.3
$x^{64} \| x^{32}$	53.0
$x^{64} \| x^4$	53.7
$x^{64} \| x^8$	51.7
$x^8 \| x^2$	44.0
$x^8 \| x^4$	52.0

Given the area information for each component, we can iterate through all possible combinations for the linear operations $op1, \ldots, op4$ (as illustrated in Fig. 2) to implement the following three subcircuits with minimal total area:

- the function $(x^{13})^{2^{k_1}}$ with two multiplications
- the function $(x^{19})^{2^{k_2}}$ with two multiplications
- the function Aff $\circ$ $x^{2^{k_3}}$

Our minimization search is subject to the additional restriction $k_1 + k_2 + k_3 = 5$ to ensure that the circuit actually computes the AES S-box. The optimal solution given our weights only uses the linear functions x^4, x^8 and a delay register. It corresponds to the choice:

$$op1(x) = x, \ op2(x) = x^8, \ op3(x) = x^4, \ op4(x) = x$$

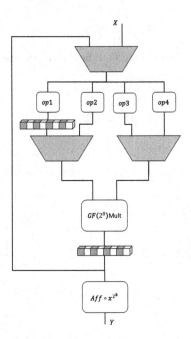

Fig. 2. Basic structure for our search algorithm.

and yields the optimal parameters $k_1 = 0$, $k_2 = 4$, $k_3 = 1$. More formally, the circuit can be expressed algebraically as the interleaved application of the following four linear functions and a multiplier

$$f_1(x) : \mathrm{GF}(2^8) \to \mathrm{GF}(2^8) \times \mathrm{GF}(2^8)$$
$$x \mapsto (x^8, x^4),\ \mathsf{mem} := x$$
$$f_2(x) : \mathrm{GF}(2^8) \to \mathrm{GF}(2^8) \times \mathrm{GF}(2^8)$$
$$x \mapsto (\mathsf{mem}, x)$$
$$f_3(x) : \mathrm{GF}(2^8) \to \mathrm{GF}(2^8) \times \mathrm{GF}(2^8)$$
$$x \mapsto (x^8, x^4),\ \mathsf{mem} := x$$
$$f_4(x) : \mathrm{GF}(2^8) \times \mathrm{GF}(2^8) \to \mathrm{GF}(2^8)$$
$$x \mapsto (\mathsf{mem}, x^4)$$

where mem denotes the last element that was stored in the delay register. The output Y is determined by applying a fifth affine function

$$f_5(x) : \mathrm{GF}(2^8) \to \mathrm{GF}(2^8)$$
$$x \mapsto \mathsf{Aff}(x^2).$$

The ANFs for all linear functions involved can be seen in Appendix A.

3.2 Domain-Oriented Masking

The mathematical description above can be turned into a first-order secure implementation with domain-oriented masking (cf. Fig. 3). To minimize area consumption our circuit is serialized along the multiplication.

Our circuit realizes $x^4 \cdot x^8 = x^{12}$ with the first multiplication. Subsequently, $x \cdot x^{12} = x^{13} =: \hat{x}$ is computed by utilizing the delay register. The third multiplication implements $\hat{x}^4 \cdot \hat{x}^8 = \hat{x}^{12}$. Finally, the circuit yields $(\hat{x}^{12})^4 \cdot \hat{x} = \hat{x}^{49}$. The subsequent application of Aff $\circ$ x^2 gives the correct result for the S-box output, as the equation $((x^{13})^{49})^2 = x^{-1}$ holds. To ensure the SCA resistance of our design, a total of sixteen bits of randomness have to be injected into the computation of the cross-domain terms, denoted as R_1 and R_2 in Fig. 3.

Further, as we re-introduce intermediate values into the same circuit, composability issues [8] have to be addressed:

Transitional Leakage. To prevent transitional leakage in any of the registers involved, we reset them to zero in between each "round-operation". This can be easily achieved in the control FSM without introducing additional latency as at any point in time either the upper ($Reg_{i,\cdot}$) or lower registers ($Reg_{o,\cdot}$) in Fig. 3 are occupied with our intermediate results while the contents of the other registers can be discarded.

Independent Sharing. As both shared inputs to the multiplier are functions depending on x, we need to re-fresh one shared input with a total of eight bits of randomness (R_1), before feeding it into the multiplier.

Note that the circuit shown in Fig. 3 is generic in the type of multiplier used. In the following, we demonstrate two designs based on serial-parallel multiplication to achieve a very low area and a fully-parallel multiplication to achieve an interesting trade-off.

3.3 Smallest Masked AES-Sbox

To obtain the smallest implementation of the AES S-box we realize the $GF(2^8)$-multiplication in eight cycles with a serial-parallel multiplier (cf. Fig. 4). It functions by applying all bits of operand a and successively shifting in one bit at a time of operand b starting with the MSB. Thereby, it computes the product of a and b in 8 cycles. The modulo reduction is based on the polynomial $(11b)_x$.

While it is clearly necessary to re-mask one input operand to use the DOM-DOM-*indep* multiplier with 8-bits of fresh randomness, this can be done at the rate of one bit per cycle by integrating the refreshing with R_1 into the shift registers $Reg_{i,1}$ and $Reg_{i,2}$. Similarly, it is required to re-mask the output of the multiplier with 8-bits of fresh randomness, which can be done during the computation of the product, one bit at a time (input wire R_2 in Fig. 4). Even though the serial-parallel multiplier contains a shift register internally, an additional register stage $Reg_{o,1}$, $Reg_{o,2}$ (cf. Fig. 3) is necessary to prevent a cross-domain term to re-enter a domain without being previously re-masked

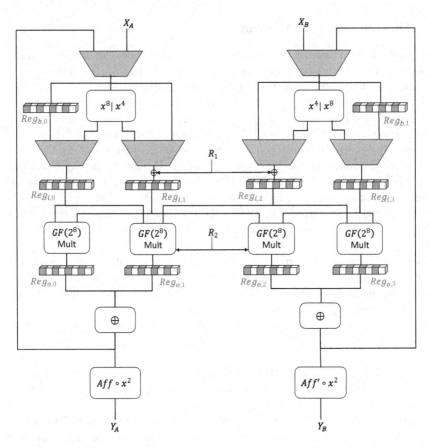

Fig. 3. First-order secure AES S-box circuit based on a $GF(2^8)$ multiplication chain. It computes two shares of x^{12}, x^{13}, $(x^{13})^{12}$ and $(x^{13})^{49}$ in the lower registers and contains a final application of $Aff \circ x^2$ to determine the shared value of the S-box output. Aff' denotes the affine function without constant terms.

with the entire 8 bits of entropy. The additional register does not incur a latency overhead as we use by-passing in cycle eight to write the multiplication result directly to the following register. This leads to a design that computes the linear functions in one cycle and the multiplication in eight additional cycles. This "round-operation" with a latency of nine cycles is executed four times. In total, our design computes an AES S-box in 36 cycles.

3.4 A Latency-Trade-Off

In the above design we can achieve a far lower latency by implementing the $GF(2^8)$-multiplication in one cycle with a fully-parallel multiplier. This straightforward design takes two cycles to compute each "round-operation". Hence, the

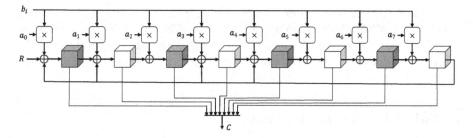

Fig. 4. Circuit of a serial-parallel $\mathbb{GF}(2^8)$ multiplier.

total latency amounts to eight cycles. The alternate usage of R_1 and R_2 allows us to connect both wires to the same source of entropy generating eight random bits per cycle.

4 Results

In this section we present area and latency results for our design and interpret them in the context of other first-order secure designs.

Comparison. We compare our design to state-of-the-art implementations of first-order secure S-boxes. More precisely, area and latency numbers for the TI(nimble) design of Bilgin *et al.* [2], the CMS design of Cnudde *et al.* [6], the multiplicative masking design of De Meyer *et al.* [7], the DOM design of Gross *et al.* [10], the CMS design of Ueno *et al.* [17] and our former TI(with guards) design [18]. It is directly apparent that our design #1 is a new area record of first-order secure S-boxes of AES. In fact, with 1378 GE we improve upon the previous record by Ueno *et al.* [17] (1656 GE) by several hundred gate equivalents. This record undoubtedly comes at the cost of huge increase in latency and does not aim to provide a beneficial area-latency trade-off. Yet, we achieved a practical solution in very special scenarios.

Our design #2 requires only eight random bits per cycle (as R_1 and R_2 are injected in alternating cycles) while its size of 2321 GE is comparable to other state-of-the-art implementations.

Practical Application. Note that our designs provide a benefit over other state-of-the-art constructions whenever the following two conditions hold: First, if the device can dedicate only a very small area to cryptographic operations our design #1 can be considered. Second, in the case of a limited peak power consumption design #1 is suitable due to its light non-linear part of only four parallel $GF(2^8)$-multiplications. Further, if a trade-off between latency and randomness is the deciding factor, our design #2 might be suitable.

Unprotected Comparison. Interestingly, an unprotected version of our S-box design with one parallel-serial multiplier occupies 520 GE, more than twice the size of the current unprotected area record by Boyar *et al.* [3] (cf. Table 3). Thereby, we demonstrated that area optimality is not necessarily maintained throughout the masking process (Table 2).

5   Side-Channel Evaluation

Measurement Setup. We evaluated our hardware design on a SAKURA-G side-channel evaluation board [1]. It is a well-established measurement platform that incorporates two Spartan-6 FPGAs separating control and target circuit to achieve a beneficial signal-to-noise ratio. We ran our implementation at a frequency of 6 MHz and sampled at a rate of 625 MS/s. Additionally, we utilized the ZFL-1000LN+ amplifier from Mini-Circuits (Fig. 5).

Table 2. Comparison of first-order secure S-boxes. IR: initial randomness, Lat: latency, RT: reciprocal throughput, R/C: rand. per cycle

Design	Shares	Lat (cyc)	crit. path (ns)	RT (cyc)	R/C (bits)	Size (GE)
Bilgin *et al.* [2]	3	3	N/A	1	16	2224
Cnudde *et al.* [6]	2	6	N/A	1	46	1872
De Meyer *et al.* [7]	2	2 + 3	N/A	1	19	1685
Gross *et al.* [10]	2	8	N/A	1	18	2600
Ueno *et al.* [a] [17]	2	5	1.5	1	56	1656
Wegener *et al.* [18]	4	16	3.3	16	0	4200
This work						
(#1)	2	36	1.5	36	2	**1378**
(#2)	2	8	1.6	8	8	2321

[a]Ueno *et al.* reported 1389 GE in the TSMC 65 library. We obtained their design and synthesized it ourselves in the UMC 0.18 μm library.

Table 3. Comparison of unprotected AES S-box implementations

Design	Lat (cyc)	crit. path (ns)	RT (cyc)	Size (GE)
Boyar *et al.* [3] [a]	1	5.6	1	205
This work				
unprotected	32	1.5	32	520

[a]We converted the equations given in their paper into VHDL and synthesized it ourselves in the UMC 0.18 μm library.

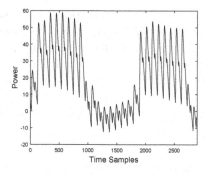
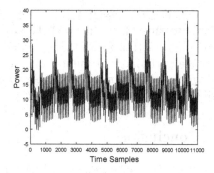

Fig. 5. Mean trace over 100 traces: parallel (left), serial (right)

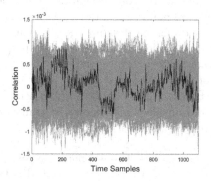
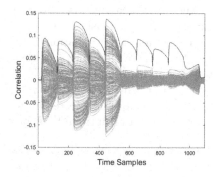

Fig. 6. Fully-parallel multiplier: MC-DPA in the first and second order with 10 million traces.

Evaluation. As recently shown by De Cnudde *et al.* [5] the common evaluation methodology of the non-specific t-test [9,16] is very sensitive to effects originating from the power distribution network if a masked implementation with only two shares is being evaluated. Hence, we deviated from the evaluation strategy based on the non-specific t-test and instead performed an evaluation based on

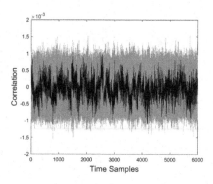
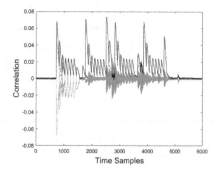

Fig. 7. Serial-parallel multiplier: MC-DPA in the first and second order with 10 million traces.

Moments-Correlating-DPA (MC-DPA) [13]. More precisely, our target consists of two sequential invocations of the S-box with several idle cycles between them to minimize both algorithmic noise and the memory effect due to amplification [12]. We performed 10 million measurements with each design and found no leakage in the first-order MC-DPA, while leakage in the second order is clearly visible (cf. Figs. 6 and 7).

6   Conclusion

First, we presented a new record for the smallest first-order SCA secure AES S-box implementation in hardware. Compared to the previous record our achievement comes at the cost of an increased latency. Yet, our design is applicable whenever small area and low power are of paramount importance. As opposed to implementing the masked inversion in one cycle, our design performs at most four serial-parallel multiplications in each clock cycle enabling a very low-power design. Second, we introduce a trade-off that achieves a lower latency than our first design and consumes only eight bits of randomness per cycle.

Finally, our contribution demonstrates that a design methodology to achieve the smallest area for unprotected implementations does not necessarily translate into a recipe for area-optimal SCA protected implementations.

Acknowledgments. The work described in this paper has been supported in part by the German Federal Ministry of Education and Research BMBF (grant nr. 16KIS0666 SysKit_HW).

A   ANFs for Linear and Affine Functions in our Design

To enhance the reproducibility of our results, we provide the algebraic normal form for all linear/affine functions used in our design.

ANF of power-map x^4 in $GF(2^8)$:

$$y_0^4 = x_0 + x_2 + x_3 + x_5 + x_6 + x_7$$
$$y_1^4 = x_2 + x_3 + x_4 + x_5 + x_6$$
$$y_2^4 = x_4 + x_5 + x_7$$
$$y_3^4 = x_2 + x_3 + x_4$$
$$y_4^4 = x_1 + x_2 + x_4 + x_5 + x_6$$
$$y_5^4 = x_3 + x_6$$
$$y_6^4 = x_4 + x_7$$
$$y_7^4 = x_3 + x_5 + x_6 + x_7$$

ANF of power-map x^8 in $GF(2^8)$:

$$y_0^8 = x_0 + x_1 + x_3$$
$$y_1^8 = x_1 + x_2 + x_3$$
$$y_2^8 = x_2 + x_4 + x_5$$
$$y_3^8 = x_1 + x_2 + x_6$$
$$y_4^8 = x_1 + x_2 + x_3 + x_5$$
$$y_5^8 = x_3 + x_4 + x_6 + x_7$$
$$y_6^8 = x_2 + x_4 + x_6$$
$$y_7^8 = x_3 + x_4 + x_5 + x_6$$

ANF of function Aff $\circ$ x^2 in $GF(2^8)$:

$$y_0^{2aff} = 1 + x_0 + x_2 + x_3 + x_6$$
$$y_1^{2aff} = 1 + x_0 + x_3$$
$$y_2^{2aff} = x_0 + x_1 + x_3 + x_6$$
$$y_3^{2aff} = x_0 + x_1 + x_4 + x_7$$
$$y_4^{2aff} = x_0 + x_1 + x_2 + x_6 + x_7$$
$$y_5^{2aff} = 1 + x_1 + x_2 + x_4 + x_5 + x_6 + x_7$$
$$y_6^{2aff} = 1 + x_1 + x_2 + x_3$$
$$y_7^{2aff} = x_2 + x_3 + x_5 + x_6 + x_7$$

References

1. Side-channel AttacK User Reference Architecture. http://satoh.cs.uec.ac.jp/SAKURA/index.html
2. Bilgin, B., Gierlichs, B., Nikova, S., Nikov, V., Rijmen, V.: Trade-offs for threshold implementations illustrated on AES. IEEE Trans. CAD Integr. Circuits Syst. **34**(7), 1188–1200 (2015). https://doi.org/10.1109/TCAD.2015.2419623
3. Boyar, J., Matthews, P., Peralta, R.: Logic minimization techniques with applications to cryptology. J. Cryptology **26**(2), 280–312 (2013). https://doi.org/10.1007/s00145-012-9124-7
4. Canright, D.: A very compact S-Box for AES. In: Rao, J.R., Sunar, B. (eds.) CHES 2005. LNCS, vol. 3659, pp. 441–455. Springer, Heidelberg (2005). https://doi.org/10.1007/11545262_32
5. Cnudde, T.D., Ender, M., Moradi, A.: Hardware masking, revisited. IACR Trans. Cryptogr. Hardw. Embed. Syst. **2018**(2), 123–148 (2018). https://doi.org/10.13154/tches.v2018.i2.123-148
6. De Cnudde, T., Reparaz, O., Bilgin, B., Nikova, S., Nikov, V., Rijmen, V.: Masking AES with $d+1$ shares in hardware. In: Gierlichs, B., Poschmann, A.Y. (eds.) CHES 2016. LNCS, vol. 9813, pp. 194–212. Springer, Heidelberg (2016). https://doi.org/10.1007/978-3-662-53140-2_10

7. De Meyer, L., Reparaz, O., Bilgin, B.: Multiplicative masking for AES in hardware. IACR Trans. Cryptogr. Hardw. Embed. Syst. **2018**(3), 431–468 (2018). https://doi.org/10.13154/tches.v2018.i3.431-468

8. Faust, S., Grosso, V., Merino Del Pozo, S., Paglialonga, C., Standaert, F.X.: Composable masking schemes in the presence of physical defaults and the robust probing model. IACR Trans. Cryptogr. Hardw. Embed. Syst. **2018**(3), 89–120 (2018). https://doi.org/10.13154/tches.v2018.i3.89-120. https://tches.iacr.org/index.php/TCHES/article/view/7270

9. Goodwill, G., Jun, B., Jaffe, J., Rohatgi, P.: A testing methodology for Side channel resistance validation. In: NIST Non-invasive Attack Testing Workshop (2011)

10. Groß, H., Mangard, S., Korak, T.: Domain-oriented masking: Compact masked hardware implementations with arbitrary protection order. IACR Cryptology ePrint Archive 2016, p. 486 (2016). http://eprint.iacr.org/2016/486

11. Moradi, A.: Advances in Side-channel Security (2016), Habilitation thesis, Ruhr University Bochum, Germany

12. Moradi, A., Mischke, O.: On the simplicity of converting leakages from multivariate to univariate - (case study of a glitch-resistant masking scheme). In: Bertoni, G., Coron, J.-S. (eds.) CHES 2013. LNCS, vol. 8086, pp. 1–20. Springer, Heidelberg (2013). https://doi.org/10.1007/978-3-642-40349-1_1

13. Moradi, A., Standaert, F.: Moments-correlating DPA. In: Bilgin, B., Nikova, S., Rijmen, V. (eds.) Proceedings of the ACM Workshop on Theory of Implementation Security, TIS@CCS 2016, Vienna, Austria, October 2016, pp. 5–15. ACM (2016). https://doi.org/10.1145/2996366.2996369

14. Nikova, S., Nikov, V., Rijmen, V.: Decomposition of permutations in a finite field. IACR Cryptology ePrint Archive 2018, p. 103 (2018). http://eprint.iacr.org/2018/103

15. Reparaz, O., Bilgin, B., Nikova, S., Gierlichs, B., Verbauwhede, I.: Consolidating masking schemes. In: Gennaro, R., Robshaw, M. (eds.) CRYPTO 2015. LNCS, vol. 9215, pp. 764–783. Springer, Heidelberg (2015). https://doi.org/10.1007/978-3-662-47989-6_37

16. Schneider, T., Moradi, A.: Leakage assessment methodology - a clear roadmap for side-channel evaluations. In: Güneysu, T., Handschuh, H. (eds.) CHES 2015. LNCS, vol. 9293, pp. 495–513. Springer, Heidelberg (2015). https://doi.org/10.1007/978-3-662-48324-4_25

17. Ueno, R., Homma, N., Aoki, T.: Toward more efficient DPA-resistant AES hardware architecture based on threshold implementation. In: Guilley, S. (ed.) COSADE 2017. LNCS, vol. 10348, pp. 50–64. Springer, Cham (2017). https://doi.org/10.1007/978-3-319-64647-3_4

18. Wegener, F., Moradi, A.: A first-order SCA resistant AES without fresh randomness. In: Fan, J., Gierlichs, B. (eds.) COSADE 2018. LNCS, vol. 10815, pp. 245–262. Springer, Cham (2018). https://doi.org/10.1007/978-3-319-89641-0_14

Jitter Estimation with High Accuracy for Oscillator-Based TRNGs

Shaofeng Zhu[1,2], Hua Chen[1(✉)], Limin Fan[1], Meihui Chen[1,2], Wei Xi[3], and Dengguo Feng[1]

[1] Trusted Computing and Information Assurance Laboratory,
Institute of Software, Chinese Academy of Sciences, Beijing, China
{zhushaofeng,chenhua,fanlimin,chenmeihui,feng}@tca.iscas.ac.cn
[2] University of Chinese Academy of Sciences, Beijing, China
[3] Southern Power Grid Science Research Institute, Guangzhou, China
xiwei@csg.cn

Abstract. Ring oscillator-based true random number generators (RO-based TRNGs) are widely used to provide unpredictable random numbers for cryptographic systems. The unpredictability of the output numbers, which can be measured by entropy, is extracted from the jitter of the oscillatory signal. To quantitatively evaluate the entropy, several stochastic models have been proposed, all of which take the jitter as a key input parameter. So it is crucial to accurately estimate the jitter in the process of entropy evaluation. However, several previous methods have estimated the jitter with non-negligible error, which would cause the overestimation of the entropy. In this paper, we propose a jitter estimation method with high accuracy. Our method aims at eliminating the quantization error in previous counter-based jitter estimation methods and finally can estimate the jitter with the error smaller than 1%. Furthermore, for the first time, we give a theoretical error bound for our jitter estimation. The error bound confirms the 1% error level of our method. As a consequence, our method will significantly help to evaluate the entropy of RO-based TRNGs accurately. Finally, we present the application of our jitter estimation method on a practical FPGA device and provide a circuit module diagram for on-chip implementation.

Keywords: TRNG · Ring oscillator · Jitter · Estimation · Entropy

1 Introduction

Ring oscillator-based true random number generator (RO-based TRNG) is a widely used kind of TRNGs for its simple implementation on logic devices such as FPGAs and smart cards. The elementary structure of RO-based TRNG is shown by Fig. 1. A slow clock signal (S_s) samples a fast oscillatory clock signal (S_o) generated by an oscillator composed of an odd number of inverters. Under the effect of correlated random noise (mainly low-frequency flicker noise) and uncorrelated random noise (mainly thermal noise) on the logic devices [6], the

© Springer Nature Switzerland AG 2019
B. Bilgin and J.-B. Fischer (Eds.): CARDIS 2018, LNCS 11389, pp. 125–139, 2019.
https://doi.org/10.1007/978-3-030-15462-2_9

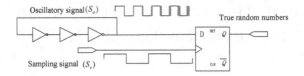

Fig. 1. Elementary structure of RO-based TRNG

periods of the oscillatory signal will vary randomly. The deviation of the periods is usually defined as the period jitter. So the jitter is mainly composed of thermal jitter and flicker jitter which are respectively contributed by the thermal noise and the flicker noise. Then the jitter is exploited by the TRNG to extract random numbers.

The randomness of a TRNG is mainly about the unpredictability of the generated random numbers. The unpredictability can be quantitatively measured by the entropy rate of the random numbers. Unfortunately, the traditional statistical test suites such as NIST SP800-22 [10], DIEHARD [9] merely evaluate the statistical properties of the output numbers, but can not answer whether the numbers to be tested hold enough entropy. In order to evaluate the entropy of RO-based TRNGs, several stochastic models have recently been proposed [1,4,7,8], all of which show that jitter is the key parameter that directly affects the entropy rate. Consequently, it is crucial to precisely estimate the jitter.

Up to now, several jitter estimation methods have been proposed. It is quite inaccurate to estimate the jitter outside the device with measuring equipments such as oscilloscopes [13], since additional jitter would be introduced by the Input/Output circuits and pins [14]. To estimate the jitter internally, Valtchanov et al. [14] designed an embedded circuit to count the rising edges of the oscillatory signal in equal-length time intervals and took the standard deviation of the counting results as an approximate measure of the accumulated jitter in the interval. Since the counting results can only be integers, this method will introduce in quantization error when estimating the jitter. Ma et al. [7] improved Valtchanov et al.'s counter-based method by counting both the rising and falling edges of the oscillatory signal. Such improvement actually reduces the quantization step size by half, thus can decrease the quantization error. Nevertheless, the quantization error is still not eliminated. Fischer et al. [2] proposed a different method based on Monte Carlo approach, which could estimate the jitter with the error smaller than 5%. Note that all the above mentioned methods are actually to estimate the total jitter containing both thermal jitter and flicker jitter. Nevertheless, most of the stochastic models for entropy evaluation are based on the common assumption that the periods of the oscillatory are independently and identically distributed (i.i.d.) under the effect of thermal noise. This requires only the jitter contributed by the thermal noise to be used to calculate the entropy. It is known that the thermal jitter is difficult to be estimated directly. Recently, Haddad et al. [3] proposed an approach to separate the thermal jitter from the total jitter and gain the ratio of the thermal jitter in the total jitter.

Nevertheless, the estimation of the total jitter in their work is also based on a counter-based method. So quantization error will inevitably be brought in, but was not considered as well.

In this paper, we provide a highly accurate jitter estimation method for RO-based TRNGs. Our method aims at eliminating the error that exists in the previous counter-based methods. Compared to the previous ones, our method can estimate the total jitter with much lower error level, which is also confirmed by theoretical analysis.

In summary, our contributions include:

- **We propose a jitter estimation method with high accuracy for RO-based TRNGs.** As we investigated, non-negligible quantization error is introduced in the previous counter-based jitter estimation methods. After eliminating the quantization error, in the meanwhile taking the waiting time in the sampling process into account, we provide a new, more accurate estimation for the jitter with the error level below 1%, which is much lower than the previous methods. This will significantly help to evaluate the entropy of a RO-based TRNG accurately.
- **For the first time, we give a theoretical error bound for the jitter estimation.** We adopt quantization error analysis approaches and present a formal upper error bound for our jitter estimation. This error bound has confirmed the 1% error level of our method in theory.
- **With our method, we provide a practical jitter estimation on FPGA device.** We demonstrate that combined with the jitter separation approach in [3], our method can be used to estimate the thermal jitter on practical hardware platforms. We also provide a circuit module diagram of our method for on-chip implementation.

The organization of this paper is as follows: In Sect. 2, we introduce the preliminaries about signal model, entropy evaluation and jitter estimation. In Sect. 3, we analyze the error of the previous counter-based jitter estimation method given by [7] and propose our jitter estimation method. In Sect. 4, we give the theoretical error analysis of our method. In Sect. 5, we conduct a practical jitter estimation on an FPGA device with our method, and we present the circuit module diagram of our method for on-chip implementation. In Sect. 6, we compare our method with the previous ones and give the conclusion.

2 Preliminaries: Signal Model, Entropy Evaluation and Jitter Estimation

In this section, we first present the signal model of an elementary RO-based TRNG, where we define symbols to describe the signals. Then we introduce the entropy evaluation methods of RO-based TRNGs. The methods take the jitter as an important parameter to calculate the entropy. As a consequence, jitter estimation is crucial and will determine the accuracy of the entropy evaluation.

128   S. Zhu et al.

2.1 Signal Model

For the RO-based TRNGs, the sampling process can be approximately treated as a stationary process, so we just consider two successive samplings. Here we define symbols to describe the oscillatory signal (S_o) and the sampling signal (S_s) by Definition 1 and Fig. 2(a).

Definition 1. *The time interval between two successive samplings SP_i and SP_{i+1} is denoted by T_s. Within T_s, the edge intervals of S_o are denoted by $T_{o1}\cdots T_{oj}\cdots T_{ok}$. The standard deviation of T_{oj} is defined as the half period jitter of S_o and denoted by σ_o. (σ_o)s will be accumulated in T_s. The mean value of T_{oj} is the half mean period of S_o and denoted by μ_o. The waiting time W is defined as the time interval between SP_i and the following closest edge of S_o. According to [4, 7], W approximately follows the uniform distribution within $[0, \mu_o]$ because of $\sigma_o \ll \mu_o$, and it is independent from the T_s in the current sampling interval.*

The μ_o can be measured from the frequency of S_o. For brevity, we normalize all the time variables with μ_o, that is $T_s \rightarrow t_s = \frac{T_s}{\mu_o}$, $T_{oj} \rightarrow t_{oj} = \frac{T_{oj}}{\mu_o}$, $\sigma_o \rightarrow \sigma = \frac{\sigma_o}{\mu_o}$, $\mu_o \rightarrow 1$ and $W \rightarrow w = \frac{W}{\mu_o} \sim U(0,1)$. The normalized variables can be transformed back to time variables by multiplying by μ_o.

Since the jitter is relative between the two signals, an equivalent model can be presented by treating S_o as stable while S_s has period jitter. The equivalent model is illustrated by Definition 2 and Fig. 2(b).

Definition 2. *The edge intervals of S_o are $t_{o1} = \cdots = t_{oj} = \cdots = 1$. The sampling interval t_s is a random variable with mean value μ_s and standard deviation σ_s. σ_s is defined as the total jitter accumulated in the interval t_s. The jitters from thermal noise and flicker noise are respectively denoted by σ_s^{th}, σ_s^{fl}. Since the two kinds of noise are mutually independent, there is $\sigma_s^2 = (\sigma_s^{th})^2 + (\sigma_s^{fl})^2$. Besides, we still have $w \sim U(0,1)$ and it is independent from the current t_s.*

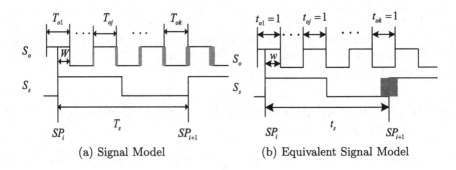

(a) Signal Model   (b) Equivalent Signal Model

Fig. 2. Signal model of RO-based TRNG

2.2 Entropy Evaluation

Previous articles such as [1,7] have given the methods to evaluate the entropy of RO-based TRNGs. In order to mathematically characterize the RO signals, the articles only take the uncorrelated thermal noise into consideration. Then under the affection of thermal noise, the edge intervals $T_{o1} \cdots T_{oj} \cdots T_{ok}$ will be i.i.d. with Gaussian distribution $N(\mu_o, \sigma_o^2)$. Correspondingly in the equivalent model, there is $t_s \sim N(\mu_s, (\sigma_s^{th})^2)$. Under the above assumption, according to [1], the min-entropy can be calculated by (1)[1].

$$H_{min} = 1 - \frac{4}{\pi^2 \ln(2)} e^{-\pi^2 (\sigma_s^{th})^2}. \tag{1}$$

The calculated entropy is actually contributed by the thermal noise and it can be a conservative estimation for the min-entropy of RO-based TRNGs.

We can see the min-entropy is determined by the σ_s^{th} in the sampling interval t_s. Hence, it is crucial to estimate σ_s^{th} precisely for entropy evaluation.

2.3 Jitter Estimation

For a practical RO-based TRNG, if the sampling frequency is high, the accumulated jitter in t_s may be too small to be estimated accurately. So we usually estimate the accumulated jitter in a larger measuring interval. Here we denote the measuring interval by t_m $(= \frac{T_m}{\mu_o}, T_m$ is time variable) with mean value μ_m and standard deviation σ_m. σ_m represents the total jitter accumulated in t_m. The thermal jitter is "sqrt" accumulated with the time interval [1,3,6]. So after estimating the total jitter σ_m and separating the thermal jitter σ_m^{th} from σ_m, we can calculate the needed thermal jitter σ_s^{th} accumulated in the sampling interval t_s by

$$\sigma_s^{th} = \sqrt{\frac{t_s}{t_m}} \sigma_m^{th}. \tag{2}$$

When the measuring interval is short enough so that the thermal jitter dominates over the flicker jitter, there is $\sigma_m^{th} \approx \sigma_m$, and the σ_s^{th} can also be estimated by

$$\sigma_s^{th} \approx \sqrt{\frac{t_s}{t_m}} \sigma_m. \tag{3}$$

Anyway, it is necessary to estimate the total accumulated jitter σ_m first and we focus on the estimation of σ_m as well.

3 Our Proposed Jitter Estimation Method

We present our jitter estimation method in this section. Firstly, we investigate the error of the previous counter-based jitter estimation method introduced by Ma et al. in [7]. Results show that non-negligible error exists in Ma's method. Our proposed method gives a new estimation for the total jitter and is able to achieve a much lower error level than the previous one.

---

[1] $(\sigma_s^{th})^2/4$ is equivalent to the quality factor Q defined in [1].

3.1   Error Investigation of Previous Counter-Based Jitter Estimation Method

We primarily investigate the previous, typical counter-based method proposed by Ma et al. [7]. Under the equivalent signal model, this method actually counts both the rising and falling edges of S_o in series of interval t_ms and approximates the variance of the counting result X to the variance of t_m:

$$\mathrm{Var}(t_m) \approx \mathrm{Var}(X). \tag{4}$$

Then the jitter σ_m is estimated by

$$\sigma_m = \sqrt{\mathrm{Var}(t_m)} \approx \sqrt{\mathrm{Var}(X)}. \tag{5}$$

The approximation between $\mathrm{Var}(t_m)$ and $\mathrm{Var}(X)$ is critical in this counter-based method, since X is measurable on the chip by edging counting.

According to Fig. 2(b) in Sect. 2, the edge-counting result X in the interval t_m is actually the flooring quantized value of $(t_m - w + 1)$ with the quantization size $q = 1$, that is

$$X = \lfloor t_m - w + 1 \rfloor_{q=1}. \tag{6}$$

Therefore, the waiting time factor of $(-w + 1)$ and the flooring quantization will definitely introduce error in Ma's method.

We investigate the error of Ma's method by Matlab simulation. The absolute error (e_a) and relative error (e_r) of the approximation (4) can be calculated with

$$e_a = \mathrm{Var}(X) - \mathrm{Var}(t_m), e_r = \frac{|e_a|}{\mathrm{Var}(t_m)}. \tag{7}$$

According to (5), the estimation error of σ_m (denoted by e_m) is equal to $\frac{1}{2}e_r$. e_m can be a measure of the error level of the jitter estimation method. With Matlab, we generate the instances of $t_m \sim \boldsymbol{N}(\mu_m, \sigma_m^2)$ with different size of σ_m and corresponding instances of X. Here the flicker noise is not considered, since to our knowledge, it is infeasible to be generated with simulation by now. Then we evaluate the e_a and e_m of Ma's method. The results are shown in Fig. 3. It can be seen that a $\frac{1}{6}$ absolute error always exists in the approximation (4) when $\sigma_m > 0.4$. While $\sigma_m < 0.4$, the absolute error e_a would be even larger and related with the fractional part of μ_m (denoted by f_{μ_m})[2]. The error e_m of this method is larger than 10% until $\sigma_m > 0.92$.

On one aspect, the error level of this method is certainly not low (10%), and non-negligible absolute error inherently exists in their estimation. Consequently, once adopted in entropy evaluation, this method will overestimate the jitter, and the entropy of RO-based TRNGs will be overestimated as well. On another aspect, this method requires $\sigma_m > 0.92$ to gain the 10% error level. For a practical RO, since the jitter can only be more accumulated by increasing the measuring interval, this method needs a large measuring interval to accumulate enough jitter for its accuracy.

---

[2] Different f_{μ_m}s are indicated by different colors as well as in following figures.

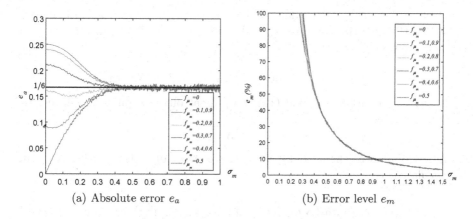

(a) Absolute error e_a (b) Error level e_m

Fig. 3. Errors evaluation of Ma's method by Matlab

3.2 New Estimation for the Jitter

In order to correct the error in Ma's method, we take a close look into the relationship between $\mathrm{Var}(t_m)$ and $\mathrm{Var}(X)$. Then we eliminate the quantization error and the effect of the waiting time factor to give an improved approximation for $\mathrm{Var}(t_m)$. Based on this approximation, we present our new, more accurate estimation for the jitter.

Firstly, we introduce the "Sheppard's correction" in quantization theory.

Sheppard's correction [11]: For a random variable v with continuous distribution, its rounding quantized value with quantization step q can be denoted by $v_q = [v]_q$. When the variance of v is large enough, the quantization error $e_q = v - v_q$ will approximately follow uniform distribution in $(-q/2, q/2)$ and be independent from v. The first-order and second-order moments of v and v_q have the following relationships [11]:

$$\mathrm{E}(v) = \mathrm{E}(v_q), \mathrm{E}(v^2) \approx \mathrm{E}(v_q^2) - q^2/12. \tag{8}$$

In the jitter estimation case, we know that the edge-counting result in the interval t_m is

$$X = \lfloor t_m - w + 1 \rfloor_{q=1} = [t_m - w + 0.5]_{q=1}. \tag{9}$$

So according to the "Sheppard correction", when $\mathrm{Var}(t_m - w + 0.5)$ is large enough, the quantization error in the jitter estimation is

$$e_q = (t_m - w + 0.5 - X) \sim \boldsymbol{U}(-0.5, 0.5) \tag{10}$$

and e_q will be independent from $(t_m - w + 0.5)$. Besides, the equivalent signal model in Sect. 2 has indicated that $w \sim \boldsymbol{U}(0, 1)$ and it is independent from the current measuring interval t_m, so we have

$$\mathrm{Var}(X) = \mathrm{Var}(t_m - w + 0.5 - e_q) \approx \mathrm{Var}(t_m) + \mathrm{Var}(w) + \mathrm{Var}(e_q). \tag{11}$$

From (11) we can see the deviation between $\text{Var}(t_m)$ and $\text{Var}(X)$ is indeed caused by the quantization error e_q and waiting time w. Consequently, we give the new approximation for $\text{Var}(t_m)$:

$$\text{Var}(t_m) \approx \text{Var}(X) - \text{Var}(w) - \text{Var}(e_q) \approx \text{Var}(X) - 1/6. \tag{12}$$

Based on the approximation (12), we present our new, more accurate estimation of σ_m by

$$\sigma_m \approx \sqrt{\text{Var}(X) - 1/6}. \tag{13}$$

In the same way, the absolute and relative errors of approximation (12) can be calculated by

$$e_a = \text{Var}(X) - 1/6 - \text{Var}(t_m), e_r = \frac{|e_a|}{\text{Var}(t_m)}, \tag{14}$$

and the error level e_m of our method is also equal to $\frac{1}{2}e_r$. By Matlab simulation, we evaluate the errors (e_a and e_m) and show them in Fig. 4. We can see our estimation has successfully eliminate e_a when $\sigma_m > 0.4$. Correspondingly, the error level (e_m) of our method gets down to lower than 1% as long as $\sigma_m > 0.4$.

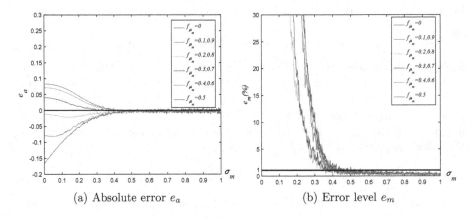

(a) Absolute error e_a (b) Error level e_m

Fig. 4. Errors evaluation of our method by Matlab

This is an obvious improvement over Ma's method. Firstly, our estimation can achieve much lower error level (1%) than Ma's method (10%). Secondly, our method can eliminate the absolute error which inherently exists in Ma's method. This will avoid overestimating the jitter. Moreover, our method needs much shorter measuring time interval, which can speed up the jitter estimation process.

3.3 An Efficient Calculation of the Variance of X

Jitter estimation should be fast for some application scenarios such as online health test. Considering that the calculation of $\mathrm{Var}(X)$ is the most time-consuming in counter-based jitter estimation method, we present an efficient approach to do this calculation.

As we know, if the samples of the counting result X are $x_1, \cdots, x_N$, then the ordinary variance calculating formula can be presented by

$$\mathrm{Var}(X) = \frac{\sum_{j=1}^{N} x_j^2}{N} - \left(\frac{\sum_{j=1}^{N} x_j}{N}\right)^2, \tag{15}$$

which needs $N + 1$ multiplications. N is the sample size.

In view of modern logic devices, the jitter accumulated in the time interval t_m is usually very small, and the edge-counting results will vary slightly around the mean value $\bar{x} = \frac{\sum_{j=1}^{N} x_j}{N}$. That is, the sample space of X is small too and we denote it by $\mathcal{S}_X = \{p_i | p_i = \lfloor \bar{x} \rfloor - I + i; 1 \leq i \leq 2I; 5 \leq I \ll N\}$. Here we recommend $5 \leq I$ so that $\mathcal{S}_X$ can cover most of the counting results. Our approach is to count the number of X's samples on each sample point p_i, and the results are denoted by $c_1, \ldots, c_{2I}$. Then $\mathrm{Var}(X)$ can be calculated by

$$\mathrm{Var}(X) = \frac{\sum_{i=1}^{2I} c_i \cdot (p_i - \bar{x})^2}{N}. \tag{16}$$

Only $4I\,(\ll N + 1)$ multiplications are needed in (16). Evidently, the efficiency of the jitter estimation is improved.

We present the corresponding Algorithm 1 for this approach.

Algorithm 1. Algorithm for the calculation of $\mathrm{Var}(X)$.

Input: The counting result $x_1, \cdots, x_N$. Parameters N and I.
Output: $\mathrm{Var}(X)$.

1: Calculating the mean value of $x_1, \cdots, x_N$: $\bar{x} \leftarrow \frac{\sum_{j=1}^{N} x_j}{N}$
2: Calculating the sample points of X:
      for $i = 1, \cdots, 2I$ do
      $p_i = \lfloor \bar{x} \rfloor - I + i$;
      end for;
3: Counting $x_1, \cdots, x_N$ on $p_1, \cdots, p_{2I}$:
      Set $c_1, \cdots, c_{2I} = 0$;
      for $j = 1, \cdots, N$ do
         for $i = 1, \cdots, 2I$ do
            if $(x_j = p_i)$ $c_i = c_i + 1$; end if;
         end for;
      end for;
4: Calculating $\mathrm{Var}(X)$: $\mathrm{Var}(X) \leftarrow \frac{\sum_{i=1}^{2I} c_i \cdot (p_i - \bar{x})^2}{N}$
5: **return** $\mathrm{Var}(X)$;

---

4   Theoretical Error Analysis

In this section, we theoretically analyze our method and give a formal error bound, which confirms the 1% error level of our method in theory.

The error e_a is affected by t_m and w. So we expand e_a in complex Fourier series based on the characteristic functions of t_m and w, then we formally express e_a and give the upper bound of the error e_m with the following steps.

Step 1. Definition of Equivalent Variable v. Firstly, we define v, its quantized value v_q ($q = 1$) and the quantization error e_q respectively by

$$v = t_m - w + 0.5 - \lfloor \mu_m \rfloor, v_q = [v] = X - \lfloor \mu_m \rfloor, e_q = v - v_q. \tag{17}$$

Step 2. Expression of e_a with v and v_q. The absolute error e_a in our estimation can be presented by

$$e_a = \mathrm{Var}(X) - \frac{q^2}{12} - \mathrm{Var}(w) - \mathrm{Var}(t_m) = \mathrm{Var}(v_q) - \mathrm{Var}(v) - \frac{q^2}{12}. \tag{18}$$

According to the "Sheppard's correction" on the first-order moment (8), mean value $\mathrm{E}(v_q)$ equals to $\mathrm{E}(v)$, so we have

$$e_a = \mathrm{E}(v_q^2) - \mathrm{E}(v^2) - \frac{q^2}{12} = 2\,\mathrm{E}(ve_q) + \mathrm{E}(e_q^2) - \frac{q^2}{12}. \tag{19}$$

Step 3. Expression of e_a in Fourier series with $W_v(\alpha)$. The characteristic function of v is

$$W_v(\alpha) = \int_{-\infty}^{\infty} f(v)e^{j\alpha v}\,dv. \tag{20}$$

Here we define $v_0 = v - \mu_v$, where $\mu_v = \mathrm{E}(v)$, then its characteristic function is

$$W_{v_0}(\alpha) = e^{-j\alpha\mu_v} W_v(\alpha). \tag{21}$$

According to [5,12], the $\mathrm{E}(ve_q)$ and $\mathrm{E}(e_q^2)$ in (19) can be expressed in the form of complex Fourier series based on $W_{v_0}(\alpha)$ and its derivation $\dot{W}_{v_0}(\alpha)$:

$$\begin{aligned}
\mathrm{E}(ve_q) &= \frac{q}{\pi} \sum_{k=1}^{\infty} \cos\left(\frac{2\pi k}{q}\mu_v\right) \dot{W}_{v_0}\left(\frac{2\pi k}{q}\right) \frac{(-1)^{k+1}}{k} \\
&+ \frac{q}{\pi} \sum_{k=1}^{\infty} \sin\left(\frac{2\pi k}{q}\mu_v\right) \mu_v W_{v_0}\left(\frac{2\pi k}{q}\right) \frac{(-1)^k}{k},
\end{aligned} \tag{22}$$

$$\mathrm{E}(e_q^2) = \frac{q^2}{12} + \frac{q^2}{\pi^2} \sum_{k\neq 0}^{\infty} \cos\left(\frac{2\pi k}{q}\mu_v\right) W_{v_0}\left(\frac{2\pi k}{q}\right) \frac{(-1)^k}{k^2}. \tag{23}$$

Step 4. Deduction of $W_v(\alpha)$. For jitter estimation, according to (17), we have

$$\mu_v = \mathrm{E}(v) = \mathrm{E}(t_m - w + 0.5 - \lfloor \mu_m \rfloor) = \mu_m - \lfloor \mu_m \rfloor = f_{\mu_m}. \tag{24}$$

Then when only considering the thermal noise, there is $t_m \sim N(\mu_m, (\sigma_m)^2)$ and $w \sim U(0, 1)$. Their characteristic functions respectively are

$$W_{t_m}(\alpha) = e^{j\alpha\mu_m} e^{-((\sigma_m)^2\alpha^2/2)}, W_w(\alpha) = e^{j\alpha/2} \sin(\alpha/2)/(\alpha/2). \tag{25}$$

According to (17) and (25), we have

$$W_v(\alpha) = \frac{2\sin(\alpha/2)}{\alpha} e^{-((\sigma_m)^2\alpha^2/2)} \cdot e^{j\alpha f_{\mu_m}}, \tag{26}$$

$$W_{v_0}(\alpha) = e^{-j\alpha\mu_v} W_v(\alpha) = \frac{2\sin(\alpha/2)}{\alpha} e^{-((\sigma_m)^2\alpha^2/2)} \tag{27}$$

and

$$\dot{W}_{v_0}(\alpha) = \left(\frac{\cos(\alpha/2)}{\alpha} - \frac{2\sin(\alpha/2)}{\alpha^2} - \frac{2\sin(\alpha/2)}{\alpha}(\sigma_m)^2\alpha \right) e^{-((\sigma_m)^2\alpha^2/2)}. \tag{28}$$

Step 5. Formal Expression of e_a. $W_{v_0}(\alpha)$ and $\dot{W}_{v_0}(\alpha)$ in Step 4 will go to zero quickly when $|\alpha| > \frac{2\pi}{q}$ because of their exponent parts [5]. For example, when $q = 1$, considering the cases of $\alpha = 2\pi$ and $\alpha = 4\pi$, we have

$$e^{-((\sigma_m)^2(4\pi)^2)/2} < 10^{-25} \cdot e^{-((\sigma_m)^2(2\pi)^2)/2}. \tag{29}$$

So we just consider the terms with $k = \pm 1$ in the sums of (22), (23). By setting $q = 1$ and combining with (18), (19), (22), (23), (27), (28), we can gain the formal expression of e_a:

$$e_a \approx -\frac{1}{\pi^2} \cos(2\pi f_{\mu_m}) \cdot e^{-2\pi^2\sigma_m^2}. \tag{30}$$

e_a will reach to its maximum when $f_{\mu_m} = 0.5$:

$$(e_a)_{max} \approx \frac{1}{\pi^2} e^{-2\pi^2\sigma_m^2}. \tag{31}$$

Figure 5(a) shows the comparison between $(e_a)_{max}$ and the evaluation results of e_a got from the Matlab simulation in Fig. 4(a). Obviously, $(e_a)_{max}$ is a reasonable upper bound of e_a.

Step 6. Upper bound of e_m. According to the above theoretical analysis, upper bound of e_m in our jitter estimation method can be formally expressed by:

$$(e_m)_{max} = \frac{1}{2}(e_r)_{max} = \frac{1}{2} \cdot \frac{|(e_a)_{max}|}{\sigma_m^2} \approx \frac{1}{2\pi^2\sigma_m^2} e^{-2\pi^2\sigma_m^2}. \tag{32}$$

As we present in Fig. 5(b), the theoretical error bound is lower than 1% as long as $\sigma_m > 0.4141$. This is in accord with the Matlab simulation results shown in Fig. 4(b). In theory, the low error level of our method has been confirmed.

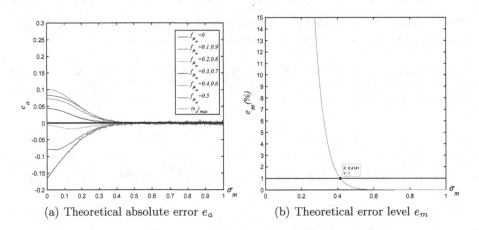

(a) Theoretical absolute error e_a (b) Theoretical error level e_m

Fig. 5. Theoretical error analysis of our method

5   Jitter Estimation on FPGA Device

In this section, we conduct a whole jitter estimation on a practical FPGA device. We adopt our method to estimate the total jitter of a RO-based TRNG and combine with the jitter separation approach in [3] to gain the part of the thermal jitter in the total jitter.

The oscillator is implemented on an Altera Cyclone IV FPGA. It is composed of 3 inverters and has about 305 MHz frequency. Firstly, we use our method to estimate the total accumulated jitter (σ_m) in different measuring intervals (T_ms), and then the results are quadratically fitted by $\sigma_m^2 = aT_m^2 + bT_m$. According to [3], the first-order term (bT_m) is the part contributed by the thermal jitter.

Specifically, we use a counter to count the edges of the oscillatory signal in multiple measuring intervals ($T_m = 0.8\,\mu s$, $1.0\,\mu s$, $1.2\,\mu s$, $1.4\,\mu s$, $1.6\,\mu s$, $1.8\,\mu s$, $2.2\,\mu s$, $2.6\,\mu s$, $3.0\,\mu s$, $4.2\,\mu s$, $5.4\,\mu s$). For each measuring interval, we calculate $\mathrm{Var}(X)$ from the edge-counting results Xs and estimate the corresponding σ_m^2 by Equation (13). Then T_m and σ_m^2 is fitted by $\sigma_m^2 = 0.0732T_m^2 + 0.087T_m$, shown in Fig. 6(a). For a chosen measuring interval $T_m(\mu s)$, the ratio of the thermal jitter in the total jitter will be

$$r_{th} = \sqrt{\frac{0.087T_m}{0.0732T_m^2 + 0.087T_m}} = \sqrt{\frac{0.087}{0.087 + 0.0732T_m}}, \tag{33}$$

and the thermal jitter can be estimated by

$$\sigma_m^{th} = r_{th}\sigma_m. \tag{34}$$

We show the estimated results of $(\sigma_m^{th})^2$ in different measuring intervals by Fig. 6(b). It can be seen that the thermal jitter $(\sigma_m^{th})^2$ increases at a near-linear trend with the growth of the measuring interval. This is consistent with the fact that thermal noise is a kind of uncorrelated noise.

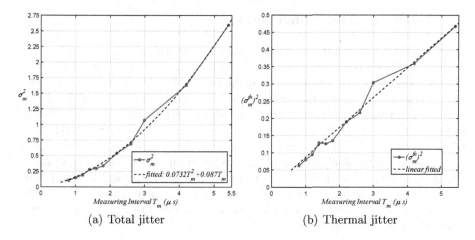

(a) Total jitter

(b) Thermal jitter

Fig. 6. Experiment results of our jitter estimation on FPGA

For some other applications such as online health test of the entropy source, jitter estimation method on the chip should always estimate the thermal jitter in a fixed time interval. In this situation, the above multi-intervals estimation and fitting work can be regarded as a pre-calculation before implementing the online health test. Based on the pre-calculation, a ratio of the thermal jitter will be obtained and set in the implementation of the online test. During the execution phase, the online test just need to estimate the total jitter in the fixed measuring interval with our method and then extract the thermal part from the total jitter according to the ratio. For example, if the measuring interval is set fixed as $1.2\,\mu s$, then the ratio of the thermal jitter pre-calculated from (33) is $r_{th} = 0.706$. σ_m is the real-time total jitter estimated by our method on the chip. Then the thermal jitter can be simply calculated by $\sigma_m^{th} = 0.706\sigma_m$.

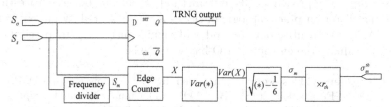

Fig. 7. Circuit module diagram for jitter estimation (the symbol $*$ represents the input of the module)

We provide the circuit module diagram of our method for on-chip implementation in Fig. 7. The sampling signal is processed by a frequency divider to generate the signal S_m which contains a series of measuring interval T_ms. Then the circuit conducts edge counting and calculates the total accumulated jitter σ_m. After multiplying σ_m by the ratio r_{th}, the circuit finally outputs the thermal jitter σ_m^{th}.

6   Discussion and Conclusion

We compare different jitter estimation methods in Table 1. The error levels of Ma's [7] and our method are gained from our analysis. The error level of Fischer's method was evaluated from their simulation results [2]. Note that the error levels presented in this table are given in the same condition that the flicker noise is not taken into account, but can still reflect the accuracy of different methods. In all of the methods, ours can achieve the lowest error level (1%), which is confirmed by theoretical analysis. For the methods in [2,7], there was no theoretical error analysis provided. Besides, compared to the method in [7], our method has reduced the requirement for the jitter σ_m, which can shorten the measuring time interval and speed up the estimation process. Taking this advantage, when our method is applied for online health test, the test can quickly assess the state of the entropy source.

Table 1. Comparisons of different methods

Methods	Error level	Theoretically confirmed	Requirement for σ_m
Ma's [7]	10%	No	0.92
Fischer's [2]	5%	No	Undefined
Our method	1%	Yes	0.4141

In conclusion, we propose a high-accurate method to estimate the jitter of RO-based TRNGs. The error level of our method can reach to 1%, which is much lower than previous jitter estimation methods. For the first time, we give a theoretical error bound for our method, and the bound confirms the low error level. Additional advantage of our method is that it requires shorter measuring time interval, which can speed up the process of jitter estimation. Our method is to estimate the total jitter in RO-based TRNGs. When combined with the jitter separation approach in [3], our method is able to be used to estimate the thermal jitter on practical logic devices, as we presented by an experiment on FPGA. Consequently, our method will significantly help to precisely and efficiently evaluate the entropy of RO-based TRNGs.

Acknowledgments. This work is supported by the Nation Key R&D Program of China (2018YFB0904900, 2018YFB0904901) and China's National Cryptography Development Fund (No. MMJJ20170214, No. MMJJ20170211).

References

1. Baudet, M., Lubicz, D., Micolod, J., Tassiaux, A.: On the security of oscillator-based random number generators. J. Cryptol. **24**(2), 398–425 (2011)
2. Fischer, V., Lubicz, D.: Embedded evaluation of randomness in oscillator based elementary TRNG. In: Batina, L., Robshaw, M. (eds.) CHES 2014. LNCS, vol. 8731, pp. 527–543. Springer, Heidelberg (2014). https://doi.org/10.1007/978-3-662-44709-3_29

3. Haddad, P., Teglia, Y., Bernard, F., Fischer, V.: On the assumption of mutual independence of jitter realizations in P-TRNG stochastic models. In: Design, Automation & Test in Europe Conference & Exhibition, DATE 2014, Dresden, Germany, March 24–28, 2014, pp. 1–6 (2014)

4. Killmann, W., Schindler, W.: A design for a physical RNG with robust entropy estimators. In: Oswald, E., Rohatgi, P. (eds.) CHES 2008. LNCS, vol. 5154, pp. 146–163. Springer, Heidelberg (2008). https://doi.org/10.1007/978-3-540-85053-3_10

5. Kollar, I.: Bias of mean value and mean square value measurements based on quantized data. IEEE Trans. Instrum. Meas. **43**(5), 733–739 (1994)

6. Lundberg, K.H.: Noise sources in bulk CMOS (2002). http://www.mit.edu/people/klund/papers/UNP_noise.pdf

7. Ma, Y., Lin, J., Chen, T., Xu, C., Liu, Z., Jing, J.: Entropy evaluation for oscillator-based true random number generators. In: Batina, L., Robshaw, M. (eds.) CHES 2014. LNCS, vol. 8731, pp. 544–561. Springer, Heidelberg (2014). https://doi.org/10.1007/978-3-662-44709-3_30

8. Ma, Y., Lin, J., Jing, J.: On the entropy of oscillator-based true random number generators. In: Handschuh, H. (ed.) CT-RSA 2017. LNCS, vol. 10159, pp. 165–180. Springer, Cham (2017). https://doi.org/10.1007/978-3-319-52153-4_10

9. Marsaglia, G.: The Marsaglia random number CDROM including the DIEHARD battery of tests of randomness. Diehard Tests (1995)

10. Rukhin, A., et al.: NIST SP800-22: a statistical test suite for random and pseudorandom number generators for cryptographic applications. http://nvlpubs.nist.gov/nistpubs/Legacy/SP/nistspecialpublication800-22r1a.pdf

11. Sheppard, W.F.: On the calculation of the most probable values of frequency-constants for data arranged according to equidistant division of a scale. Proc. London Math. Soc. **29**(1), 353–380 (1897)

12. Sripad, A.B., Snyder, D.L.: A necessary and sufficient condition for quantization errors to be uniform and white. IEEE Trans. Acoust. Speech Signal Process. **25**(5), 442–448 (1977)

13. Sunar, B., Martin, W.J., Stinson, D.R.: A provably secure true random number generator with built-in tolerance to active attacks. IEEE Trans. Comput. **56**(1), 109–119 (2007)

14. Valtchanov, B., Aubert, A., Bernard, F., Fischer, V.: Modeling and observing the jitter in ring oscillators implemented in FPGAs. In: Proceedings of the 11th IEEE Workshop on Design & Diagnostics of Electronic Circuits & Systems (DDECS 2008), Bratislava, Slovakia, April 16–18, 2008, pp. 158–163 (2008)

Electromagnetic Activity vs. Logical Activity: Near Field Scans for Reverse Engineering

Marc Lacruche[✉] and Philippe Maurine

LIRMM, Université de Montpellier, Montpellier, France
marc.lacruche@lirmm.fr

Abstract. Electromagnetic Near Field Scanning has formerly been proposed to guide side channel and fault injection attacks. However very few studies support its use for reverse-engineering. This absence could be explained by difficulties linked to the diffusion of currents in the power supply network, which are the root of EM radiations. This diffusion has for consequence that a local electrical activity in an IC can be observed quite far from its origin point, thus limiting the interest of EM near field scans for reverse engineering. This paper proposes a solution to this problem by describing a method to extract the source areas of an IC where electrical activity is occurring from EM near field scans. Experimental results are given for an ARM based microcontroller designed in a 90 nm process.

1 Introduction

Electromagnetic (EM) side channel [11] and fault injection attacks [2] are major concerns in hardware security. However, within the context of security evaluations limited in time, one practical problem of these attacks is to place at the right coordinate tiny EM probes. To avoid time consuming exhaustive searches of hotspots, EM Near Field Scans of ICs [10] have been proposed in the last decade as a way of guiding Side Channel Attacks (SCA) [3] or fault injection attacks [7].

The scanning process is usually performed in the following manner: an EM probe (usually a copper coil) connected to an oscilloscope through a low noise amplifier is used to scan a grid of points over the surface of an IC using a motorized XY stage. At each position of this XY grid $N_{executions}$ traces of a same IC processing are acquired with a Digital Sampling Oscilloscope. Each acquired trace, composed of $N_{samples}$ time samples, is an EM view of the IC processing perceived from a (X, Y) position. Of course, the perception of the computation performed by the IC varies from one coordinate to another because of the locality of EM measurements but also because of the vectorial nature of the magnetic field. These measurements are then used to draw maps using a criterion (an image contrast) chosen according to the target purpose.

© Springer Nature Switzerland AG 2019
B. Bilgin and J.-B. Fischer (Eds.): CARDIS 2018, LNCS 11389, pp. 140–155, 2019.
https://doi.org/10.1007/978-3-030-15462-2_10

Among the advantage of EM near field scanning, one can identify:

– its low cost: the required equipment is the same as for performing EM attacks,
– its non invasivity: EM scans can be non-invasive (i.e. done without removing the IC package) or semi-invasively (done after removal of the package) to get a higher spatial resolution.

While many papers have been published on the subject, most focus on improving the tools used to perform the scans [6,8] or on post processing methods to find Points of Interest (PoI) for SCA [3,12,13]. However, and despite the obvious advantages of EM near field scans, only one paper (to the best of our knowledge) focuses on a reverse-engineering technique [9] and does so by introducing a different technique based on injecting low amplitude EM pulses and measuring the variations induced on the power network of the chip instead of passive EM measurements. In addition none of the former works discuss or consider the diffusion of the currents in the power/ground network, diffusion impeding the usage of EM scans for reversal engineering or for guiding side-channel and fault injection attacks.

Other related works use EM side-channel as a method of reverse engineering, however they focus on single point measurements instead of full chip scans. Their applications include code disassembly [5] or reverse engineering of cryptographic algorithms [1]. Finally a comparable technique to EM near field scans is photonic analysis [14]. While extremely precise, this technique is also more expensive, and requires long exposure times.

The rest of the paper is organized as follows. Section 2 first elaborates on the limitations of EM near field scans for reverse engineering or for attacks guidance. A special attention is paid to the diffusion of currents in the power/ground networks and its effects on the interpretation of EM near field scans. Then a criterion is introduced in Sect. 3. It allows deciding if the EM field acquired with a probe at a given coordinate is effectively due to an electrical activity located below the probe or is due to an electrical activity source located further away. In the latter case, the observed magnetic field is due to the passing of the current consumed by this distant source below the probe position. Section 3 ends by the proposal of an algorithm, derived from the proposed criterion, allowing to detect real electrical activity areas. This algorithm is derived from the criterion. A textbook example is used to illustrate both the criterion and the algorithm all along this section. Section 4 gives a concrete application example: the detection of electrical activity spots during the execution of piece of code by a 90 nm microcontroller. Finally a conclusion and perspectives are given in Sect. 5.

2   Limitations of EM Near Field Scans

EM near field scanning has a few characteristics, that are not necessarily problematic when used for optimizing SCA (the objective being to find out probe positions yielding a high Signal to Noise Ratio (SNR), the signal being in this case the leakage [4]), but can be misleading for functional or physical reverse-engineering purposes. Among these characteristics one can cite:

- The non uniformity of the EM coupling between the EM probe and the IC which varies with the EM probe position above the its surface because the routing and the integration density are not uniform. This is especially true while performing EM scans above the IC front side. This non uniformity could for instance affects the EM perception of a same electrical activity source placed in different areas of an IC and partially explain why a same hard IP macro integrated in two different ICs radiates differently.
- The heterogeneity of emissions that can alter the interpretation of EM maps. This unavoidable problem is due to the heterogeneous nature of the blocks integrated in ICs. For instance, a RAM, an embedded clock generator, a pump charge and a combinational block do not have the same EM emissivity and some blocks can hide the emission of other blocks if activated simultaneously.
- The diffusion of currents. This effect is undoubtedly, in conjunction with the heterogeneity of EM emissions, the most impeding problem for the exploitation of EM scans. It is therefore the topic of next paragraphs.

In order to explain this limitation let us consider that ICs are made up of several functional blocks, each one emitting EM radiations proportionally to the derivative of the current they consume.

When one of these blocks is turned on, it starts consuming current. This power consumption creates a voltage drop and a ground bounce in the close vicinity of the block. These drops and bounces, which are due to the resistive and capacitive nature of the internal supply wires, persists the time until a sufficient amount of current is conveyed to the block by the power/ ground networks. Thus the power consumed by the block travels from its originating point towards the power and ground pads and generates EM emissions all along its path.

The EM emissions radiated all along the current paths are of course similar in nature (and thus statistically linked) to those observed at the originating point and this despite the damping factor of the power and ground network; damping factor which is, by design, low to ensure the correct operation of the IC. As a result, even an electrical activity confined in a tiny area of the IC can be observed over a large circuit area. This forbids a precise and safe localization of an electrical activity source by direct analysis of EM near field scans.

Figure 1 gives an illustration. It shows the propagation of the current consumed by an activity source $S1$ through an hypothetical supply path toward the power and ground pads. It also shows the related EM radiations all along this path.

One can argue that in practice the EM emissions observed all along the travel path of the current are not visually similar. This is often right. Hence the interest of high spatial resolution EM probe. However, if they do not look like similar, this is mainly due to two effects that do not suppress the statistical link between the emissions observed at the originating point and those observed all along the propagation path.

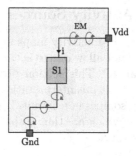

Fig. 1. Illustration of the diffusion of the current consumed by an activity source $S1$ and its related EM emissions.

The first effect is the position of the EM probe relatively to the travel path. For instance, moving the EM probe from one side of the path to the other side inverses the shape of the measured signal because of the reversal of the magnetic field orientation.

The second effect, illustrated Fig. 2, is the merging of current travel paths. This figure shows two independent activity sources, $S1$ and $S2$ sharing part of their current propagation paths. At the meeting points of the two paths, the associated currents i_1 and i_2 pile up and produce an EM radiations with a different shape which remains however still correlated with those observed above the two originating points.

This piling up effect is a main concern when interpreting EM cartographies. Indeed, it can lead to mistaking the meeting points for electrical activity sources. This can occur (not always the case) if one uses the maximum (or mean) amplitude or the variance of EM emissions as image contrast to localize activity sources. Hence the need for an improved technique to interpret EM near field scans for identifying areas where IC computations are done.

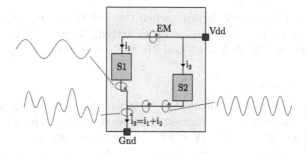

Fig. 2. Propagation path for multiple sources of activity

3   Searching for the Activity Sources

For all aforementioned reasons, EM activity maps may be misleading for reverse engineering purposes and may not allow one to accurately distinguish the spatial origin of logical activity in an IC. This section proposes a method (an image contrast and an algorithm) to limit misinterpretations of EM maps while aiming at locating the logical activity sources in a circuit. It allows to find areas that are probably under operation and which are thus responsible for the EM emissions measured above the all the IC surface.

3.1   Activity Influence Criterion

The image contrast defined below is an influence criterion. It quantifies if EM emissions measured above a position are likely to be the result (the residue after propagation) of EM emissions observed at another position.

Let i and j be two positions at which EM measurements are done and A_{ij} be the influence criterion:

$$A_{ij} = \frac{|Cov(X_i, X_j)|}{Var(X_i)} \tag{1}$$

where X_i and X_j are the EM traces acquired during a chosen time window at the i and j positions, respectively. As one can observe A_{ij} is the coefficient of the simple linear regression between the measurements at i and j : $E(X_j) = A_{ij} \cdot X_i + a_{ij} + \varepsilon$. It is herein used to evaluate the strength of the link between two signals, but compared to Pearson's correlation it has the advantage of not being symmetric depending on the amplitudes of the signals:

– if X_j and X_i are strongly correlated but X_j has a higher amplitude than X_i then $A_{ij} > 1$. This indicates the EM trace measured at position i is a potential propagation residue of the EM trace measured at position j.
– However if $A_{ij} < 1$, this does not mean that the EM trace measured at position i is the source of the EM radiations measured at j, as it can either be the result of lower variance of X_j or the result of poor correlation between X_i and X_j.

Thus A_{ij} is a measure indicating when the EM traces measured at a given position are the propagation residue of an activity at another position. A_{ij} is thus called influence coefficient of j on i in the rest of the paper.

3.2   Influence Matrix

Let us consider a dataset associated to N measurement positions above an IC. By calculating all influence coefficients associated to each pair of positions, one obtains a square matrix of $N \times N$ which is similar to a covariance matrix. In this matrix, the ith row represents the influence of the EM measurements done at every position on the EM measurements done at position i. Similarly the jth column quantifies the influence of the EM measurements done at j on all other positions.

Since $A_{ii} = 1$, if the maximum of the ith row is equal to 1 then no position has a significant influence on i. This means that i is likely to be the position of an activity source.

3.3   A Simple Example

In order to illustrate the above definition, this section provides an example on arbitrary signals detailed Fig. 3. In this figure, $S1$, $S2$ and $S7$ are positions of activity sources. $S3$ and $S4$ are positions along the propagation paths of current consumed by sources at $S1$ and $S2$, respectively. As such they have EM radiations similar in shape to those observed at $S1$ and $S2$ but with lower amplitudes. $S5$ is a position at which the currents consumed by sources at position $S1$ and $S2$ meet. As such, EM radiations at position $S5$ are close to be the damped sum of the signal observed at $S3$ and $S4$. Finally, $S6$ is a position away from all propagation paths. EM radiations measured at this position consists of small residues of all sources. Figure 4 shows the same signals with some measurement noise.

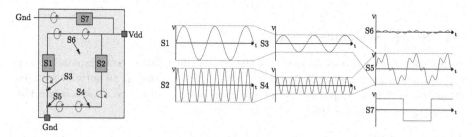

Fig. 3. A simple example. Left part: illustrative supply network and positions ($S1$ to $S7$) at which are done EM measurements. Right part: EM signals measured at positions $S1$ to $S7$; only $S1$, $S2$ and $S7$ are positions associated to an electrical activity.

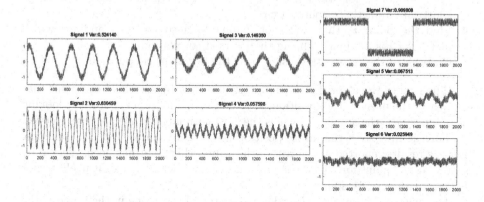

Fig. 4. Examples Signals generated with random noise

All of A_{ij} values computed from the signals reported Fig. 4 are given Table 1. Values in green (> 1 or $\simeq 1$) show that EM measurements done at $S3$ and $S4$ are propagation residues of $S1$ and $S2$, respectively. This table also shows that EM measurements done at position S5 are influenced by that of $S1$, $S2$ and $S3$. Finally, as highlighted in red, $S3$ is not linked to $S2$, $S4$ is not impacted by $S1$ and no signal is impacted by $S7$ besides itself.

Table 1. Influence matrix calculated from generated noisy signals of Fig. 4

A	S1	S2	S3	S4	S5	S6	S7
S1	1.0000	0.0012	0.4851	0.0015	0.2673	0.0677	0.0143
S2	0.0010	1.0000	0.0105	0.2393	0.1059	0.0593	0.0437
S3	1.7023	0.0442	1.0000	0.0085	0.4764	0.1175	0.0632
S4	0.0135	2.6197	0.0220	1.0000	0.3008	0.1417	0.0483
S5	2.0755	0.9891	1.0539	0.2567	1.0000	0.2056	0.0078
S6	1.3680	1.4405	0.6764	0.3144	0.5350	1.0000	0.0636
S7	0.0083	0.0303	0.0104	0.0031	0.0006	0.0018	1.0000

Influence of other positions on S4

$A_{S4,S6}$: Influence of S6 on S4

Influence of S4 on other positions

3.4   Source Searching Algorithm

In practice, for high resolution scans, the size of the influence matrix can be very large. Consequently, a way to extract positions corresponding to activity sources from the matrix is required. Many solutions are possible, we chose to use the following algorithm for this:

1. Select a starting position i_0.
2. Find the point j_0 for which $A_{i_0 j}$ is maximum. j_0 is then considered to be the position influencing the most EM measurements done at i_0, i.e. as the potential activity source of what is being observed at i_0.
3. Find all points for which $A_{j_0 j} > (1 - \epsilon)$. These points, together with j_0 constitute an activity source area.
4. Find the point i_1 that does not belong to a source area and for which $\rho(X_{i_1}, X_{j_0})$ is minimal, ρ being the Pearson correlation.
5. Go back to the second step using i_1 as the new starting position.

The goal of the algorithm is to identify a source by searching the point that influences the most a given position, and then search for other sources by looking at points where the activity profile is the least correlated to the previous sources.

For the first step, the initial position i_0 does not matter much in practice. For the results reported in the rest of the paper, this point has been selected by searching the point for which $Var(X_{i_0})$ is minimal, which makes it likely to not belong to an activity source.

For high resolution scans (displacement step of the probe in the range of the micrometer), activity sources cannot be pinpointed to a single point of the map. Thus the goal of the third step is to determine a source area from the source origin point found at the previous step. This is done by relaxing the constraint ($A_{ij} > 1$) for a point to be a source (an influencing point) or be part of a source. This latter constraint becomes at this step $A_{ij} > 1 - \epsilon$ where ϵ is a constant chosen by the user. The greater ϵ is, the larger the source areas are. In practice values of ϵ close to 0.05 worked well, and this value is used in the rest of the paper.

The fourth step aims at finding the point the least influenced by the already found sources, in order to maximize the chances that it is influenced by a undisclosed source.

When applied to the signals of the example of Fig. 4, the algorithm works as described below:

1. Start from the measurement with the smallest variance: $S6$
2. Finding the position influencing the most $S6$: $S2$ becomes the first source origin.
3. No point sufficiently influences $S2$ to be considered part of the same source area.
4. Finding the point with the lowest correlation with $S2$: $S7$ becomes the next starting position.
5. Finding the position influencing the most $S7$: $S7$, the next source origin.
6. No point sufficiently influences $S7$ to be considered as part of the same source area.
7. Finding the point with the lowest correlation with $S7$: $S5$ becomes the next starting position.
8. Finding the position influencing the most $S5$: $S1$, becomes the next source origin.
9. No point sufficiently influences $S1$ to be considered as part of the same source area.

At the end of the algorithm execution, $S2$, $S7$ and $S1$ are thus identified as measurement positions corresponding to an activity source location. The number of iterations the algorithm must perform to disclose all source areas should be theoretically be equal to the number of sources sought. However, in practice, because of the amplitude disparity of sources, new source origins are sometimes found in the periphery of an already discovered source area. It is thus preferable to set the number of iterations to a value slightly greater than the number of expected source areas. Another possibility is to modify the algorithm so that to ignore newly found origin points which are contiguous and highly correlated with an already disclosed source.

4   Practical Application

An EM activity mapping of a recent 32-bits 90 nm microcontroller was performed using a grid of 90 by 110 points with a displacement step of 50 μm between each points (9900 total positions covering a surface of 4.5×5.5 mm). For each point of the grid 100 EM traces were acquired. Each acquired trace corresponds to one execution by the microcontroller of the following sequence of operations:

1. Generate a 32bits number using the TRNG peripheral and store it in an array A in RAM four times.
2. Copy the array A into an array B at another address in RAM,
3. Load the 128 bits of the array A into the input FIFO of the hardware AES,

4. Encrypt the 128 bits using the hardware AES,
5. Overwrite the array B with the ciphered text provided by the AES.

For each execution an EM trace was recorded using a custom hand-made single coil probe and an oscilloscope. The diameter of the coil is approximately 400 μm. The measurement was done through the backside of the chip after removal of the package and thinning of the substrate down to 140 μm.

4.1   Traces and Code Execution Timing

An EM trace acquired during the scanning process is shown Fig. 5. One can observe that not much can be identified regarding the timings of operations besides the AES execution towards the end of the trace (around samples 31000–32000).

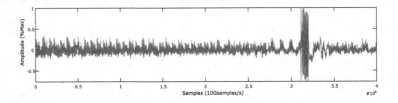

Fig. 5. A sample EM trace obtained

In order to get a better idea of when each part of the code is performed along the EM trace, a correlation EM analysis has been performed between the measurements and the hamming weight of the generated 32-bits random values and ciphered texts so that to disclose the timings of the different operations. The correlation traces giving the timings are given Fig. 6. The operations corresponding to each correlation spike are annotated on this figure as well as three clock periods (between the pairs of vertical red lines); these three windows of time being used as testcases for the proposed source searching algorithm. Among all clock periods of the EM trace, period (a) corresponds to a period during which the fourth random number is generated, period b corresponds to the writing of this number in the RAM and finally during period c the hardware AES is under operation.

4.2   Micocontroller Floorplan

Finally, to help reading the maps in the following sections, Fig. 7 outlines the few informations about the floorplan of the microcontroller at our disposal: two flash memory blocks are located at the top of the die, with the flash controller in between, the analog part with voltage regulators and clock PLLs are in the bottom right and the RAM is in the bottom left. The rest is mostly filled with logic, including the hardware AES in the corner between the bottom of the flash and the left edge of the chip.

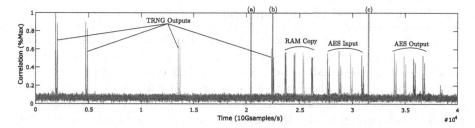

Fig. 6. CPA traces obtained during the timing analysis. Spikes are likely to correspond to the end of each executed operation; the three clock periods (a), (b) and (c) highlighted as there are used as examples in the rest of this section. (Color figure online)

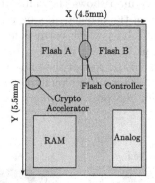

Fig. 7. Microcontroller floorplan informations (Color figure online)

5   Results

5.1   Activity Propagation

The EM radiations generated above the IC surface during the operation of the hardware AES provide a good illustration of the current propagation effect described in Sect. 3. Indeed, Fig. 8 shows traces acquired at different positions (including positions close to the four corners of the IC) above the IC surface during the course of this block. As one can observe, the operation of the AES is clearly visible at the end of these traces. However, on the last trace, measured over the lower middle of the chip (35,95), the activity is barely visible despite the distance to the hardware AES being shorter than for the top right (80,10) and bottom left (15,100) measurements.

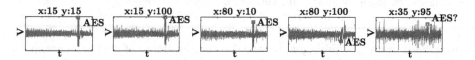

Fig. 8. Traces measured over different positions of the IC surface, with the activity of the hardware AES highlighted.

5.2   Influence Matrices Computation

To calculate the influence matrices associated to all clock periods, the mean trace (40000 samples) of the 100 measurements acquired at each position has been first computed to reduce the noise. According to the SNR of traces, this step is not mandatory. The resulting traces have been divided in 481 segments (of 83 samples) corresponding each to a clock period (120 MHz clock frequency, 10 GS/s sampling rate). The 481 influence matrices of associated to the 481 segments, featuring each 9900×9900 coefficients, were then computed. Then the proposed source searching algorithm was applied to these matrices.

As an example, Fig. 9 shows the maps of the A_{ij} values for the point i_0 indicated by a cross. The left map shows the value of the i_0^{th} row $(A_{i_0 j})$ which corresponds to the influence of the other points on i_0, and the right map shows the values of the i_0^{th} column $(A_{j i_0})$ which corresponds to the influence of i_0 on the other points. These maps illustrate why the rows of the matrix (influence towards i_0) will be the focus of the rest of the paper: since the columns depend on $Var(X_j)$, the values in a column can't really be compared with one another and tend to mostly highlight the positions where $Var(X_j)$ is small (ie. where signal amplitude is low).

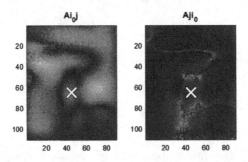

Fig. 9. Maps of a row (influence on i_0) and a column (influence of i_0) corresponding to a same position (Color figure online)

5.3   Algorithm Progression

Figure 10 displays the results of the first eight iterations of the search algorithm for clock period c. On each map, the source origin (point j_n in the algorithm description) is indicated by a cross. The first iteration found a source originating in the flash memory, and the second iteration found the cryptographic-accelerator. The high amplitude of the EM activity measured in these two locations then caused the algorithm to bounce between them for a few iterations, until iteration 7 during which the dedicated memory of the cryptographic-accelerator has been detected. Finally, iteration 8 detects a source in the analog block of the circuit, this block appears to be a source on nearly every clock period of the acquisitions and is likely to be the on-chip voltage regulator or

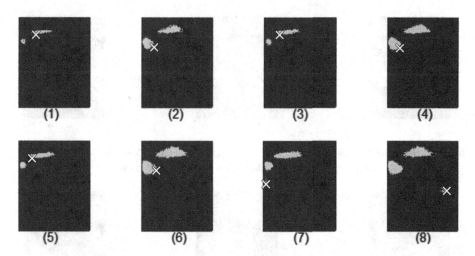

Fig. 10. Activity areas found at the end of the first 8 iterations of the source searching algorithm for period c (AES under operation) (Color figure online)

the clock generator. The following iterations (up to 20) did not highlight more activity sources and continue to expand the already found ones.

6   Overlapped Sources Maps

This section shows maps for the clock periods (a), (b) and (c). For each figure, the left map shows the values of $Var(X_w)$ with X_w the samples for the selected clock period w (since EM traces have a mean equal to zero, variance is equivalent to the mean EM power over that window).

The middle map shows $Var(X_w)/Var(X_{trace})$ with X_{trace} the samples for the whole acquisition. These middle maps are thus visualizations of the mean EM power over time period w normalized by the mean EM power of the whole acquisition. Thus they highlight points at which there is during the time window w more activity than usual.

Finally, the third map corresponds to the results of the searching algorithm introduced in Sect. 3. To obtain these maps, 20 algorithm iterations were performed and the 20 recovered areas were superimposed. Yellow points are points that were selected during two or more iterations and green points were selected by the algorithm during a single iteration.

Figure 11 shows the maps for clock period a, the highlighted areas correspond to the Flash B block, and a part of the analog block that is almost always active, as well as two unknown areas in the left and top left of the die. This pattern of sources is typical of the RNG activity periods, unfortunately as no information on the location of the TRNG on the chip is available, it is difficult to reach further conclusions.

 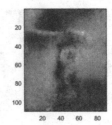 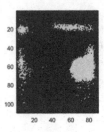

Fig. 11. Results for clock period a, from left to right: $Var(X_w)$, $Var(X_w)/Var(X_{trace})$, and the activity sources found by the algorithm (Color figure online)

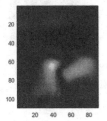 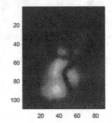 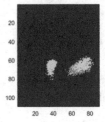

Fig. 12. Results for clock period b, from left to right: $Var(X_w)$, $Var(X_w)/Var(X_{trace})$, and the activity sources found by the algorithm (Color figure online)

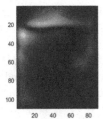 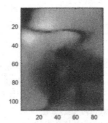 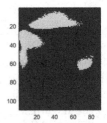

Fig. 13. Results for clock period c, from left to right: $Var(X_w)$, $Var(X_w)/Var(X_{trace})$, and the activity sources found by the algorithm (Color figure online)

Figure 12 shows the maps for clock period b. The same analog block appears again and the source in the center is active during each clock period that coincides with a correlation spike on the CPA trace at the end of each code part where the RAM is read or written, as such it can be suspected to be a RAM bus or controller.

Figure 13 shows the maps for clock period c, for which the first algorithm iterations were detailed previously. As discussed above, two source areas near the cryptographic hardware accelerator appear, as well as the flash and the usual analog block area which is the expected result.

6.1   Current Propagation Paths

Another possible use of the influence matrix is to draw the current propagation path from one point to the influencing source. To do so, starting from a point on the circuit, one can draw a path by selecting the point with the maximum influence on it among its direct neighbors and then doing the same with this new point. With the restriction that a point can't be selected twice (no backtracking or looping). The path stops when it either becomes trapped (all the neighbors are already part of the path) or hits an edge of the map.

The paths displayed in Fig. 14a and b are drawn for clock period c, starting from the point indicated by a cross. On both figures, the left map is drawn using the influence coefficient to guide the propagation path, while the right map uses Pearson correlation for comparison. The difference between the obtained maps is important.

The first path, on Fig. 14a, goes from the starting point to the cryptographic-accelerator following first a vertical and then an horizontal line that may be a result of the power supply grid. Meanwhile, the path drawn by the correlation coefficient goes towards the analog block following a chaotic path.

Similarly, on Fig. 14b, the path drawn from the influence matrix goes to the cryptographic-accelerator memory, then towards the cryptographic-accelerator itself following horizontal and vertical lines.

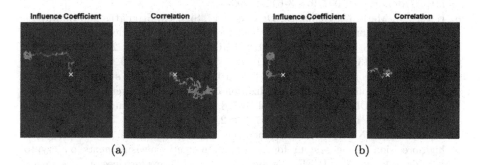

Fig. 14. Propagation path examples for clock period c (Color figure online)

7   Conclusion

In this paper we have proposed a method for finding the electrical activity sources of the EM emissions measured when performing EM near field scans and presented experimental results obtained on a microcontroller. To do so an EM activity influence coefficient has been introduced. This coefficient is based on simple linear regression used to evaluate how much the electrical activity in one point of a circuit contributes to the EM measurements performed at another position. While the results presented are interesting, there is room for improvement in many directions to make EM near field scans a better tool for reverse engineering of ICs. A particular improvement would be a version of the coefficient less sensitive to the synchronization of signals. Another step will be to test this method on FPGAs, where we will have a better knowledge of the positions of each function of the circuit for better validation of the results.

References

1. Clavier, C.: Side channel analysis for reverse engineering (scare)-an improved attack against a secret A3/A8 GSM algorithm (2004)
2. Dehbaoui, A., Dutertre, J.M., Robisson, B., Orsatelli, P., Maurine, P., Tria, A.: Injection of transient faults using electromagnetic pulses -Practical results on a cryptographic system-. IACR Cryptology ePrint Archive **2012**, 123 (2012)
3. Dehbaoui, A., Lomné, V., Ordas, T., Torres, L., Robert, M., Maurine, P.: Enhancing electromagnetic analysis using magnitude squared incoherence. IEEE Trans. VLSI Syst. **20**(3), 573–577 (2012)
4. Doget, J., Prouff, E., Rivain, M., Standaert, F.X.: Univariate side channel attacks and leakage modeling. J. Crypt. Eng. **1**(2), 123 (2011)
5. Eisenbarth, T., Paar, C., Weghenkel, B.: Building a side channel based disassembler. In: Gavrilova, M.L., Tan, C.J.K., Moreno, E.D. (eds.) Transactions on Computational Science X. LNCS, vol. 6340, pp. 78–99. Springer, Heidelberg (2010). https://doi.org/10.1007/978-3-642-17499-5_4
6. Heyszl, J., Merli, D., Heinz, B., De Santis, F., Sigl, G.: Strengths and limitations of high-resolution electromagnetic field measurements for side-channel analysis. In: Mangard, S. (ed.) CARDIS 2012. LNCS, vol. 7771, pp. 248–262. Springer, Heidelberg (2013). https://doi.org/10.1007/978-3-642-37288-9_17
7. Madau, M., Agoyan, M., Maurine, P.: An EM fault injection susceptibility criterion and its application to the localization of hotspots. In: Eisenbarth, T., Teglia, Y. (eds.) CARDIS 2017. LNCS, vol. 10728, pp. 180–195. Springer, Cham (2018). https://doi.org/10.1007/978-3-319-75208-2_11
8. Mai-Khanh, N.N., Iizuka, T., Yamada, M., Morita, O., Asada, K.: An integrated high-precision probe system for near-field magnetic measurements on cryptographic LSIs, pp. 1–4. IEEE, October 2012. http://ieeexplore.ieee.org/document/6411173/
9. Omarouayache, R., Maurine, P.: An electromagnetic imaging technique for reverse engineering of integrated circuits, pp. 352–357. IEEE (2016). http://ieeexplore.ieee.org/document/7916459/
10. Ordas, T., Lisart, M., Sicard, E., Maurine, P., Torres, L.: Near-field mapping system to scan in time domain the magnetic emissions of integrated circuits. In: Svensson, L., Monteiro, J. (eds.) PATMOS 2008. LNCS, vol. 5349, pp. 229–236. Springer, Heidelberg (2009). https://doi.org/10.1007/978-3-540-95948-9_23
11. Quisquater, J.J., Samyde, D.: Eddy current for magnetic analysis with active sensor. In: Proceedings of ESmart 2002, pp. pp 185–194. Eurosmart (2002)
12. Real, D., Valette, F., Drissi, M.: Enhancing correlation electromagnetic attack using planar near-field cartography, pp. 628–633. IEEE, April 2009. http://ieeexplore.ieee.org/document/5090743/

13. Sauvage, L., Guilley, S., Flament, F., Danger, J.L., Mathieu, Y.: Blind cartography for side channel attacks: cross-correlation cartography. Int. J. Reconfigurable Comput. **2012**, 1–9 (2012). http://www.hindawi.com/journals/ijrc/2012/360242/
14. Schlösser, A., Nedospasov, D., Krämer, J., Orlic, S., Seifert, J.-P.: Simple photonic emission analysis of AES. In: Prouff, E., Schaumont, P. (eds.) CHES 2012. LNCS, vol. 7428, pp. 41–57. Springer, Heidelberg (2012). https://doi.org/10.1007/978-3-642-33027-8_3

An In-Depth and Black-Box Characterization of the Effects of Laser Pulses on ATmega328P

Dilip S. V. Kumar[1], Arthur Beckers[2(✉)], Josep Balasch[2], Benedikt Gierlichs[2], and Ingrid Verbauwhede[2]

[1] SEAL, Department of Computer Science and Engineering,
IIT Kharagpur, Kharagpur, India
[2] imec-COSIC, KU Leuven, Kasteelpark Arenberg 10,
3001 Leuven-Heverlee, Belgium
{arthur.beckers,josep.balasch,benedikt.gierlichs,
ingrid.verbauwhede}@esat.kuleuven.be

Abstract. Laser fault injection is a complex, physical process with many parameters that influence the success of the injection. Some parameters are difficult to control. While many works have established *that* focused laser light can inject seemingly random faults in electronic devices such as microcontrollers, FPGAs and ASICs, only few works explain precisely *why* a specific fault can be observed. We narrow this gap and characterize in detail the effects of laser pulses on an 8-bit microcontroller in a black-box fashion, with access to only public documentation. With our setup and settings we can inject faults only in the read-out circuitry for the on-chip flash memory. As result of our analysis we are able to inject bit-reset faults in individual bits of opcodes and data words stored in flash with *100%* accuracy and repeatability. This allows us to easily demonstrate well known attacks on cryptographic software, e.g. manipulation of a block cipher implementation's number of rounds. At the same time our study informs the targeted development of countermeasures.

Keywords: Laser fault injection · Microcontroller · Black-box characterization · Flash memory

1 Introduction

After the publication of the first fault attack by Boneh et al. [6] a vast body of work has been accumulated regarding fault attacks, countermeasures and fault injection methods. A fault attack aims to inject a fault during a device's nominal operation, and to analyze the faulty output, in order to retrieve secret information stored on the device. The most common fault analysis methods are Differential Fault Analysis (DFA) [4], Collision Fault Analysis (CFA) [14] and Ineffective Fault Analysis (IFA) [5,11]. Each of these attacks requires the fault

© Springer Nature Switzerland AG 2019
B. Bilgin and J.-B. Fischer (Eds.): CARDIS 2018, LNCS 11389, pp. 156–170, 2019.
https://doi.org/10.1007/978-3-030-15462-2_11

introduced into the device to have certain properties, the introduced faults need to behave according to a desired fault model. To counter these fault attacks countermeasures usually rely on some form of redundancy [3] or on sensors [16].

To achieve the required fault model different fault injection methods can be employed. These fault injection methods are often classified according to their invasiveness. Common fault injection methods include voltage glitching [15], clock glitching [2], electromagnetic pulses [19] and laser fault injection [21]. Of these injection methods, laser fault injection is the most invasive since it requires the exposure of the bare die. However, laser fault injection is also very precise and can target a specific area of an integrated circuit (IC) and introduce faults controlled both in time and space.

Laser fault injection is a powerful method to disrupt an IC's operation. Laser light, with the correct wavelength, can penetrate an IC's substrate and reach the transistor layer. The coherent light produced by the laser source is directed at the IC's circuitry and causes transistors to toggle. Due to the small spot size, the area illuminated by the laser light, very precise faults can be introduced into the circuit. The spot size can be in the μm range and depends on the used wavelength, the quality of the laser source and the optics. For this reason laser fault injection was used first to simulate the effect of single event upsets [13] on ICs and later to perform fault attacks on cryptographic implementations [21].

With shrinking technologies it is no longer possible to target a single transistor. Instead clusters of transistors are illuminated by the laser light, making the outcome of a laser fault harder to predict. A multitude of parameters can be varied all of which can influence the outcome of a laser fault injection.

Laser fault injection can be applied to every platform ranging from ASICs or FPGAs to microcontrollers (μCs). In this paper we will focus on laser fault attacks on μCs. Previous works have already demonstrated the vulnerability of μCs to laser fault attacks. The first laser fault attack on a μC was published by Skorobogatov et al. [21]. They managed to set bits in SRAM using a laser pointer and some optics. Later a more in-depth study into faulting the SRAM of μCs was done by Agoyan et al. [1]. Courbon et al. demonstrated that besides SRAM the registers of a μC are also vulnerable to laser fault injection [12]. Note that these results were not obtained on the μC that we use in our study.

We chose the ATmega328P as our target μC. The susceptibility of the ATmega328P to laser fault injection was already demonstrated by Breier et al. [8,9]. In their work the authors demonstrate that meaningful faults, i.e. program flow or data is corrupted but the chip does not reset, can be introduced into the ATmega328P. The region on chip where they achieved these faults corresponds to one of the regions also found sensitive to laser pulses in our experiments. For our experiments we use a setup similar to the one used by Breier et al.

In their experiments they achieved three types of faults: instruction skip faults, register disturbance faults and address change faults. Under register disturbance faults they understand faults that influence the values stored in registers. Address change faults are faults where data from a different register than intended is written to memory. Breier et al. describe the type of faults they observe but give no explanation for the underlying mechanism.

Contribution. We characterize in detail the effects of laser fault injection on the 8-bit μC ATmega328P while it reads from program memory. This includes the pre-loading of operations in the fetch stage and the loading of data in the execute stage. We not only locate the regions sensitive to laser fault injection, but also describe the physical effects causing the fault model. The different fault types observed by Breier et al. can be unified under the fault model resulting from our characterization. As result of our analysis we are able to inject bit-reset faults in individual bits of opcodes and data words stored in flash with *100%* accuracy and repeatability.

2   Experimental Design

In this section we describe our experimental setup for fault injection as well as our methodology to characterize and understand the injected fault.

2.1   Target Device

In this work we target an 8-bit AVR microcontroller, the Atmel ATmega328P [17]. It has 32 kB of flash memory, 1 kB of EEPROM and 2 kB of RAM. It operates on a two stage pipeline with fetch and execution stages: the next instruction is fetched during execution of the current instruction. In our experiments the target device (DUT) runs at 4 MHz. The ATmega328P was chosen for several reasons. The fault sensitivity of the μC has already been demonstrated, but not described in depth, in previous works. The ATmega328P is also used in the Arduino UNO platform, making it easy to program and interface with the target device. Another important advantage of the ATmega328P is its availability in DIP packages. This allows to easily decapsulate the target device and should the device be damaged by the laser fault injection it can easily be replaced.

Laser fault injection is a semi-invasive attack where the adversary needs line-of-sight to the bare die. Therefore the backside of the chip's package together with the copper paddle was removed using a cheap hobbyist mill. After removing the thermal paste with acetone the bare die is exposed. Our characterization is performed from the backside. Thus the laser first has to penetrate the chips substrate before it reaches the transistor layer. The backside of the IC is chosen as a target since the topside holds the metal routing wires. These are not transparent to light and would therefore block or hinder the laser light from reaching the transistor layer.

The DUT is mounted on a modified Arduino UNO board. Since the laser fault injection is performed through the backside of the DUT a DIP socket was soldered to the Arduino UNO PCB, such that the exposed die is pointing "upwards" towards the microscopic lens of the laser fault injection setup.

In order to better understand which part of the µC was faulted, we took a through substrate image of an ATmega328P using a near infrared (NIR) camera (Fig. 1). The original substrate thickness of the chip is around 500 µm making it impossible to make a clear image due to the high absorption coefficient of Si for NIR light. Therefore the substrate of the µC was thinned down mechanically to 50 µm. After thinning a complete image of the 3 by 3 mm die was taken. No thinning was done on the chip used for our characterization experiments.

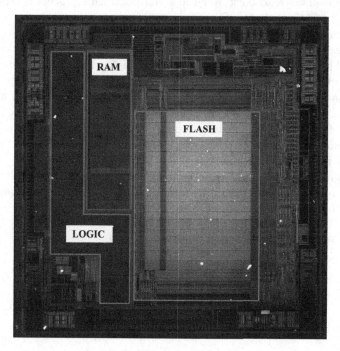

Fig. 1. Through substrate image of an ATmega328P.

2.2   Laser Fault Injection Setup

The laser fault injection setup used to perform the characterization employs a diode pumped laser source with a 1064 nm wavelength. The laser source has a maximal output power of 2 W and a minimal pulse width of 1 ns. The laser beam is focused using a 50X microscope objective. The microscope objective is mounted on a XYZ stepper table that has a minimum step size of 0.1 µm. A NIR camera in combination with NIR LEDs is used to focus the laser source on the target µC.

With the stepper table we control the position of the laser relative to the DUT. The trigger for the laser fault injection setup is generated by the DUT on one of its output pins. Communication with the DUT is done through a serial interface. All the components of the setup (steppers, communication, etc.) are controlled with a PC.

2.3 Methdology

Our black-box analysis follows the methodology of Balasch et al. [2]. Before injecting a laser pulse, the device is reset and initialized in order to bring it to a fully known state. Under a known state we understand that all registers and memories contain the same values before every pulse injection. After resetting the device, the target code is executed, a fault is injected and the content of all working registers is read back over the serial port. This process is repeated for every target location on the µC.

After collecting the data for every target location we examine the difference between the expected register values and the ones received after laser pulse injection. The goal is to reverse-engineer what instruction was executed instead of the target instruction, which in turn reveals which bits of the opcode have changed, and how. *This manual process is extremely time consuming and at the heart of our study.*

By carefully selecting the target instructions and analyzing the different faults we obtain for each of them we can get an understanding of the underlying cause for the obtained faults.

To ensure that the fault injection affects only a single instruction and hence to simplify our task, we surround the target instruction with several *nop* instructions. Our test code is shown in Table 1.

Table 1. Test code.

Cycle	Instruction
1	sbi 0X0B, 7 // trigger
2	nop
3	nop
4	target
5	nop
6	nop

2.4 Locating Sensitive Regions

In a first step we scanned the entire chip area for regions that are sensitive to laser fault injection. We applied laser pulses with large pulse width, twice the clock period, while executing different target instructions such as *brne* and *ldd*. We used a relatively large step size of 20 µm for these scans. During these initial scans we only checked if the program was correctly executed or not, by comparing the content of the registers after normal and faulted execution.

The initial scans revealed that only laser pulses directed at flash memory caused meaningful faults in the program's execution. This region will therefore be the focus of the characterization.

3   Faulting the Flash Memory

The initial scanning of the chip to find sensitive regions showed that flash memory was the only region that demonstrated meaningful faults during the program execution. Note that *no permanent faults* were introduced. The content of the flash memory cells remained the same before and after the laser fault injection. This observation suggests that we inject faults in the read-out circuitry. Flash memory has different components that can be faulted. The flash found in the ATmega328P most likely has a NOR-type structure where flash memory cells can be accessed individually. Each memory cell can be addressed separately by enabling its word-line and bit-line as can be seen in Fig. 2. Some control logic is required to enable the correct word-line drivers and select the correct bit-line. The content of the addressed memory cell is read out by one or several sense amplifier(s). There are also analog components to generate the high voltages needed to program the flash cells, to generate reference voltages for the sense amplifiers, etc. Each of these components might be sensitive to laser pulses. The fact that flash memory can be faulted by laser fault injection has been demonstrated by Skorobogatov [20].

The characterization is done in a black-box setting thus we can never be completely sure about the effects the laser pulses have on the targeted circuit. Our initial scan of the chip showed that the entire flash region was sensitive to laser pulses. Besides the flash memory cells themselves another region in the bottom left corner proved to be sensitive to laser pulses. Based on the image taken through the chips substrate we can observe that this is most likely an analog component.

In the next sections the effects of laser pulses on the ATmega328P's flash memory will be discussed in more detail.

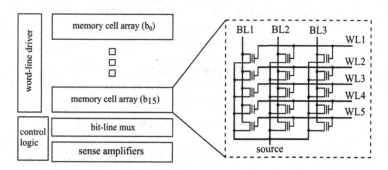

Fig. 2. Flash memory structure.

3.1   Effect of Laser Pulses on Program Flow

In order to analyze the effects of laser pulses on program flow, we set our target instruction to be *muls r23, r27* (Multiply Signed). Figure 3a illustrates the sensitive regions in flash memory that are vulnerable to laser fault injection for our

(a) Fault Sensitive Regions on flash memory

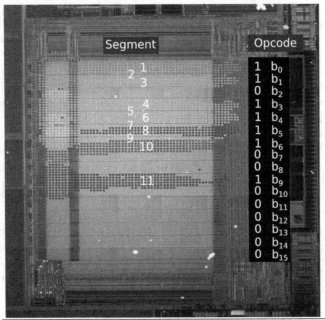

Segment	Cycle	Instruction	Opcode(bin)	Bit(s) Reset
	i	nop	0000 0000 0000 0000	
	i+1	muls r23, r27	0000 0010 0111 1011	
1	i+1	muls r23, r26	0000 0010 0111 1010	b_0
2	i+1	muls r23, r24	0000 0010 0111 1000	b_0 & b_1
3	i+1	muls r23, r25	0000 0010 0111 1001	b_1
4	i+1	muls r23, r19	0000 0010 0111 0011	b_3
5	i+1	muls r22, r19	0000 0010 0110 0011	b_3 & b_4
6	i+1	muls r22, r27	0000 0010 0110 1011	b_4
7	i+1	muls r20, r27	0000 0010 0100 1011	b_4 & b_5
8	i+1	muls r21, r27	0000 0010 0101 1011	b_5
9	i+1	muls r17, r27	0000 0010 0001 1011	b_5 & b_6
10	i+1	muls r19, r27	0000 0010 0011 1011	b_6
11	i+1	nop *(Invalid)*	0000 0000 0111 1011	b_9

(b) Instructions replacing the target instruction.

Fig. 3. *muls r23, r27.* (Color figure online)

target instruction. The heat map consists of 11 different fault sensitive regions, enumerated in Fig. 3a, and in each of these regions, our target instruction is replaced with the execution of a different instruction. The instructions executed in place of our target instruction are shown in Fig. 3b. The sensitive regions are colour-coded in the heat map in order to distinguish them from each other.

Based on the instructions that replace the target instruction in Fig. 3b, we could observe that the fault segments are correlated with the *opcode* of *muls r23, r27* and the *opcode* of all the erroneous instructions differ from our target instruction by only one or two consecutive bit resets. Let us represent the bits of the *opcode* as $b_{15}b_{14}\cdots b_0$. As we traverse the memory from top to bottom in Fig. 3a, we can notice a gradual advancement in the bit positions that are reset. Fault injection in Segment 1 resets the bit b_0 and in Segment 11 resets the bit b_9. And the segments that reset two bits of the *opcode* are formed from the overlap of the segments immediately above and below them. It is also interesting to note that the relative positions of the fault segments in Fig. 3a resemble the bit positions in the target instruction's opcode. For instance, Segments 3 and 4 are separated from each other by a fault free-region as they represent non-adjacent bits b_1 and b_3. Note that these two bits are equal to 1 in our target instruction whereas the bit between them, b_2 is equal to zero in our target instruction. From this, we can be certain that the fault model is *bit-reset* and not *bit-flip*.

We repeated our experiments on more instructions such as *ldd*(Load Indirect from data space), *breq*(Branch if Equal),*mov*(Copy Register) etc. and observed very similar results. Figure 4 illustrates the results we obtained on targeting the instruction *ldd r11,z +0x1c*.

Flash memory in ATmega328P is organized as 16-bit words. Every instruction in AVR assembly language has a unique 16-bit opcode (Operation code) representing it. On programming the chip, all the instructions of our program are stored in the flash memory as 16-bit operation codes. In the pre-fetching phase, the opcode of the instruction pointed to by the Program Counter (PC) is loaded through the 16-bit Program Bus. Hence injecting a laser pulse during fetch disturbs the opcode, thereby replacing the target instruction with a different instruction.

Overlapping of fault segments does indeed create specific regions near the left margin of the memory that can even reset more than 2 bits in the instruction *opcode*. But these regions are hard to generalize for all instructions as the level of overlap would depend on many parameters such as the pulse width, laser intensity and the instruction's opcode. The size of the regions influenced by the laser pulses depends on the settings of the laser source. For our experiments we used a pulse width of 150 ns and a laser power of 0.6 W. Relatively high laser power is required since there was no thinning of the IC's 500 μm thick substrate. An increase in laser power or pulse width will up to a point increase the size of the sensitive regions as can be seen in Fig. 5. This suggests that a certain amount of energy is required to inject a fault into flash memory. Furthermore, the regions are obviously much larger than any single flash memory cell. This supports our assumption that we are injecting faults into the read-out circuitry. More precisely, we seem to affect a part that is shared for many bits.

At the bottom-left corner of flash memory, there exist some fault sensitive regions as depicted in Fig. 6. These regions form concentric rings, and in each of these regions the target instruction is always replaced with a fixed instruction irrespective of the target instruction. Based on the through substrate image we can observe that this region most likely contains analog circuitery. One possible

(a) Fault Sensitive Regions on flash memory.

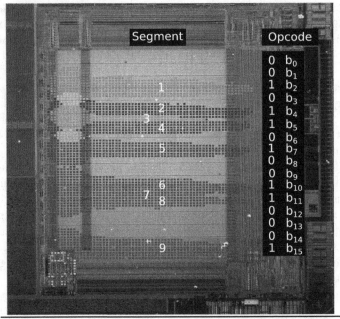

Segment	Cycle	Instruction	Opcode(bin)	Bit(s) Reset
	i	nop	0000 0000 0000 0000	
	i+1	ldd r11, z+0x1c	1000 1100 1011 0100	
1	i+1	ldd r11, z+0x18	1000 1100 1011 0000	b_2
2	i+1	ldd r10,z+0x1c	1000 1100 1010 0100	b_4
3	i+1	ldd r8, z+0x1c	1000 1100 1000 0100	b_4 & b_5
4	i+1	ldd r9, z+0x1c	1000 1100 1001 0100	b_5
5	i+1	ldd r3, z+0x1c	1000 1100 0011 0100	b_7
6	i+1	ldd r11, z+0x14	1000 1000 1011 0100	b_{10}
7	i+1	ldd r11, z+0x04	1000 0000 1011 0100	b_{10} & b_{11}
8	i+1	ldd r11, z+0x0c	1000 0100 1011 0100	b_{11}
9	i+1	add r11, r4	0000 1100 1011 0100	b_{15}

(b) Instructions replacing the target instruction.

Fig. 4. *ldd r11, z + 0x1c.*

explanation for this behaviour would be that injecting faults in these locations produce *stuck-at* faults during opcode fetch. The instructions executed instead of our target instruction in some of these regions are:

- nop (Opcode : 0000 0000 0000 0000)
- muls r16, r16 (Opcode : 0000 0010 0000 0000)
- and r0, r16 (Opcode : 0010 0010 0000 0000)
- or r0, r18 (Opcode : 0010 1010 0000 0010)
- or r0, r16 (Opcode : 0010 1010 0000 0000)

(a) Width = 70ns & Power = 0.6W

(b) Width = 150ns & Power = 0.6W

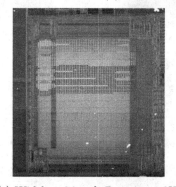

(c) Width = 70ns & Power = 1.2W

Fig. 5. Influence of the laser parameters on the size of the sensitive regions.

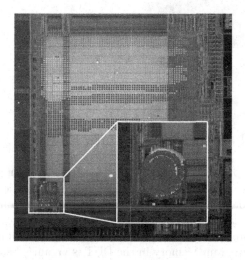

Fig. 6. Concentric fault sensitive rings.

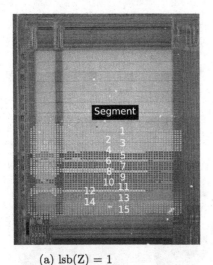

(a) lsb(Z) = 1

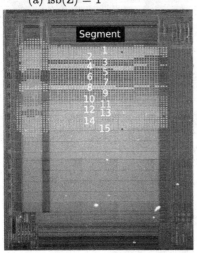

(b) lsb(Z) = 0

Segment	Value $r9$	Bits Reset
	255	None
1	254	v_0
2	252	v_1 & v_0
3	253	v_1
4	249	v_2 & v_1
5	251	v_2
6	243	v_3 & v_2
7	247	v_3
8	231	v_4 & v_3
9	239	v_4
10	207	v_5 & v_4
11	223	v_5
12	159	v_6 & v_5
13	191	v_6
14	63	v_7 & v_6
15	127	v_7

(c) Data Faults in Register $r9$

Fig. 7. Faults in the data flow

4   Effects of Laser Pulses on Data Flow

From the observations we have made on the effects of laser fault injection on program flow, we can be fairly certain that fault injection does indeed disturb the 16 bits of opcode fetched from flash memory. In this section, we demonstrate how fault injection can also affect the execution stage of target instructions that read values from program memory, thereby inducing data faults.

As discussed, Program Memory in the DUT is organized and accessed as 16-bit words. However, the lpm (Load from Program Memory) instruction uses a byte address pointer (Z) to load a single byte to the destination register. Selecting between low or high byte of the 16-bit word is most likely determined by the least significant bit of the Z pointer. This characteristic enables the following experiment. We store a table of 8-bit constants with the value 0xff in program memory. We use the command lpm r9,z as our test instruction, to load an element from the table. The constants being 8-bit wide, two adjacent elements of the table are stored together as a 16-bit word in Program Memory. To verify this assumption, we load two constants stored at consecutive memory locations using lpm instructions. If our assumption is right, one constant should be a low byte and the other a high byte. We perform a step-wise scan throughout flash memory and monitor if the value getting stored in Register $r9$ matches the expected value (0xff). Figure 7b and a show the heat maps for the cases when the least significant bit of Z is 0 and 1 respectively. The fault pattern in both Figs. 7b and a are identical, as depicted in Fig. 7c, indicating every bit of the 16-bit word can be reset. In other words, there exists a dedicated region on flash memory that can be targeted to reset a particular bit of the 16-bit word.

Additionally one can notice that fault sensitive regions for both cases are present in only one half of flash memory. This observation implies that the low byte of the 16-bit word from which the constant 0xff was fetched is present in the top half of the flash memory and the high byte in the bottom half. We can now conclude that the bits of flash memory word are arranged in flash memory cells in a vertical arrangement, with the least significant bit placed near the top margin of flash memory and the most significant bit near the bottom margin. The fault sensitive region for a certain bit of a target instruction or data, e.g. the least significant bit, comprises that bit of all words in flash memory, e.g. all LSBs. This suggests that (part of) the read-out logic is shared among all bits that have the same position in a word.

5   Application

In this section, with the knowledge we have acquired so far, we demonstrate a couple of threats laser fault injection could pose to an implementation of AES on our platform. Figure 8a illustrates a snippet of AES-128 encryption, where _rcon indicates the round counter. Now suppose we target the Branch If Not Equal (brne) instruction in this snippet and inject a laser fault in the location shown in the Fig. 8, highlighted in red. The opcode bit b_{10} of brne RoundFunction would be reset changing the instruction type of the target instruction from Branch if Not Equal (brne)(Opcode : 1111 01kk kkkk k001) to Branch if Equal (breq)(Opcode : 1111 00kk kkkk k001). If brne were to be replaced with breq in the encryption algorithm, it would prevent the control from branching and would drastically reduce the number of rounds executed during encryption, thereby enabling key-recovery through simple cryptanalytic attacks [10].

Additionally, look-up tables such as the S-box would likely be stored as constants in flash memory and frequently accessed during encryption (resp. decryption). As this would require the usage of the *lpm* (Load from Program Memory) instruction, an adversary could target this instruction in order to inject faults in the data flow. This would allow to mount classical DFA attacks such as Piret and Quisquater [18].

When countermeasures or tools [7] are developed to defend against fault attacks, particularly DFA, the assumption is often that only the operands are vulnerable to fault injection. Or if an attacker manages to fault an instruction it will only lead to an instruction skip. These assumptions might hold for most devices, but as demonstrated in this paper, they do not hold for all of them. Therefore, when developing countermeasures, it is safer to assume a fault model where an attacker is able to manipulate the opcode bits up to a certain degree.

```
...

RoundFunction:
...
inc _rcon
cmp _rcon, 0x0a
brne RoundFunction
...
```

(a) AES encryption snippet

(b) Fault Injection Location

Fig. 8. Faulting AES round counter. (Color figure online)

6   Conclusion

In this work we described the effects of laser pulses on the flash memory of an 8-bit microcontroller, the ATmega328P. We target the read out of data from flash memory and are able to reset one or multiple bits of the fetched data or opcode to zero. We have full control over which of the 16 bits is reset. Being able to reset arbitrary bits in the opcode is a very powerful fault model which allows us to perform any of the many well known published attacks. For instance, the opcode of instructions can be faulted such that the program flow is altered, or data read from memory is faulted in order to enable a classical DFA attack. The acquired fault model is supported by the physical layout of the flash memory.

Understanding the underlying cause for a fault model does not only allow us to mount powerful attacks, it also helps us in understanding which countermeasures need to be taken in order prevent these attacks. In order to detect faults in the flash memory, error detecting codes that detect at least two bit resets can for instance be added. However, to detect the faults that we observed in our experiments, it may not be necessary to protect the memory itself, but only the readout circuitry.

Acknowledgment. This work was supported in part by the Research Council KU Leuven: C16/15/058 and through the Horizon 2020 research and innovation programme under Cathedral ERC Advanced Grant 695305.

References

1. Agoyan, M., Dutertre, J.-M., Naccache, D., Robisson, B., Tria, A.: When clocks fail: on critical paths and clock faults. In: Gollmann, D., Lanet, J.-L., Iguchi-Cartigny, J. (eds.) CARDIS 2010. LNCS, vol. 6035, pp. 182–193. Springer, Heidelberg (2010). https://doi.org/10.1007/978-3-642-12510-2_13
2. Balasch, J., Gierlichs, B., Verbauwhede, I.: An in-depth and black-box characterization of the effects of clock glitches on 8-bit MCUs. In: Breveglieri, L., Guilley, S., Koren, I., Naccache, D., Takahashi, J. (eds.) FDTC 2011, pp. 105–114. IEEE Computer Society (2011)
3. Bar-El, H., Choukri, H., Naccache, D., Tunstall, M., Whelan, C.: The sorcerer's apprentice guide to fault attacks. Proc. IEEE **94**(2), 370–382 (2006)
4. Biham, E., Shamir, A.: Differential fault analysis of secret key cryptosystems. In: Kaliski, B.S. (ed.) CRYPTO 1997. LNCS, vol. 1294, pp. 513–525. Springer, Heidelberg (1997). https://doi.org/10.1007/BFb0052259
5. Blömer, J., Seifert, J.-P.: Fault based cryptanalysis of the advanced encryption standard (AES). In: Wright, R.N. (ed.) FC 2003. LNCS, vol. 2742, pp. 162–181. Springer, Heidelberg (2003). https://doi.org/10.1007/978-3-540-45126-6_12
6. Boneh, D., DeMillo, R.A., Lipton, R.J.: On the importance of checking cryptographic protocols for faults (extended abstract). In: Fumy, W. (ed.) EUROCRYPT 1997. LNCS, vol. 1233, pp. 37–51. Springer, Heidelberg (1997). https://doi.org/10.1007/3-540-69053-0_4
7. Breier, J., Hou, X., Liu, Y.: Fault attacks made easy: differential fault analysis automation on assembly code. IACR Trans. Cryptogr. Hardw. Embed. Syst. **2018**(2), 96–122 (2018)
8. Breier, J., Jap, D.: Testing feasibility of back-side laser fault injection on a microcontroller. In: Proceedings of the WESS 2015: Workshop on Embedded Systems Security, WESS 2015, pp. 5:1–5:6. ACM, New York (2015)
9. Breier, J., Jap, D., Chen, C.-N.: Laser profiling for the back-side fault attacks: with a practical laser skip instruction attack on AES. In: Proceedings of the 1st ACM Workshop on Cyber-Physical System Security, CPSS 2015, pp. 99–103. ACM, New York (2015)
10. Choukri, H., Tunstall, M.: Round reduction using faults. In: 2005 Workshop on Fault Diagnosis and Tolerance in Cryptography, pp. 13–24 (2005)
11. Clavier, C.: Secret external encodings do not prevent transient fault analysis. In: Paillier, P., Verbauwhede, I. (eds.) CHES 2007. LNCS, vol. 4727, pp. 181–194. Springer, Heidelberg (2007). https://doi.org/10.1007/978-3-540-74735-2_13
12. Courbon, F., Loubet-Moundi, P., Fournier, J.J.A., Tria, A.: Adjusting laser injections for fully controlled faults. In: Prouff, E. (ed.) COSADE 2014. LNCS, vol. 8622, pp. 229–242. Springer, Cham (2014). https://doi.org/10.1007/978-3-319-10175-0_16

13. Habing, D.H.: The use of lasers to simulate radiation-induced transients in semi-conductor devices and circuits. IEEE Trans. Nucl. Sci. **12**(5), 91–100 (1965)
14. Hemme, L.: A differential fault attack against early rounds of (Triple-)DES. In: Joye, M., Quisquater, J.-J. (eds.) CHES 2004. LNCS, vol. 3156, pp. 254–267. Springer, Heidelberg (2004). https://doi.org/10.1007/978-3-540-28632-5_19
15. Kim, C.H., Quisquater, J.-J.: Fault attacks for CRT based RSA: new attacks, new results, and new countermeasures. In: Sauveron, D., Markantonakis, K., Bilas, A., Quisquater, J.-J. (eds.) WISTP 2007. LNCS, vol. 4462, pp. 215–228. Springer, Heidelberg (2007). https://doi.org/10.1007/978-3-540-72354-7_18
16. Matsuda, K., et al.: A $286f^2$/cell distributed bulk-current sensor and secure flush code eraser against laser fault injection attack. In: International Solid-State Circuits Conference - ISSCC 2018, pp. 352–354. IEEE (2018)
17. Microchip. Atmega328p, July 2018. https://www.microchip.com/wwwproducts/en/ATmega328P
18. Piret, G., Quisquater, J.-J.: A differential fault attack technique against SPN structures, with application to the AES and KHAZAD. In: Walter, C.D., Koç, Ç.K., Paar, C. (eds.) CHES 2003. LNCS, vol. 2779, pp. 77–88. Springer, Heidelberg (2003). https://doi.org/10.1007/978-3-540-45238-6_7
19. Quisquater, J.-J., Samyde, D.: ElectroMagnetic Analysis (EMA): measures and counter-measures for smart cards. In: Attali, I., Jensen, T. (eds.) E-smart 2001. LNCS, vol. 2140, pp. 200–210. Springer, Heidelberg (2001). https://doi.org/10.1007/3-540-45418-7_17
20. Skorobogatov, S.: Flash memory 'bumping' attacks. In: Mangard, S., Standaert, F.-X. (eds.) CHES 2010. LNCS, vol. 6225, pp. 158–172. Springer, Heidelberg (2010). https://doi.org/10.1007/978-3-642-15031-9_11
21. Skorobogatov, S.P., Anderson, R.J.: Optical fault induction attacks. In: Kaliski, B.S., Koç, K., Paar, C. (eds.) CHES 2002. LNCS, vol. 2523, pp. 2–12. Springer, Heidelberg (2003). https://doi.org/10.1007/3-540-36400-5_2

Breaking All the Things—A Systematic Survey of Firmware Extraction Techniques for IoT Devices

Sebastian Vasile[✉], David Oswald, and Tom Chothia

University of Birmingham, Birmingham, UK
sxv512@student.bham.ac.uk, {d.f.oswald,t.p.chothia}@bham.ac.uk

Abstract. In this paper, we systematically review and categorize different hardware-based firmware extraction techniques, using 24 examples of real, wide-spread products, e.g. smart voice assistants (in particular Amazon Echo devices), alarm and access control systems, as well as home automation devices. We show that in over 45% of the cases, an exposed UART interface is sufficient to obtain a firmware dump, while in other cases, more complicated, yet still low-cost methods (e.g. JTAG or eMMC readout) are needed. In this regard, we perform an in-depth investigation of the security concept of the Amazon Echo Plus, which contains significant protection methods against hardware-level attacks. Based on the results of our study, we give recommendations for countermeasures to mitigate the respective methods.

1 Introduction

Extracting the firmware from IoT devices is a crucial first step when analysing the security of such systems. From a designer's point of view, preventing the firmware from falling into the hands of an adversary is often desirable: for instance, to protect cryptographic keys that identify a device and to impede product counterfeit or IP theft. The large variety of IoT devices results in different approaches to firmware extraction, depending on the device in question.

Past work has looked at the state of security of IoT devices, e.g. [1–3]. Past work on the analysis of IoT firmware has found a wide range of vulnerabilities [4–6], and such vulnerabilities have been widely exploited [7]. Much of this work looks at firmware downloaded from the Internet, rather than taken from a device.

In contrast, not so much attention has been given to the hardware security of these devices. Having access to an embedded device's firmware can provide valuable insight into how the device operates and potential vulnerabilities it might have. Sensitive information, such as passwords and static keys can often be found in a firmware, which is indicative of insecure design and bad overall security. Besides, vectors used for firmware extraction also give write access to the device, enabling firmware *modification* as well.

Firmware extraction is not an exact science. The market is filled with a variety of IoT devices, each using one of the many embedded processors, with their own

© Springer Nature Switzerland AG 2019
B. Bilgin and J.-B. Fischer (Eds.): CARDIS 2018, LNCS 11389, pp. 171–185, 2019.
https://doi.org/10.1007/978-3-030-15462-2_12

settings and software stacks, making each device unique in its own way. Because of this, there is no one-glove-fits-all scenario when it comes to firmware extraction of IoT devices. At DEFCON 25, techniques to extract firmware from a range of IoT devices were presented [8], while Etemadieh et al. focused on the use of the eMMC interface (cf. Sect. 3.2). This work culminated into the Exploitee.rs project [9]. We include certain devices from [9] as part of our survey (cf. Sect. 4), but would like to note that we are not affiliated with that project.

The topic has only received relatively limited academic attention, with a first step towards a more systematic approach given by Schwartz et al. [10]. However, the authors of [10] focus on a relatively narrow class of low-cost devices (IP/baby cameras and doorbells). In this paper, we consider a significantly wider range of device types as well as extraction methods. Our case studies include popular smart voice assistants like the Amazon Echo product range and other extremely wide-spread IoT devices. Out of the devices included in the survey, our research suggests that UART is currently the most common and exploitable debugging interface found in IoT devices, with over 45% of the considered devices being vulnerable to firmware extraction via UART. However, direct access to flash memories (e.g. eMMC) is also becoming important for modern devices. Notably, in almost all cases where a hardware method is available for firmware extraction, the method also enables firmware modification and hence "rooting" of the device.

Contrary to the common opinion that security in the IoT is a lost cause, we also observed positive developments, with newer high-profile devices like the Amazon Echo offering a better level of protection compared to most other vendors.

· The remainder of this paper is structured as follows: in Sect. 2, we present background information about the technologies and debugging interfaces in use in embedded systems. In Sect. 3, we present methodologies for firmware extraction using different techniques and interfaces. Then, in Sect. 4 we present case studies for the described methods. Particularly, in Sect. 4.4, we describe various measures implemented in new Amazon Echo devices, that—while they do not prevent firmware extraction—significantly raise the bar for malicious firmware modifications. Based on the case study, we recommend countermeasures for securing devices against firmware extraction and modification in Sect. 5, before concluding in Sect. 6.

2   Technical Background

Unlike the PC market, embedded systems are very diverse, each suited for particular applications of these devices. Such devices usually employ microcontrollers, that consist of one or more CPUs, along with their own memory and I/O peripherals. Common microcontroller architectures for IoT devices include ARM, MIPS, Freescale and Texas Instruments TI MSP.

Firmware. In the context of embedded IoT devices, the firmware usually refers to the entire OS image that incorporates the kernel and file system, together with different binaries and scripts running together, making up the device's functionality. On very low-end devices, such as TV remotes for example, the firmware can be a single binary handling the entire functionality of the device, from booting to transmitting RF signals. A full firmware image usually consists of bootloader(s) (2nd/3rd stage, often U-Boot), the kernel, and one or multiple file system images (e.g. SquashFS, JFFS2, UbiFS, etc.) containing custom binaries and scripts. While there are many custom operating systems made for specific devices, by far the most common is embedded Linux. There are many different distributions of embedded Linux currently used in embedded devices, but they are all very similar in functionality. Another notable commonly found OS in embedded devices is Android (cf. Sect. 4.4). There are also new operating systems specifically made to address the security and performance requirements of the IoT devices of today. These include Windows IoT Core, Kaspersky OS and Google Brillo OS (Android Things).

Bootloaders. The bootloader is the first piece of software that runs on a system. The bootloader initializes hardware components such as RAM, flash storage, and I/O, and loads the kernel into memory for execution. In embedded systems, the boot process can be set up in one, two, or three stages, each stage having a different role during boot. In a three-stage process, the initial bootloader, which is usually located in ROM and is microcontroller-specific, handles the basic initialization of hardware components, and loads the second stage bootloader. The second stage bootloader, which typically resides on flash storage and is board-specific, handles the initialization of board-specific hardware. After the initialization, it loads the final bootloader, which copies the kernel into main memory, loads device drivers for the found hardware components, and runs the kernel code. One of the most widely used bootloader for embedded systems is U-Boot [11], which is used as a second stage bootloader. Aside from the booting process, U-Boot also has a command line interface.

Debug Interfaces. Most microcontrollers offer on-chip debugging functions, usually used for IC fault-testing, direct memory access, and for programming integrated flash chips. Common interfaces include UART, JTAG, Serial Wire Debug (SWD) for ARM processors, as well as Background Debug Mode (BDM) in automotive processors. Other serial interfaces include SPI and I2C.

3   Firmware Extraction Techniques

Firmware extraction presents a couple of challenges for IoT device manufacturers. First, there is a risk of potential IP loss. More importantly however, firmware extraction can often lead to the discovery of new vulnerabilities in such devices. In some cases, this can have an effect not only on the analyzed device, but on all devices belonging to the manufacturer, due to critical vulnerabilities being discovered. We classify firmware extraction methods into three main categories:

- Leveraging debug interfaces to get local shell access or read memory contents;
- Performing a flash chip hardware memory dump;

– Using software methods to gain access to firmware (e.g. firmware updates, network services, etc.).

The execution of these methods usually varies from one device to another, adapting to the particularities of each device. Apart from the aforementioned methods, there is also a hardware method called bus snooping. This method inspects in-transit data between caches and controllers on a bus. A well-known example of this is the original XBox hack [12], which used hypertransport bus snooping to extract the firmware decryption key of the XBox. Aside from the hardware extraction methods, there are also software methods that can be leveraged for firmware extraction. One example are code execution vulnerabilities, which can be exploited to get shell access on the device. As most software runs as root on embedded devices, a successful exploit results in a root shell. In most cases where firmware extraction is possible, firmware modification can also be achieved using the same methodology [13]. In some cases, this can be even more harmful than firmware extraction [14]. Even if no vulnerabilities are found, an attacker might still implant a backdoor on a device such as the Amazon Echo and sell it online. An unsuspecting buyer would get a backdoored device, capable of spying via the microphone, or using the linked Amazon account to make fraudulent purchases. Besides, firmware modification is useful when dynamically analysing the firmware's behaviour, for instance by enabling live debug capabilities (e.g. through a disabled UART or `adb` interface).

3.1   Debug Interfaces

UART Firmware Extraction. UART is often a straightforward way (see also [10]) of gaining access to an embedded device's firmware. An unrestricted root shell can often be found by simply connecting to UART. On Android-based devices, a root shell is sometimes accessible via the Android debug interface `adb`. Another method is to utilize the shell of a bootloader to enable root access or obtain a firmware image in cases where a root shell is not present during operation or is password-protected. With root access, one way to dump the firmware is to perform a live internal dump of the entire filesystem, with all files bundled together in a tar or zip archive, or to dump the block devices available on the device using `dd` or `cat`. However, dumping block devices can cause problems since embedded systems use different types of flash storage with different filesystems. In general, we recommend to follow the following steps when performing UART firmware extraction:

1. Identify the UART interface through visual inspection, oscilloscope probing, and trial-and-error;
2. If an unprotected shell is available, image the device or download all files. Files can be downloaded using `netcat` (or similar tools) and a PC connected on the same network;
3. If the shell is password-protected, try common username/password pairs from a list (e.g. `root/root` etc.). If no shell is available or the credentials cannot be determined, attempt to interrupt the boot process and enter bootloader shell;

4. If the bootloader shell cannot be entered, try to temporarily disturb the flash interface (e.g. by grounding a data or clock pin) when the bootloader loads the kernel in order to fallback to the bootloader's shell. Image the device from the bootloader shell (e.g. using **nand dump** or **nand read** and **md** under U-Boot).

JTAG Firmware Extraction. The JTAG port used during manufacturing for loading firmware can in some cases be used for reading the full memory of the chip. Reading the memory of a device via a JTAG port requires a suitable programmer that can receive the memory dump and transmit it to a computer. Some manufacturers lock the device from being read or reprogrammed after manufacturing. Leaving the JTAG interface connected and unlocked exposes the device to firmware extraction and firmware injection attacks. The general process of JTAG firmware extraction is:

1. Visually identify possible JTAG/SWD (and other) debug interfaces. SWD requires only two pins, while JTAG has a variety of different pin arrangements, ranging from 8 pins to 20. As a general rule, two rows of four or more pins are likely candidates for JTAG;
2. As with UART, first identify the ground pin using a multimeter;
3. To identify the pinout, the data sheet for the particular microcontroller is needed. If the data sheet is not available, use a tool like the JTAGulator [15] to identify possible pinouts;
4. After identifying all pins, a suitable JTAG/SWD programmer can be used to dump the internal memory if no readout protection is enabled.

Due to the large variety of different pinouts and proprietary pins, as well as different JTAG debuggers for different microprocessors and architecture types, firmware extraction via JTAG requires more effort than UART, as specialized hardware and software and information gathering are required.

3.2 Raw Flash Dump

The third and final hardware-based firmware extraction method considered in this paper is directly reading the flash storage. Reading older flash chips with parallel interfaces requires many connections to the target device, as well as a specialized programmer. Newer technologies such as eMMC however, require less connections and can be read with a standard SD card reader. Alternatively, specialised tools like easyJTAG Plus[1] or RiffBox[2] can be used. A deeper description of eMMC extraction can be e.g. found in [16]. The general steps for performing flash dumps are:

1. Identify the flash chip (by label, package type, number of connections to processor) and obtain a data sheet if possible;

---

[1] http://easy-jtag.com/.

[2] http://www.riffbox.org/.

2. Identify the pins, either by data sheet or oscilloscope. eMMC uses DAT0, CMD and CLK pins, as well as power and ground. CLK is a repetitive signal, while the CMD line has short data bursts, generally preceding data reads/writes on the DAT0 pin.
3. For eMMC: Disable access to eMMC from the processor, and connect pins to a generic SD card and use an SD reader to interface with it;
4. For other flash chips: Use a suitable adapter and programmer to read the chip contents, e.g. the MiniPro TL866[3];
5. If in-circuit dump is not possible, de-solder the flash chip and perform the dump with a suitable reader.

For in-circuit dumps, it is required to prevent accesses from the board's CPU while reading the memory. This can e.g. be achieved by temporarily cutting the clock line and re-connecting after the dump is completed. Sometimes, simply connecting an eMMC interface (e.g. easyJTAG Plus) prevents the CPU from booting, cf. Sect. 4.4. Alternatively, one can attempt to keep the processor in reset through the respective pin.

3.3   Software Methods

Software methods are a form of firmware extraction that does not require physical access to the device in some cases. Examples include:

1. Check the device manufacturer website for publicly available firmware;
2. Follow direct download links to firmware updates, analyzing the device's network traffic;
3. Intercept network traffic for firmware updates. If TLS is used, attempt to perform a man-in-the-middle attack using self-signed certificates to decrypt the traffic;
4. Identifying and using running services on the device, and exploiting known vulnerabilities in such software (e.g. default credentials).

Often, firmware update services provide packages containing only modified files. Therefore, this results in an incomplete image. There are however cases where firmware updates consist of full firmware images, making this method a simple and effective firmware extraction solution. In addition, it should be noted that in many cases, firmware images are packed or encrypted, sometimes in proprietary formats. Unpacking or decrypting such images is a challenge on its own.

4   Case Studies

Table 1 summarizes the results of the case studies presented in this paper together with other devices we analyzed (that are not described here for the

---

[3] http://minipro.txt.si/.

Table 1. Survey of firmware extraction and modification techniques

Device	Reference	Debug Interfaces			HW Dump	SW Methods	Root achieved
		UART	JTAG	Other			
Accu-Chek Insulin Pump	[17], this paper		✓				?
Amazon Echo	[18,19], this paper			SD+UART	✓	✓	✓
Amazon Echo Dot	[19,20], this paper				✓	✓	?
Amazon Echo Plus	this paper				✓		?
DroiBOX MXG	this paper	✓					✓
Hive Nano V2 Hub	this paper				✓	✓	✓
Infotainment ECU	this paper	✓					✓
KONX Video Doorbell	this paper	✓					✓
Phillips Hue Lights	[21], this paper	✓					✓
Samsung SHS-5230 Lock	this paper		✓				?
Smart-I Doorbell	this paper	✓					✓
Smart Rear View Mirror	this paper			adb			✓
Swann OneTouch Hub	this paper	✓					✓
WD My Cloud NAS	this paper					✓	✓
Yale Alarm	this paper		✓				?
Amazon Fire TV Stick	[9]				✓		✓
Amazon Fire TV	[9]				✓		✓
Amazon Tap	[9]	✓					✓
Asus OnHub	[9]	✓					✓
Google Nest	[9]					✓	✓
Google Chromecast	[9]	✓					✓
Google OnHub	[9]			USB			✓
LG Smart Refrigerator	[9]	✓			✓		✓
Samsung Allshare Cast	[9]	✓					✓
Total #	24	11	3	3	7	5	18
Total %		45.83%	12.50%	12.50%	29.16%	20.83%	75%

sake of space) and devices from other sources as indicated. We also indicated whether obtaining root access via a hardware method is possible, or if this has not been tested but should be possible (marked as "?"). These devices were not tested due to various reasons, as some devices are running monolithic firmware without an OS, or running Windows CE. The Amazon Echo Dot is very similar to the Amazon Echo Plus, so results from the Plus should transfer to the Dot.

For the devices from [9], we list a selection of popular devices where (i) a hardware method can be used to extract the firmware and (ii) where it is clear that a firmware binary was actually obtained. We chose devices from the following major manufacturers: Google, Samsung, LG, Asus, and Amazon.

4.1   Custom Debug Interface: Amazon Echo

On the bottom of the device, a group of test points is exposed for debugging purposes. The pinout of the debug port has been documented in [18].

The Echo pinout shows the device has a UART interface and an MMC interface, which allows an external SD card to be connected. Connecting to the UART interface and booting up the device, we observe that the Echo uses a three-stage booting process. In the first stage, X-Loader tries to locate U-Boot in the boot partition of the internal memory card. Once U-Boot is loaded, it starts the final bootloader, found in the storage partition under the /boot directory. In the case of the Echo, the booting process cannot be stopped by sending UART characters, and any input after booting has finished is ignored. Since firmware extraction purely via UART is not possible, the debug interface is marked as "other" (combination of SD and UART) in Table 1.

The initial bootloader tries to boot from the external `mmc-0` (which fails) and then boots from `mmc-1`, the internal memory. As detailed in [18] and also explained in [22], it is possible to build a bootable SD card that can be connected to `mmc-0`. Then, the device can be configured to boot into a root shell, and imaged with `cat /dev/mmcblk1 > image.img`. Alternatively, we found that it is also possible to create an SD card that only contains U-Boot (but does not attempt to boot the kernel). This was also reported by independent research in [23]. From this card, we can drop into a U-Boot shell, from where the device can be imaged or configured to enable root access (by injecting an SSH service and running it on boot).

4.2   UART: Smart-I Doorbell

The Smart-I WiFi Doorbell is a WiFi-enabled unit that is installed outside the front door of a house. It has a camera, which is activated when a visitor presses the button, and can also be equipped with an optional door release. Using an Android/iOS app, the user can see and speak to the visitor and open the door remotely (Fig. 1).

Fig. 1. Smart-I PCB with UART interface attached

Opening up the device, a UART port can be easily found, to which we can connect. Using the UART interface of the device (baud rate of 38400), we identified the presence of U-Boot as bootloader, and found an enabled root shell as well. Furthermore, U-Boot has the bootdelay left at the default value of 3, which allows us to interrupt the booting process and drop to the U-Boot shell. The firmware can be extracted via the live filesystem using the root shell or via the U-Boot shell. For this device, the latter approach was used. The flash dump can be obtained with the commands in Listing 1.1:

Listing 1.1. Dumping Smart-I SPI flash from U-Boot

```
=> sf probe 0:0; sf read 0x8000000 0x0 0x800000; md.b    0x8000000 0x800000
#SF: Got idcode ef 40 17
8192 KiB W25Q64CV at 0:0 is now current device
########################
08000000: 47 4d 38 31 32 36 00 00    GM8126..
          00 60 00 00 00 60 00 00    .'...'..
08000010: 00 60 0a 00 00 00 0e 00    .'......
          00 00 00 00 00 00 00 00    ..........
```

In order to save and process the dump, the serial output needs to be saved to a file. A simple Python script can then be used to convert the dump into a binary file. Further analysis with Binwalk [24] revealed that the image is LZMA-compressed. Decompression using Easylzma [25] results in a readable firmware image.

4.3 JTAG: Yale Easy Fit Smartphone Alarm

The Yale Easy Fit Smartphone Alarm is a wireless home alarm system that can be fully controlled from a mobile app. The alarm kit consists of motion sensors, wireless cameras, a keypad, a wireless remote, a central unit and a siren. We focused on the central unit as depicted in Fig. 2.

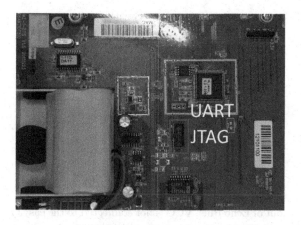

Fig. 2. Yale Easy Fit central unit PCB with UART and JTAG (Color figure online)

Inspecting the disassembled device, we observe that the board employs an ARM Freescale MK60 CPU. The board has both UART and JTAG interfaces, highlighted in blue and red, respectively, in Fig. 2. A UART interface was enabled on the device (baud rate 115200) but did not respond to user input. Its only purpose appears to be to output proprietary debug data. As user input was disabled, the bootloader could also not be bypassed. A standard JTAG header was found on the board, so further pinout reverse engineering was not needed. As the JTAG interface was not locked or disabled, the J-Link [26] programmer could be used to extract the complete firmware image using the J-Link proprietary software.

4.4   eMMC: Amazon Echo Plus

The new Echo Plus is similar to the second generation Echo Dot, as it runs an Android system, compared to the previous Amazon Echo, which runs a custom embedded Linux system (Sect. 4.1). We selected the Echo Plus as the most extensive case study in this paper, as it (in contrast to most other devices) employs a variety of rather effective security measures and is an example for best practices in the IoT. As with the previous Echo, debug pins are available on the bottom of the device. A UART interface is available, but only used for diagnostic output during the boot process, instead of giving shell access on the device. There are two different levels of debugging output, a lower level for the first stage ROM bootloader with a baud rate of 115200, as well as output for the following bootloaders with a baud rate of 912000. Booting from a custom SD card image is no longer possible for the Echo Plus. Besides, we also could not find an adb shell on the device, consistent with the findings of [20]. However, in [19], the eMMC interface of the Echo Dot is documented. With minor modifications, we could connect to this interface using the easyJTAG Plus programmer. The pinout and the necessary connections are shown in Fig. 3. It is noteworthy that the easyJTAG, when connected, prevents the Echo Plus from booting.

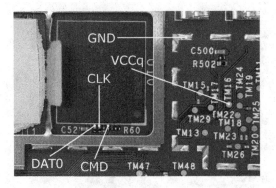

Fig. 3. eMMC pinout of Echo Plus. VCC is not connected to the easyJTAG; the eMMC chip is powered via the normal power supply of the board.

Therefore, we used an interface board (plugged into the easyJTAG), to which thin wires to the eMMC pads are soldered. The interface board can stay permanently connected; to boot the Echo Plus, the board is simply unplugged from the easyJTAG—yielding the ability to repeatedly read and write the firmware without (re-)soldering wires. Extracting the firmware via eMMC results in 16 separate partitions (following the Android standard layout). The Echo Plus has two separate _a and _b partitions each for the Little Kernel (LK), the actual kernel, and the system partition. The reason for having redundant partitions is the software update: the device e.g. boots from the *_a partitions, but then updates the *_b ones and switches to those when fully updated.

Secure Boot. The boot process on the Echo Plus consists of three stages. The Boot ROM (BROM) embedded in the MT8163 processor boots the first stage bootloader. The preloader is present in the *bootloader_rom2.bin* partition. In the second stage, the preloader loads the LK, which resides in the *lk_a* and *lk_b* partitions. LK is the standard Android bootloader, which loads the kernel (version 3.18.19+) in the final stage. The kernel, which is present on the *boot_a* and *boot_b* partitions, loads the file system and initializes all system services. The kernel image holds all Android startup scripts, SELinux domain definitions, service definitions, kernel boot parameters and all other system configuration files. As evident from the boot log, the Echo Plus employs a secure boot process, where each bootloader verifies the subsequent stage. Furthermore, SELinux is enabled in *enforcing* mode [27]. To enable dynamic analysis of the running device (as achieved for the previous generation, see Sect. 4.1), we attempted to obtain shell access with full root privileges.

Our first attempt was to modify the kernel image to implant our own startup service with full root access. However, the Echo Plus employs a trusted boot chain, where each bootloader verifies a signature of the next boot stage. This means that we were unable to boot the device when changing the kernel image, LK, or preloader on the eMMC. The first stage (BROM) is stored in ROM and hence unchangeable.

Modifying the System Partition. In contrast to the boot process, the system partition is not signed, and we did not find evidence for the use of cryptographic verification methods like `dm-verity`[4]. Having write access to the system partition, we first attempted to start a reverse shell from one of the several scripts (in the system partition) that get executed at boot time. For this, we added an ARM `netcat` binary in the `/system/bin` partition, as well as adding debug commands in each `.sh` file found, outputting different files to the `/cache` partition so we could identify which script files are executed on boot. After identifying the startup scripts, we found that SELinux was preventing us from running the `netcat` binary. The reason for this is that shell scripts on boot run in the restricted *init_shell* SELinux context. We are currently exploring further methods to run a binary with full admin privileges (SELinux context `su_exec`). Work on this subject has recently been published at DEFCON 26 [28], where researchers have been able to successfully root the Echo Plus. We will examine this research in order to obtain root access on the Echo Plus.

5   Countermeasures

Based on the findings from our survey, we propose a set of countermeasures against firmware extraction (and sometimes modification). These measures increase the cost to an adversary per device analyzed to prevent wide-reaching, low-cost attacks. Although increasing the cost to an adversary might stop low-level attackers, the model of "security by obscurity" is never an adequate defense

---

[4] https://source.android.com/security/verifiedboot/dm-verity.

strategy against well-resourced attackers. As pointed out by Dullien [29], removing "inspectability" usually does not deter malicious adversaries, while creating obstacles for benign security researches and defenders. On the other hand, when physical access to a device is part of the threat model, leaving debug interfaces open may allow straightforward extraction of secrets and user data as well as malicious modifications. It is an open problem to balance these two aspects. A potential solution might be to provide device-specific debugging credentials to the device owner, or to implement an *auditable* mechanism (e.g. using write-once fuse bits) to put the device into a debugging mode.

UART, Bootloader, and Software Methods. Debug interfaces can be disabled or protected post-production. For UART, the bootloader and kernel can be configured to disable the console to prevent access (as e.g. implemented in the Echo Plus). If a UART shell or remote SSH/Telnet access is required post-production, it should be password-protected, with a password unique for each device. This password could be made available in a secure way to the device owner to provide inspectability. All network communication with back-end services should be encrypted using TLS or a similar protocol, especially for firmware updates.

JTAG and Other Debug Interfaces. On most microcontrollers, JTAG (and other interfaces) can be either permanently disabled or protected with a password (if JTAG is not to be fully disabled for debugging or fault analysis). While these protections have been repeatedly shown to be vulnerable to fault injection (e.g. voltage and clock glitching) and similar physical attacks as well as logical attacks [30–36], simple read-out with an off-the-shelf programmer is prevented. Again, in case of password use, this password could be made available to the device owner.

Raw Flash Dump. It is hard to prevent the direct dump of external flash memory, especially eMMC, which only requires a few connections and a low-cost SD card reader. Some processors provide means to encrypt the firmware stored in external flash, e.g. the ESP32 [37]. If such features are available, they should be activated. Otherwise, it may be at least possible to mitigate straightforward in-circuit dumps by routing all flash connections on inner layers of the PCB (without test pads) when BGA packages are used. Alternatively, the entire PCB can be covered in epoxy or other materials to prevent access to the flash chip as shown in Fig. 4. This thwarts direct access, but can still be removed with more effort using heat or chemicals.

Secure Boot and SELinux. The Echo Plus is an example of an IoT device with stronger security measures compared to most other devices. Through the use of Android, trusted boot and SELinux, even though the firmware can be extracted, obtaining root access is difficult compared to other devices. It appears that SELinux, which is often considered hard to properly configure for a desktop system, might be suitable for IoT devices, which usually only provide limited and defined functionality. This is especially in light of the worrying practice to run all

Fig. 4. Covered PCB of an industrial IoT device

services with `root` permissions, which we encountered on many IoT devices. In addition, techniques to cryptographically verify the filesystem (e.g. `dm-verity`) or possibly also firmware encryption (if supported by the underlying processor, see e.g. [37]) should be considered for future IoT devices.

6   Conclusion

As shown in this paper, extracting firmware from IoT devices is possible through a variety of low-cost methods, with over 45% of the considered devices vulnerable to extraction through a simple UART connection. This problem exists throughout the industry, affecting high-profile devices like the first generation Echo as well as home hubs and alarm systems with significant security and privacy implications. Further details of all analyzed devices (notes, photographs, boot logs, etc.) are available at https://github.com/david-oswald/iot-fw-extraction.

We considered whether our work requires responsible disclosure to the affected manufacturers. However, our survey did not focus on the discovery of vulnerabilities in the considered devices. Furthermore, in some cases, a similar technique had already been disclosed by a third party (e.g. [19,21,23]). Therefore, we decided not to engage in a formal disclosure process. We plan to widen our survey, analysing additional devices and developing new methods for firmware extraction where necessary. An interesting approach in this regard is to analyse the low-level bootloaders integrated in the ROM of most modern processors w.r.t. to undocumented functions or implementation errors. Besides, it would also be interesting to better understand the susceptibility of firmware encryption mechanisms to physical attacks, e.g. side-channel analysis.

References

1. Zhang, Z.-K., Cho, M.C.Y., Wang, C.-W., Hsu, C.-W., Chen, C.-K., Shieh, S.: IoT security: ongoing challenges and research opportunities. In: SOCA 2014. IEEE, pp. 230–234 (2014)
2. Riahi, A., Challal, Y., Natalizio, E., Chtourou, Z., Bouabdallah, A.: A systemic approach for IoT security. In: DCOSS 2015. IEEE, pp. 351–355 (2013)
3. Hwang, Y.H.: IoT security & privacy: threats and challenges. In: IoTPTS 2015. ACM, p. 1 (2015)
4. Costin, A., Zaddach, J., Francillon, A., Balzarotti, D.: A large-scale analysis of the security of embedded firmwares. In: 23rd USENIX Security Symposium (USENIX Security 14), pp. 95–110. USENIX Association, San Diego (2014)
5. Thomas, S.L., Chothia, T., Garcia, F.D.: Stringer: measuring the importance of static data comparisons to detect backdoors and undocumented functionality. In: Foley, S.N., Gollmann, D., Snekkenes, E. (eds.) ESORICS 2017. LNCS, vol. 10493, pp. 513–531. Springer, Cham (2017). https://doi.org/10.1007/978-3-319-66399-9_28
6. Thomas, S.L., Garcia, F.D., Chothia, T.: HumIDIFy: a tool for hidden functionality detection in firmware. In: Polychronakis, M., Meier, M. (eds.) DIMVA 2017. LNCS, vol. 10327, pp. 279–300. Springer, Cham (2017). https://doi.org/10.1007/978-3-319-60876-1_13
7. Herzberg, B., Bekerman, D., Zeifman, I.: Breaking Down Mirai: An IoT DDoS Botnet Analysis. https://www.incapsula.com/blog/malware-analysis-mirai-ddos-botnet.html. Accessed 25 May 2018
8. Zenofex, 0x00string, CJ_000, Maximus64: All Your Things Are Belong To Us (2017). Presentation at Defcon 2017
9. exploitee.rs: Exploitee.rs Wiki. https://www.exploitee.rs/. Accessed 20 May 2018
10. Shwartz, O., Mathov, Y., Bohadana, M., Elovici, Y., Oren, Y.: Opening Pandora's box: effective techniques for reverse engineering IoT devices. In: Eisenbarth, T., Teglia, Y. (eds.) CARDIS 2017. LNCS, vol. 10728, pp. 1–21. Springer, Cham (2018). https://doi.org/10.1007/978-3-319-75208-2_1
11. Glass, S.: Das U-Boot - the Universal Boot Loader. https://www.denx.de/wiki/U-Boot. Accessed 20 May 2018
12. Huang, A.: Hacking the Xbox: An Introduction to Reverse Engineering. No Starch Press, San Francisco (2002)
13. Cui, A., Costello, M., Stolfo, S.J.: When firmware modifications attack: a case study of embedded exploitation. In: NDSS 2013. The Internet Society (2013)
14. Basnight, Z., Butts, J., Lopez Jr., J., Dube, T.: Firmware modification attacks on programmable logic controllers. Int. J. Crit. Infrastruct. Prot. 6(2), 76–84 (2013)
15. Grand, J.: JTAGulator. http://www.grandideastudio.com/jtagulator/. Accessed 20 May 2018
16. Etemadieh, A., Heres, C., Hoang, K.: Hacking Hardware with a $10 SD card reader (2017). Presentation at BlackHat USA 2017
17. EthicalHacker523: Hardware Hacking of Accu-Chek Performa Insight. https://hackaday.io/project/41162-hardware-hacking-of-accu-chek-performa-insight/. Accessed 20 May 2018
18. Clinton, I., Cook, L., Banik, S.: A survey of various methods for analyzing the Amazon Echo (2016). https://vanderpot.com/Clinton_Cook_Paper.pdf. Accessed 25 May 2018

19. Hyde, J., Moran, B.: Alexa, are you Skynet? Presentation at SANS DFIR Summit 2017 (2017)
20. Micaksica: Exploring the Amazon Echo Dot, Part 2: Into MediaTek utility hell. https://medium.com/@micaksica/exploring-the-amazon-echo-dot-part-2-into-mediatek-utility-hell-b452f62e5e87. Accessed 10 May 2018
21. OpenWRT forum: Philips Hue Bridge v2 hacked (root access). https://forum.openwrt.org/viewtopic.php?id=66346. Accessed 20 May 2018
22. Texas Instruments: How to Make 3 Partition SD Card. http://processors.wiki.ti.com/index.php/How_to_Make_3_Partition_SD_Card. Accessed 20 May 2018
23. Barnes, M.: Alexa, are you listening? (2017). https://labs.mwrinfosecurity.com/blog/alexa-are-you-listening. Accessed 25 May 2018
24. Binwalk (2017). https://github.com/devttys0/binwalk Accessed 20 May 2018
25. Easylzma. https://github.com/lloyd/easylzma. Accessed 20 May 2018
26. Segger: J-Link Debug Probes (2017). https://www.segger.com/jlink-debug-probes.html, Accessed 20 May 2018
27. SELinux Wiki: Guide/Mode – SELinux Wiki. https://selinuxproject.org/w/?title=Guide/Mode&oldid=808. Accessed 28 May 2018
28. Yuxiang, L., Wenxiang, Q., Huiyu, W.: Breaking Smart Speaker - Exploit Amazon Echo. https://github.com/tencentbladeteam/Exploit-Amazon-Echo. Accessed 10 June 2018
29. Dullien, T.: Closed, heterogenous platforms and the (defensive) reverse engineers dilemma (2018). Presentation at SSTIC 2018. https://www.sstic.org/2018/presentation/2018_ouverture/
30. Skorobogatov, S.: Copy protection in modern microcontrollers. https://www.cl.cam.ac.uk/~sps32/mcu_lock.html. Accessed 05 May 2018
31. Goodspeed, T.: Side channel timing attacks on MSP430 microcontroller firmware (2008). Presentation at BlackHat USA 2008
32. Strobel, D., Oswald, D., Richter, B., Schellenberg, F., Paar, C.: Microcontrollers as (In)Security devices for pervasive computing applications. In: Proceedings of the IEEE, vol. 102, pp. 1157–1173, August 2014
33. Obermaier, J., Tatschner, S.: Shedding too much light on a microcontroller's firmware protection. In: WOOT 2017. USENIX Association (2017)
34. Pareja, R., Wierma, N.: Automotive microcontrollers. Safety != Security. Presentation at SHA2017 (2017)
35. Nedospasov, D.: NXP LPC1343 Bootloader Bypass. https://toothless.co/blog/bootloader-bypass-part1/. Accessed 10 May 2018
36. Scott, M.E.: The FaceWhisperer for USB Glitching; or, Reading RFID with ROP and a Wacom Tablet. PoC||GTFO 0x13 (2016)
37. ESP-IDF: ESP32 Flash Encryption. https://esp-idf.readthedocs.io/en/latest/security/flash-encryption.html. Accessed 20 May 2018

Exploiting JCVM on Smart Cards Using Forged References in the API Calls

Sergei Volokitin$^{(\boxtimes)}$

Riscure B.V., Delft, The Netherlands
volokitin@riscure.com

Abstract. This paper presents a novel style of attack which compromises the applet isolation implemented by modern smart cards built on the Java Card platform. System calls (APIs) implemented by all cards tested during our research – from several different manufacturers – fail to perform (sufficient) checks on the ownership of the objects provided by applets, compromising the security of the applet firewall. The practical impact of these vulnerabilities is platform-specific; we show that disclosure of critical private data including secure channel protocol keys is possible on some cards, and that even Secure Elements – with dedicated hardware support for memory isolation – fail to prevent memory disclosure of objects owned by the Java Card Runtime Environment, despite preventing all other known state-of-the-art logical attacks. We demonstrate that physical attacks can also be used to exploit this vulnerability on some smart cards, removing the need for an attacker to first install an applet on the card. Finally, we propose a potential countermeasure for preventing these classes of attacks.

Keywords: Java Card · Logical attacks · Physical attacks ·
Secure element · Memory isolation · Fault injection

1 Introduction

Being the most widespread smart card platform, Java Card has been a target of numerous studies aimed at the security of all aspects of the platform including logical robustness of the platform and resilience to physical attacks.

One of the distinctive features of the Java Card platform is the support for multiple applets on a single card and an availability of post-issuance of the applets. This feature makes it possible for an attacker, who has the ability to load malicious code on a card, to compromise the security of the platform if logical vulnerabilities are present.

Logical attacks, being extremely cheap to exploit in a scalable fashion, are not simple to apply in the field. In most cases, an attacker does not have card management keys to load malicious code and execute it. Nevertheless, logical attacks can reveal a lot about the architecture of the platform and internal

© Springer Nature Switzerland AG 2019
B. Bilgin and J.-B. Fischer (Eds.): CARDIS 2018, LNCS 11389, pp. 186–199, 2019.
https://doi.org/10.1007/978-3-030-15462-2_13

design, which can be used by an attacker in order to find weak spots of the platform and combine it with other techniques in a successful attack.

Physical attacks, on the other hand, do not require an attacker to be able to load and execute malicious code which makes such attacks much more dangerous. There were a number of papers proposing physical attacks on Java Card platforms [1, 10, 11] showing their effectiveness, but the limiting factor of physical attacks is the price of the equipment and scalability of the attack [12]. Although the price of physical attacks is traditionally much higher than logical attacks, in recent years availability and price of basic equipment for physical attacks decreased significantly.

Section 2 presents state-of-the-art logical and physical attacks on the Java Card platform. Section 3 discusses the applet firewall and additional countermeasures used to ensure applet isolation on a card as well as common attack techniques used to break applet isolation and its limitations. Section 3.3 introduces a logical attack which uses forged references to break applet isolation using API calls provided by the platform. Section 3.4 reveals results of the evaluation of the logical attack on five different cards from multiple manufacturers. Section 4 presents a physical attack based on a single electromagnetic fault injection allowing an attacker to corrupt code on the card to break applet isolation and read the memory of other applets. Finally, Sect. 5 discusses some of the countermeasures presumably implemented on some of the cards and proposes a few improvements which could make the Java Card platform more secure.

2   Related Work

Various attacks on Java Card platform were published in recent years presenting a number of different ways to perform logical, physical and combined attacks.

The main focus of logical attacks is to break applet isolation assuming that an attacker has or can load malicious code on a card.

The paper of Mostowski and Poll presents a number of logical attacks on the Java Card platform which use ill-formed applets [9]. The authors proposed to break applet isolation by means of type confusion between arrays of different types, arrays and objects and the use of pointer arithmetic to create references to create fake array metadata.

Faugeron proposed a novel attack on an operand stack implementation of a Java Card platform and in particular insufficient checks of dup_x instruction, which allows an attacker to copy a number of bytes under the stack bottom which might lead to the disclosure of data belonging to a different context [4]. The proposed attack allowing to read 8 bytes of the stack under the stack bottom was limited to Java Card virtual machine implementation which supports optional in Java Card specification int type.

Bouffard and Lanet proposed a number of attacks to break applet isolation and get a memory dump containing code and data of other applets and the runtime environment and even the native code [2]. First proposed technique abuses the getstatic_b instruction provided by the virtual machine which lacks checks on the index to the constant pool. The second attack abused the metadata of a transient array object which had a pointer to the physical memory which could be corrupted in order to read other parts of memory.

Finally, Farhadi and Lanet present an attack which allows reversing internal representation of multiple data structures provided by Java Card virtual machine, key objects in particular, by providing a reference to them in the Java Card API call arrayCopyNonAtomic [3]. Authors proposed the use of the API calls to reverse object internal representation but did not attempt to break applet isolation. An attack on applet firewall using API calls is described later in Sect. 3.3.

There were a number of publications discussing physical and combined attacks on the Java Card platform [1,10,11]. The combined attacks on the Java Card platform are used to bypass bytecode verifier present on some of the cards by using a fault injection [1] to corrupt loaded applet or its execution to make it malicious. Physical attacks designed to corrupt the execution flow of an applet [7]. The physical attack described Sect. 4 does not require an attacker to load any code on a card since it relies on a weakness of the platform implementation itself.

With regard to the logical attack approach, there are a number of publications presenting how similar attack method can be applied to a Trusted Execution Environment (TEE). Machiry et al. presented an attack allowing an attacker in control of a user application in Rich Execution Environment to abuse the fact that there are not sufficient checks on the TEE side to leverage the privileged rights of the TEE to escalate privileges in the REE side. As a result, so called confused deputy attack allowed an attacker to break memory isolation.

3   Logical Attack

This section introduces a novel logical attack allowing an attacker to break applet isolation enforced by the firewall. The proposed attack is successful even on some of the most modern and protected Java Card platforms such as Secure Elements which have a memory protection unit for memory isolation. Section 3.1 describes memory allocation and management on most of the modern implementations of Java Card platform. Section 3.2 will discuss some of the published state-of-the-art attacks and countermeasures present on modern cards preventing the attacks. Section 3.3 will present a novel attack which uses Java Card and Global Platform API calls with forged references in order to bypass applet firewall. In this section only the logical attack, which requires an attacker to be able to load and execute code on a Java Card using a set of card management keys, will be discussed. Section 4 will introduce a physical attack which does not require an attacker to be able to execute arbitrary code on a card to read some parts of memory belonging to other applets or the Java Card Runtime Environment.

3.1   Java Card Applet Isolation

Due to the limited resources of typical Java Card cards, applets installed on a card are running in a single Java Card Virtual Machine and share the EEPROM or flash memory for storing data and code. A dedicated feature defined in the Java Card specification, the applet firewall, is required to ensure that an applet cannot access an object owned by another applet. The firewall is designed to ensure that no malicious or erroneous applet can compromise separation between applets and the Java Card virtual machine and get read or write access to other parts of memory.

In order to be able to learn more about the way a Java Card platform is implemented on a card a simple ill-formed applet, as shown in the code fragment below, can be used to get a value of a reference. Such a code cannot be compiled due to type mismatch, but it can be created by manipulating bytecodes of a CAP file.

```
public static short addr( byte[] ptr ) {
    return (short) ptr;
}
```

Such a malicious applet is effective and works on most available Java Card implementations since the operand stack is untyped, and there is no cost-effective way to detect malicious code execution at runtime. The code may be prevented from being loaded onto a card if a full bytecode verifier has been provided on the card. However, this is not the case for most of the implementations on the market.

Execution of the malicious code on a card can reveal information about the way the references are created and handled internally by the virtual machine. Most of the old implementations of Java Card virtual machines have a reference value equal to the physical address in memory where the object is stored. In contrast, most of the modern cards implement a table where the reference value is an index to the table which stores a physical address and, optionally, metadata of an object. The use of an index table allows preventing a lot of attacks published before, such as the creation of fake metadata using pointer arithmetic [2,9,12]. The actual location of the index table in memory and internals depends on the implementation and is not required for the attacks described in this paper.

Despite the fact that it is possible on most of the cards to get the value of a reference and convert it back from short to reference using ill-formed code described below, any use of such a reference will fail with a security exception or with a card mute.

```
public static byte[] ptr( short addr ) {
    return addr; \\ ill-formed, patched after compilation
}
```

```
byte[] p1 = ptr(0x0001);    \\ no exception
p1[0] += 1;                 \\ security exception or a mute
len = p1.length;           \\ security exception or a mute
```

When access to a content of a reference is attempted, the applet firewall performs checks of the ownership of the object and makes a decision to deny access or not.

3.2 Limitations of State-of-the-Art Attacks

The logical attacks published so far, which rely on type confusion, were mostly focused on type confusion between byte arrays and short arrays owned by the applet [2,9,12]. Such an attack can allow an attacker to break memory isolation by reading twice as many bytes due to the fact that a lot of old implementations would not check an array type and resolve memory address based on the access operation, namely load byte or load short, and an index. Then metadata of the following in memory objects of the applet can be corrupted, leading to reading out or writing to big parts of EEPROM memory, including code and data of other applets. Although this attack was quite successful in the past on older implementations of Java Card virtual machine, modern virtual machines often implement some additional runtime checks which prevent this attack from a successful memory isolation break. There are a number of different ways in which such a countermeasure can be implemented in a virtual machine, for example, checks of a type of an array stored in metadata of an object and the instruction used to access it. A different address resolution of array elements and/or storage of bytes and short array elements using two bytes of memory for each can make the attack useless and in fact, most of the modern solutions implement some of them and as a result, classical type confusion logical attacks do not work anymore.

Another state-of-the-art attack uses lack of checks on `getstatic_<t>` common for a lot of old Java Card virtual machines, which allows an attacker to execute a malicious code with `getstatic_<t>` and incorrect index to the constant pool and read the memory of other applets and JCRE [2]. Such an attack is easy to prevent since a simple runtime check can be added which performs a check of the index to be within constant pool index range.

As it can be seen from modern Java Card implementations, card manufacturers have improved virtual machine implementations and made them more robust against logical attacks. Additionally, there is an increasing number of Java Card platforms which have hardware support of memory isolation, such as Secure Elements with memory protection units. These units, if configured correctly, mean that any logical attack cannot break memory isolation since access to memory is controlled by the hardware. In this section, we will introduce a new logical attack which uses a different approach to break memory isolation of Java Card applets even when additional runtime checks or memory isolation hardware support are present.

3.3 Attack Based on API Calls

The Java Card runtime environment specification states that the Java Card runtime environment is executed as a privileged process which should have unrestricted access to all the memory of the virtual machine. A common way to exploit a system with kernel and user space separation is to use system calls provided by the kernel which do not have enough checks on the parameters of the system call [6]. This exploitation technique, despite being widely used on traditional systems, has not been applied to Java Card platforms in the research published so far. The implementation of such an attack will be discussed in this section in detail.

There are over one hundred API calls defined in the Java Card API and Global Platform API, and they are fully or partially supported by most smart cards [5,8]. There are API calls providing cryptographic operations, communication, exception support, card management and more. Depending on the parameters and returned types there are different types of API calls. Some API calls do not take references as parameters and they are not vulnerable to the attack proposed in this paper. Some other API calls take a reference or a number of them to applet objects as a parameter and return a data as a result of an operation over the provided data. As an example, the objects of type javacardx.crypto.Cipher have a method doFinal with the following signature:

```
doFinal(byte[] inBuff, short inOffset, short inLength,
byte[] outBuff, short outOffset)
```

The API call has two references in the parameters, namely inBuff and outBuff, pointing to byte arrays with input and output data. Finally, there are some API calls which take a reference as a parameter and change a state of the virtual machine or perform some kind of operation. For example, an API call sendBytesLong takes a reference and the virtual machine sends the data at the byte array to the terminal.

It is expected that a reference given as a parameter to an API call is to an object owned by the applet or to a global buffer, but in fact, as it was shown above a simple ill-formed method can be used to create a reference which would point to any record in the index table. Some ill-formed code which can be used to read out the memory of other applications is presented in the following listing:

```
public static byte[] getRefBA( short addr ) {
    return addr; // ill-formed code, patched after compilation
}
...
case INS_API_TEST_1:
    bufPtr = Util.getShort(buffer, ISO7816.OFFSET_P1);
    len = Util.getShort(buffer, ISO7816.OFFSET_CDATA);
    apdu.sendBytesLong(getRefBA(bufPtr), (short) 0, len);
    break;
```

The ill-formed code above allows an attacker to request the Java Card virtual machine to send an APDU response with data referenced by getRefBA(bufPtr) and offset and length controlled by an attacker. The Java Card virtual machine

has to check that the type of the object is as expected by the API call and
that the object at the reference is owned by the applet. In case the check is not
present or not complete the content of a byte array owned by another applet or
JCRE is returned in the APDU response.

In a similar way, a number of API calls can be used to write to the objects
which belong to other contexts. For example, the same API call doFinal,
exploited to read memory by providing a forged reference of the source buffer,
can be used to write to them by using the forged reference for the destination
buffer parameter. Since the key used by the method doFinal is controlled by
the caller an arbitrary write can be achieved by encrypting a buffer and then
decrypting the ciphertext to the buffer at the forged reference. Additional, not
only Java Card API calls can be used to bypass the applet isolation, for example,
most of the Java Cards also support Global Platform specification and there are
a number of API calls which can be invoked by an applet, given the privileges,
such as setATRHistBytes which takes a reference to a byte array, offset and
length and sets historical bytes returned as part of the card's ATR.

It is important to note that the proposed attack in this paper, unlike previously published attacks, will work even in the case that there is a memory
protection unit on a card. The Java Card runtime environment is supposed to
have access to all of the memory regions, including the memory which belongs
to JCRE and all the applets, and so insufficient checks of the parameters of the
API calls will result in the hardware protection being useless.

3.4   Evaluation

In order to evaluate the applicability and scalability of the attack, it was executed
on multiple cards from different manufacturers and the results were analyzed.
The Java Card specification does not require a virtual machine to be implemented in a specific way and every manufacturer is free to decide how it needs
to work internally and what additional countermeasures are in place. As a result,
the applicability of an attack may differ a lot depending on the internals of a
virtual machine. The cards used in the evaluation are listed in Table 1.

Table 1. Specification of the cards

Card	Global Platform	Java Card
card_a_1	GP 2.1.1	JC 2.2.1
card_a_2	GP 2.1.1	JC 2.2.1
card_b_1	GP 2.2.1	JC 3.0.4
card_b_2	GP 2.1.1	JC 2.2.1
card_c_1	GP 2.1.1	JC 2.2.1

The letter in the card name identifies a unique manufacturer, and the number
distinguishes between different cards made by the same manufacturer. The cards

with the same letter in the name are made by the same manufacturer – for instance, card_a_1 and card_a_2, may have similar internal implementations since they are produced by the same manufacturer, but are not identical.

Three different API calls of different kinds were used for the evaluation of the attack. First, apdu.sendBytesLong() method was tested as a Java Card defined call commonly used in the real-life applets and one of the easiest for an attacker to exploit. Second, cipher.doFinal() API call which normally uses a crypto-engine to perform the operation. And finally, an API call defined in the Global Platform specification, GPSystem.setATRHistBytes(), which takes a reference to an object and sets the historical bytes sent with an ATR of the card.

The values of references in the Java Card virtual machine implementation grow incrementally from 0x0000. In our evaluation, the values of all references which are lower than the first object of our test applet (between 0 and the reference of this first object) were tested with the API calls described above. In Table 2 the first number in a cell is a number of successful calls, meaning that the card did not mute or give an exception and returned an expected result. The second number in a cell is the total number of reference tested. Since the goal of the attack is to break isolation of applets, the total number of references tested is different on different cards, since the number of references belonging to other applets is JCRE-specific.

Table 2. The results of the attacks on the cards

Attack	Card				
	card_a_1	card_a_2	card_b_1	card_b_2	card_c_1
apdu.sendBytesLong()	40/139	2/181	38/183	37/125	3/195
cipher.doFinal()	40/139	4/181	34/183	37/125	3/195
GPSystem.setATRHistBytes()	82/139	136/181	151/183	✗	137/195
SCP keys identified	✓	✓	✓	✗	✓

As can be seen from Table 2, the number of successful calls of apdu.sendBytesLong() and cipher.doFinal() is close but not identical. This might be explained by similar but not identical checks of the objects provided at the references. In particular, it can be seen that there are some type checks and references to short arrays result in a fail when provided to both calls.

The results for Global Platform API calls differ a lot from the tested Java Card API calls. On one of the cards, namely card_b_2, a Global platform API call GPSystem.setATRHistBytes() failed for all references including legal values, which indicates rather a functional issue with the API call. For all other cards it was possible to call GPSystem.setATRHistBytes() for bigger number of objects in the index table which might be explained by the fact that the checks of the Global Platform calls is implemented in a different way and there are less or no checks on the type and ownership of the object provided.

For all of the cards but one, it was possible to identify the default Secure Channel Protocol keys stored in one of the objects in plain text.

In order to confirm that the objects found on card_a_1 correspond to the Issuer Security Domain keys and not just a data with the same content, a new key with value 1011...1E1F was added to the Issuer Security Domain using put key command and the following data was identified at object reference 0x0099:

```
0x81 0x31 0x80 0x45 0x10 0x11 0x12 0x13 0x14 0x15 0x16 0x17
0x18 0x19 0x1A 0x1B 0x1C 0x1D 0x1E 0x1F
```

It is worth noting that the key send to the card has to be encrypted using the key encryption key to prevent man-in-the-middle attacks as required by the Global Platform specification, but it is stored in plain text in the card.

Applet Class Object

A large number of objects in memory are of substantial length, and so an attacker can read significant parts of the memory of the card containing code and data. It was identified during tests that there is an object preceding the test applet class objects which points to the beginning to the applet instance and contains data objects with metadata and code. An example of such an object of length 0xB0 on the card card_a_1 is given below:

```
0x01 0x00 0x00 0x88 0x20 0x00 0x00 0x01 0x08 0x00 0x00 0x09
0x00 0x89 0x07 0x08 0x80 0x82 0x00 0x08 0x01 0x02 0x03 0x04
0x05 0x06 0x07 0x08 0x80 0x82 0x00 0x08 0x01 0x02 0x03 0x04
0x05 0x06 0x07 0x08 0xA0 0x82 0x00 0x10 0x00 0x00 0x00 0x11
0x00 0x00 0x00 0x22 0x00 0x00 0x00 0x33 0x00 0x00 0x00 0x44
0x00 0x00 0x00 0x55 0x00 0x00 0x00 0x66 0x00 0x00 0x00 0x77
0x00 0x00 0xFF 0x88 0x80 0x82 ...
```

The test applet code corresponding to the obtained memory dump starts with the following declarations of class variables:

```
static byte[] in  =   {0x01,0x02,0x03,0x04,0x05,0x06,0x07,0x08};
static byte[] out =   {0x01,0x02,0x03,0x04,0x05,0x06,0x07,0x08};
static short[] sbuf = {0x11,0x22,0x33,0x44,0x55,0x66,0x77,0x88};
```

There are a number of class objects at the beginning of the memory chunk and it is clear to see that, apart from the data itself, there is metadata of the objects as well. An attacker can use these objects as the first step for corrupting the metadata of the objects of a malicious, or benevolent, applet. This allows them to read large parts of the memory following the object, as described in previous work [9,12].

4   Physical Attack

The logical attack above successfully breaks applet isolation on multiple modern cards from various manufacturers, despite the presence of software and hardware countermeasures. An attacker with ability to execute arbitrary code on the platform can get read and write access to the objects of other applets and Java Card runtime environment. However, in many cases, an attacker has no means of installing arbitrary code on cards in the field, which means that the logical attack described above is not possible. In this section, we propose a physical attack which relies on the logical weakness of all of the observed Java Card virtual machine implementations, namely insufficient checks of the ownership of objects passed as a parameter to an API call provided by the virtual machine, such as sendBytesLong() or setATRHistBytes() as described in Sect. 3. This physical attack removes the requirement for an attacker to be able to execute arbitrary code on a card. All the attacker needs is to know – or be able to guess – which command is executing on a card.

For our proof-of-concept example of this physical attack, a reference assignment was chosen as a target for a fault injection. In practice, there are many more places where a successful glitch can result in a corruption of a reference value. Below, we provide an example of the type of code which could be targeted by this attack:

```
byte[] ref1;
byte[] ref2 = {...}
...
ref1 = ref2;   //<- GLITCH HERE to corrupt a reference assignment

res = anyApiCall(ref1);
send(res);
```

Code which can be targeted using this physical attack needs to have an operation on a reference – an assignment in this case – which can be corrupted using fault injection, and an API call of Java Card or Global Platform which uses the reference. Such code is standard for a Java Card implementation and can be found in virtually all applets.

Evaluation

We performed an evaluation of the effectiveness of this attack on card_a_1. We used electro-magnetic fault injection, since the card has a voltage sensor. The card was not decapped, which increases the probability of an attack being successful because it is less likely to damage the card while decapping.

The code which we used for the evaluation of the physical attack is shown in the listing below:

```
byte[] ref1;
byte[] ref2 = {}

ref1 = ref2;
ref2 = ref1;
 <200 times to ease timing>  // <- GLITCH HERE
ref1 = ref2;
ref2 = ref1;

apdu.setOutgoing();
apdu.setOutgoingLength(len);
apdu.sendBytesLong(ref2, offs, (byte) len);
```

An attacker performing fault injection attack has little control over the value of a reference after a fault introduced in the assignment and in most cases the reference value will be arbitrary and the API call **sendBytesLong()** returns the content at the reference back in the APDU.

We performed a fine-grained scan of the chip. In total, we attempted the attack two million times, with a success rate of around 1%. The results of this scan, with the successful glitches marked as red dots, are shown in Fig. 1.

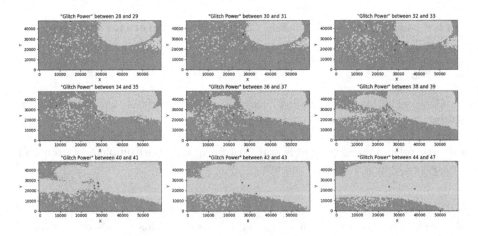

Fig. 1. EMFI results on **card_a_1** (Color figure online)

The initial value of the reference before corruption was equal to 0x0091. As a result of the test, the reference was corrupted to 13 unique values, providing a different delay, location, and length of the glitch. The obtained values of the reference are shown below:

```
0x0000, 0x0001, 0x0002, 0x0004, 0x0006, 0x0014, 0x0018,
0x0019, 0x001A, 0x0089, 0x0094, 0x009C, 0x00A0
```

Obviously, not all these corruptions could be used by an attacker to get access to other objects in memory of a card. For example, the most common fault injection corruption outcome is 0x0000 which will result in Null Pointer Exception when passed to the API call. On the other hand, some of the values correspond to the objects of other applets and JCRE itself.

As shown in Table 2 for card_a_1 and setOutgoingAndSend() API call, there were 40 unique references which could be used with this API call on this card. This means that if the value of a reference is corrupted to any of these identified values, an attacker can break applet firewall isolation and read data of another applet on the card with a single glitch and no malicious code running on the card. In fact, one of the values of the corrupted reference is equal to 0x001A which corresponds to an object of length 184 bytes apparently containing an applet AID along with both code and data. This physical attack allowed us to successfully obtain the contents of this object, with potentially serious impact since the RID of an applet belongs to a bank.

The physical attack introduced in this section serves as a proof-of-concept of an attack which relies on a logical weakness in the way modern Java Card virtual machines are handling and checking the parameters provided in the API calls. This physical attack shows how an attacker can exploit the vulnerability of a virtual machine using single fault injection to break applet isolation. Although it is difficult to control the address of a pointer after a successful glitch, a number of attempts can allow an attacker to read memory of other applets and Java Card Runtime environment and in some cases, if the corrupted value corresponds to the Secure Channel Protocol keys as it was shown for the logical attack, potentially, can reveal the key values and get full control over a card. Although the fine-grained scan above was performed using two million attempts, a real-world attacker would be able to choose optimized parameters and obtain success with far fewer attempts.

5   Conclusions

In the past years, the security of Java Card implementations has greatly improved. Many vulnerabilities allowing logical attacks have been fixed, and and as a result, there are a number of Java Card virtual machine implementations which are not vulnerable to type confusion attacks. The usage of index tables was one of the countermeasures which lead to a number of logical attacks becoming impossible.

The novel attack proposed in this paper introduces a way to exploit the API calls provided by the platform. The evaluation of the attack on multiple cards from different manufacturers revealed that all of them are vulnerable to some extent to this attack, including the most protected implementations with hardware support for memory isolation.

Additionally, the evaluation of the attack with different API calls showed that the way parameters are checked is not consistent and in most cases the checks on the parameters in the Global Platform API is much less strict and a bigger number of objects of other applets can be read and modified. On all but one card it was possible to identify the objects containing the Secure Channel Protocol keys stored in plain text. Finally, one of the objects identified contains the beginning of the test applet class file with data and metadata of class owned objects which allow an attacker to corrupt metadata of objects of the malicious applet and read and modify most of the card memory.

Logical attacks prove to be useful to identify weaknesses of the platform, but they are difficult to use in real life because in many cases an attacker has no means of loading and executing malicious code on a card. The physical attack proposed in this paper shows a way an attacker can exploit a weakness in the platform using single fault injection to corrupt a reference value used in an API call and as a result bypass the applet firewall.

The Java Card virtual machine specification requires the applet firewall to perform checks of the objects when access to the objects is performed using one of the virtual machine memory access bytecodes, meaning that all of the Java Card virtual machines already have ownership checks implemented and all of the objects in a virtual machine already have to have labels indicating an owner of the object which makes implementation of the countermeasures a trivial task. Having consistent checks of the reference parameters provided in the API calls would solve the issue and make it impossible for attackers to bypass applet firewall using such an attack.

References

1. Barbu, G., Duc, G., Hoogvorst, P.: Java card operand stack: fault attacks, combined attacks and countermeasures. In: Prouff, E. (ed.) CARDIS 2011. LNCS, vol. 7079, pp. 297–313. Springer, Heidelberg (2011). https://doi.org/10.1007/978-3-642-27257-8_19
2. Bouffard, G., Lanet, J.-L.: Reversing the operating system of a Java based smart card. J. Comput. Virol. Hacking Tech. 10(4), 239–253 (2014)
3. Farhadi, M., Lanet, J.-L.: Chronicle of a Java Card death. J. Comput. Virol. Hacking Tech. (2), 1–15 (2017)
4. Faugeron, E.: Manipulating the frame information with an underflow attack. In: Francillon, A., Rohatgi, P. (eds.) CARDIS 2013. LNCS, vol. 8419, pp. 140–151. Springer, Cham (2014). https://doi.org/10.1007/978-3-319-08302-5_10
5. GlobalPlatform. GlobalPlatform Card Specification 2.2, March 2006. http://www.win.tue.nl/pinpasjc/docs/GPCardSpec_v2.2.pdf

6. Machiry, A., et al.: Boomerang: exploiting the semantic gap in trusted execution environments. In: Proceedings of the 2017 Network and Distributed System Security Symposium (NDSS) (2017)
7. Mesbah, A., Mezghiche, M., Lanet, J.-L.: Persistent fault injection attack from white-box to black-box. In: 2017 5th International Conference on Electrical Engineering - Boumerdes (ICEE-B), pp. 1–6 (2017)
8. Sun Microsystems. The Java Card application programming interface (API), 3.0.5, October 2015. https://docs.oracle.com/javacard/3.0.5/api/index.html
9. Mostowski, W., Poll, E.: Malicious code on java card smartcards: attacks and countermeasures. In: Grimaud, G., Standaert, F.-X. (eds.) CARDIS 2008. LNCS, vol. 5189, pp. 1–16. Springer, Heidelberg (2008). https://doi.org/10.1007/978-3-540-85893-5_1
10. Rothbart, K., Neffe, U., Steger, C., Weiss, R., Rieger, E., Mühlberger, A.: Power consumption profile analysis for security attack simulation in smart cards at high abstraction level. In: Proceedings of the 5th ACM International Conference on Embedded Software, pp. 214–217 (2005)
11. Vermoen, D., Witteman, M., Gaydadjiev, G.N.: Reverse engineering java card applets using power analysis. In: Sauveron, D., Markantonakis, K., Bilas, A., Quisquater, J.-J. (eds.) WISTP 2007. LNCS, vol. 4462, pp. 138–149. Springer, Heidelberg (2007). https://doi.org/10.1007/978-3-540-72354-7_12
12. Witteman, M.: Java Card security. Inf. Secur. Bull. 8, 291–298 (2003)

Author Index

Printed in the United States
By Bookmasters